Cairo Pop

Cairo Pop

Youth Music in Contemporary Egypt

Daniel J. Gilman

University of Minnesota Press
Minneapolis • London

Published by the University of Minnesota Press
111 Third Avenue South, Suite 290
Minneapolis, MN 55401–2520
http://www.upress.umn.edu

Library of Congress Cataloging-in-Publication Data
Gilman, Daniel J.
Cairo pop : youth music in contemporary Egypt / Daniel J. Gilman.
Includes bibliographical references and index.
ISBN 978-0-8166-8927-9 (hc : alk. paper)
ISBN 978-0-8166-8928-6 (pb : alk. paper)
1. Popular music—Egypt—Cairo—History and criticism. 2. Music—Social aspects—Egypt—Cairo—History—21st century. 3. Popular culture—Egypt—Cairo—History—21st century. 4. Music and youth—Egypt—Cairo—History—21st century. I. Title.
ML3503.E3G55 2014
306.4'84230962—dc23

2014001552

Printed in the United States of America on acid-free paper

20 19 18 17 16 15 14 10 9 8 7 6 5 4 3 2 1

Contents

Preface

I arrived in Cairo to start my first long-term research trip in the middle of December 2006. I last left the city in the middle of June 2011. It is no exaggeration to say that the changes that the inhabitants of *umm al-dunya,* "the Mother of the World," have seen during that time period have been unprecedented in all of Egypt's extremely long history. Some of these changes have been heartening for those who hope to see Egyptians build a better, happier, and more peaceful society than the one foisted upon them for decades; others have been cause for despair, not only for the loss of life and destruction of property but also for the suggestion that the great majority of Egyptians will never gain any more freedom, political accountability, or even the necessities of survival without a long and bloody struggle.

The revolution and its counterrevolution have continued throughout the preparation of this book, a progression that has been exhilarating and sometimes frightening to observe, even as it has been intellectually frustrating for an anthropologist attempting to present a coherent analysis of events. Anthropologists are, as a rule, creatures of synchronicity, and even the most exhaustive monograph must be received as only a snapshot of a particular moment of historical time. I therefore offer the caveat to readers that some of the information I present on more recent events may seem inaccurate by the time of reading; if this is so, then I assure you that I strove for complete accuracy with the best information available at time of writing.

For the same reasons, it is possible that some of my analysis may be out of date or dissonant with the latest news by the time this book sees print. It grieves me to think that perhaps the optimism I express for Egypt and particularly its youth to enact positive political change and to settle accounts with an aging and entrenched power-wielding elite may be what will strike readers as out of date. This book went to press at the end of August 2013, just after an especially horrifying outburst of state violence (el-Ghobashy et al. 2013) and an equally horrifying chorus of approval of such violence by more Egyptians than my friends, colleagues, or I ever expected to voice such sentiments. The fact that some of these people held legitimate grievances against the supporters of the ousted president Muḥammad Mursi, including Christians grieving the destruction of their churches, did not lessen the horror. It has been hard to witness people turning on each other with such ferocity, no less with words than with guns and tear gas. I can only hope that all of my friends and colleagues in Egypt will receive this book in better circumstances than those that they endured when I completed the manuscript.

Acknowledgments

The initial research for this book was funded by a Fulbright-Hays Doctoral Dissertation Research Abroad award, a research grant that, most regrettably, has since ceased to exist. It is a travesty for scholars, for the academy at large, and for the United States that the latter seeks to maintain global influence while eliminating one of the few means of promulgating sound scholarship about the world beyond its borders. I consider myself doubly fortunate to have received a DDRA award when it was still a possibility, and I hope that someday it will be reestablished for the benefit of future scholars and all who seek to learn from them. The second research period for the book was funded by the American Research Center in Egypt, in partnership with the National Endowment for the Humanities. I am eternally grateful to both institutions, not only for underwriting my research but also for providentially choosing me as an ARCE fellow for the fateful 2010–2011 academic year. It was truly a once-in-a-lifetime opportunity. At ARCE, I am grateful for the assistance and facilitation of the entire staff, but especially Djodi Deutsch and Amira Khattab, both of whom made superhuman efforts to keep our fellowships up and running, even when many other research programs pulled out of the country. The final revision of the manuscript was partially subsidized by a Faculty Development Summer Stipend Award, given by DePauw University.

Many of the other ARCE fellows and I came to know each other and each other's work well through the 2010–2011 year, and a number of them offered me useful critiques and insights as I set about theorizing the developments around us. Among this group I wish to thank Mohammed Bamyeh, Sinem Adar, and Eric Schewe, as well as Hakem Rustom and Valentine Edgar, whom I met through Sinem and Eric, respectively. I owe especial thanks to two ARCE fellows in particular, Walter Armbrust and Carolyn Ramzy, both of whom considerably enriched my understanding of the theoretical issues afoot and gave freely of their time outside our regular meetings. Carolyn was of enormous help to me in thinking through questions of martyrdom in particular, but also the musical landscape of Cairo in general, aided in both at times by her husband, Marcus Zacharia.

I was also fortunate enough to become acquainted with a number of colleagues living in Cairo that year unaffiliated with ARCE, some of whom not only talked shop with me but occasionally provided a bit of *wasṭa* to reach interlocutors. My thanks go to Aaron Jakes, Emma Trentman, Rashad Mahmood, and most of all Jessica Winegar, who not only encouraged me to pursue this book but has also been a source of invaluable critique and guidance at many points throughout the writing process. Several old friends by then employed at the American University in Cairo with whom I caught up during my ARCE fellowship proved themselves sources of crucial emotional support in tense times as well as of professional collegiality: these are Mark Westmoreland and John Schaefer, along with their families.

Once I returned to the United States, several more colleagues contributed to my thinking on various ethnographic matters during the writing process. I am grateful for the questions, critiques, and support that I received from Vivian Ibrahim, Mona Bhan, Ted Swedenburg, and Amira Mittermaier. I am equally grateful for the efforts of my editor Jason Weidemann at the University of Minnesota Press, who has been a strong advocate for this book from its inception, and for the thoughtful critiques by my two anonymous outside readers.

My heartfelt thanks go to my dear friend Andrea Petranyi, who offered me a safe harbor in Nicosia when I decided to evacuate from Cairo, and who patiently and brilliantly played the dual roles of facilitator and host to me for a month. Old friends truly are golden: her kindness and generosity under such uncertain and chaotic circumstances cannot be repaid. Finally, I thank my family for their continued patience with and emotional support for their wayward son. (I gather that my research for this book was cause for more than a few of their gray hairs.) Writing can be an intensely lonely endeavor, and those phone calls home were badly needed. I hope I will be lucky enough to research and write the next book in circumstances less trying for my loved ones, and for me.

The analysis and conclusions I present herein are my attempt to do justice to my interlocutors and the ideas they shared with me. I hope I have succeeded in this aim; and, if I have not, then the fault is entirely my own, and none of theirs.

Note on Transliteration and Pseudonyms

In general, I have followed a modified form of the transliteration system of the *International Journal of Middle Eastern Studies (IJMES)*. Names that have a commonly accepted English transliteration, such as Hosni Mubarak, have been given as such. In the interest of consistency, I have used a relatively formal system of transcription for artists' names, since some can be (and are) transliterated in a multitude of ways from one medium to another. This may seem superfluous or even condescending for artists such as 'Amr Diyab (Amr Diab), whose names are relatively easy to transcribe and may even have a preferred English spelling for commercial purposes, but, given the proliferation of idiosyncratic transcriptions for names like Shirin 'Abd al-Wahhab, it seemed a necessary resort. For ease of reading, I have dispensed with the diacriticals over long vowels.

More often than not, I have transcribed Egyptian Colloquial Arabic utterances with many, although not all, of the Modern Standard Arabic sounds, in order to clarify the speaker's meaning. I presume that Arabic speakers can intuit the nuances of pronunciation that characterize ECA in general and Cairene Arabic in specific. This choice has sometimes yielded uncanny results, since song texts are heavily dependent on the interplay of phones and musical composition, and are often voiced according to the accent of the songwriter rather than the singer. I encourage interested readers to seek out the recordings mentioned in the book so that they may hear for themselves the actual pronunciation.

In accordance with standard ethnographic practice, I refer to people by pseudonyms to protect their privacy, except for a select few individuals whose celebrity was part of the rationale for interviewing them. As much as possible, I have assigned people pseudonyms that carry the same socio-religious resonance, or lack thereof, as their real names. Thus, the reader should understand that interlocutors such as Huda and Bushra bear Arabic names that do not clearly index a religious identity, and may be found among both Muslims and Christians. In contrast, other interlocutors such as Alice and Giselle bear names of recognizably non-Arabic European origin that, in contemporary Egypt, index their identity as Christians.

Introduction

Good Music, Bad Music, and Youth Music

In late December 2010, I sat in a café with Zayn, an Egyptian professor of music at one of Cairo's state universities. "Originally," he declaimed to me between sips of Turkish coffee and deep inhalations of tobacco, "there was no Arab music. Arabs originally had poetry, though, which was like music to them as auditory culture. But there *is,* however, Egyptian music, going back thousands of years."[1] This was not a practice lecture but foreground for his larger point: that contemporary Egyptian pop music does not deserve to be called "Egyptian." He indicated the wall-mounted television set in a corner, which was playing the video clip of 'Amr Diyab's song *Khalik fakirni* ("Keep remembering me"), and sighed to me, "Listen to this song. You hear the melody? That's the Beatles, really, that melody. There's nothing Egyptian at all about that song but the language, and if you swapped that out with a European language, you wouldn't even hear that vaguely Egyptian sound you believe that you hear." The professor took a long drag on his cigarette, and thought for a moment. He languidly gestured in the general direction of the television, and mused, "I'm not free when I have to listen to this stuff everywhere I go. Freedom means freedom of choice, right? But I have no choice. This is all there is nowadays. There's only one producer."

On Sunday, February 6, 2011, the Egyptian television host Muna al-Shadhli made an unusual choice for her evening broadcast. It was nearly two weeks into the mass uprising that we now recognize as the beginning of the 2011 Egyptian revolution; in another five days, President Hosni Mubarak would be ousted in disgrace by his own military brass, forced from office by widespread public protests of his rule. Al-Shadhli, who was already well known as a critic of the regime and whose show was occasionally yanked from the airwaves for refusing to obey state propaganda directives, explained that she had received a video clip[2] from the popular singer Muḥammad Munir presenting his perspective on the protests taking place across the country. The song, she explained to her viewers, had been composed and recorded several months before, but the state censors forbade its publication: the song struck the censors as too politically provocative to air. When the nationwide protests and the government's repressive reactions became everyone's daily television viewing, Munir gave the song to a videographer to create a suitable video clip. The result was a combination of anonymous people singing the song in a studio and news footage that Egyptians already knew through television and the Internet.[3] The song itself, entitled *Izzay* ("How"), was angry, accusing the government of ignoring the needs of its people, and the imagery tied that individual anger to the mass anger concurrently being expressed in huge demonstrations. When al-Shadhli aired the video clip (al-Baguri 2011) in its entirety on her show, the revolution began to acquire its own pop music soundtrack.

Why This Book?

It may seem strange to readers of this book that I pursue a link between commercial pop music and politics in Egypt. From the historical vantage point of 2013, with Egypt's recent—and arguably, ongoing—revolution against the Mubarak regime and its associated issues of neoliberal economic policies, abuse of political power, and torture (to name only a few major topics that have made international headlines), it may seem beside the point to worry about how Egyptians listen to popular music. As I shall discuss throughout this book, however, connections between music and politics in Egypt are both long-standing and deep.

I am keenly interested in the phenomenon of emotional evocation in pop music, not only as a fascinating subject in its own right but also as a means of comprehending this linkage between music and politics. Music—of any variety, not just commercial pop—is capable of moving listeners by playing on their emotions on a mass-media scale, and thereby inspiring them to commit one act or another. Such exhortation is, of course, also a common goal of political rhetoric. In this regard, music and politics are not only potential allies but also potential oppositional forces.

In the case of pop music, there has perhaps always been a relationship between music's ability to move a listener and its ability to seduce someone: indeed, these phenomena are two sides of the same coin. Conservative orthodox Islam has been cited for its uneasiness with music, partly on such grounds of uncontrolled eroticism but, more importantly, because the potentially amoral pleasure of music can distract (or, if you will, seduce) a person's attention away from obedience to God. In both regards, however, Islam is not alone. America in the 1950s was frequently a hostile place toward contemporary pop music, and commentators expressed the paramount fear that rock 'n' roll would literally seduce young people away from their studies and responsibilities to both God and man toward a constant state of sexual arousal and mindless gratification of the physical self.

A permutation of this anxiety about the seductive potential of music is that it can distract people from a political aim. This anxiety, although applicable in a wide variety of scenarios, is well documented in projects of nationalist modernity. Such anxiety derives from the sensibility that nationalist modernists tend to have concerning popular expressive culture: that it must serve societal goals for collective betterment (whether Islamic, socialist, capitalist, or otherwise), and that cultural mandarins must ever be watchful for "bad art" manifestations that fail to measure up to standards or actively oppose and attack their vision of national modernity. In this regard, music is equally threatening to the Egyptian Salafist and the Russian Communist: Lenin was famously ambivalent about his admiration for Beethoven's music, saying that its beauty soothed and comforted him, rather than putting him in the angry, uncompromising mood needed to complete the Bolshevik Revolution.

I am primarily interested in the aural material of pop music and secondarily interested in music videos, a subject that has occupied anthropologists and other social scientists who study the Middle East more than pop music itself. Music videos, to be sure, are a fascinating subject of study; so fascinating that I consider them seductive to scholars. They are available to anyone with a satellite dish or a relatively fast Internet connection and, for those who assume that sound is always subjugated to vision in pop culture, they can appear the richer topic. But, as has long been the case in ethnographic anthropology generally (Stoller 1989, 25–32) and especially in analyses of nationalism and popular culture, scholars have tended toward a methodological "ocularcentrism" even when examining media that people do not encounter only through visual stimuli (Z. Fahmy 2011, 13–17). Although I do not quarrel with the idea that people may trust what they see more than what they hear, it is neither useful nor even possible to posit such a hierarchy in popular culture: sound is no less important than sight, even when the images of a music video seek to monopolize one's attention.

I recognize that many writers on Egyptian pop music have focused on music videos to the near-exclusion of other phenomena. I do not believe that the best response to this tendency is to ignore a salient phenomenon but to contextualize it within the larger music industry. I am sensitive to the irony that it is not possible to discuss most contemporary Egyptian pop songs of note without devoting some attention to their visual presentation as well as the aural. It is an inescapable fact that pop musicians working in Cairo at almost all levels of prestige and media exposure assume that they will disseminate their work partly by means of video clips that may contain messages that correspond, contradict, or even ignore utterly the form and content of the song itself. Indeed, many of my interlocutors' comments to me will not make sense to readers without some understanding of how central music videos are as a medium of dissemination and consumption. Since the preponderance of my Cairene interlocutors indicated to me that they frequently received contemporary pop music through the medium of the music video clip, and that they gave this medium some thoughtful consideration as they consumed it, I have attempted to present holistic analyses of these songs, drawing on all aspects of their production and presentation.

When I had formulated some guesses about what mattered to Cairenes about popular music and why, I went off to Egypt, living in Cairo during and just after the last years of Mubarak's rule. I have tried to bring out in this book the city-bound nature of my ethnographic work; thus I frequently refer to my interlocutors as Cairenes specifically rather than as Egyptians in general. The metropolitan area of Greater Cairo constitutes an enormous population center, and confining my ethnographic work to the city and its exurbs still afforded me a potential pool of interlocutors over 20 million strong.[4] The city is also the locus of most of Egypt's culture industry output, which, until recent years, was close to coterminous with the culture industry output of the entire Arab world; as I shall discuss, this long-standing industry is a source of nationalist pride to some of my interlocutors. Moreover, since I can make no ethnographically informed claims as to how Egyptians living in the provincial cities, towns, and rural areas of the country receive pop music, I have emphasized the Cairo-focused scope of my research.

I spent several years in total in Cairo, listening to, speaking with, and even arguing on occasion with Cairenes about pop music. As I imagine is the case for a great many ethnographers, I learned that some of my guesses were accurate, others wrong, and still others irrelevant. At this point, I must lay out for the reader the epistemological framework through which Cairenes experience pop music, rather than approaching the topic through a preconceived Western theoretical framework. As it turned out, taxonomy has loomed large in my research, and the terminology must be unpacked with some care.

Taxonomy and Its Discontents

As I discuss in chapter 3, to engage in questions of musical taxonomy is to some degree to accept the terms of debate in a very real and sometimes brutal class struggle. This fact presents the ethnographer with a discomfiting irony when attempting to explain music to people who may never have heard it, since any discussion of taxonomy immediately raises the question of its intrinsic value and the larger questions of power that lurk beneath the terminology. Since it is impractical to discard taxonomy altogether, I implore the reader to keep in mind that the system of classification discussed throughout this book is not a neutral hypothetical thing but reflects power relations within a system of class domination, relations obscured but not entirely erased by the terms of classification.

The genre of popular music, vocal and instrumental, which has traditionally defined the Arabic-language music industry is, oddly enough, difficult to name precisely in Arabic. In her biography of Umm Kulthum, Virginia Danielson notes the proliferation of terms used by different sources, with accordingly different implications: "*aṣil* (authentic), *turath* (heritage), *klasiki* (classical), and *mutaṭawwir* (advanced or developed)" were all used by various informants of hers to describe the repertoire of Umm Kulthum (1997, 14). I have encountered a similar proliferation in my own field research, albeit with fewer academic overtones than the corpus of phrases that Danielson heard. Some people whom I know refer to this music as *al-musiqa al-qadima* (old music); others say *al-musiqa al-klasikiyya* (classical music); still others, especially professional musicians of my acquaintance, prefer *musiqa al-turath* (the music of heritage).

The last term, *turath* or heritage, is most expressive of the feelings of many toward this genre, which, for reasons I shall discuss below, is strongly associated with an earlier epoch of Egyptian cultural history and the heyday of pan-Arab nationalism as well. In fact, those acquaintances who used the term *turath* tended to slip freely and confusingly between connotations of Egyptian national heritage and pan-Arab ethno-linguistic heritage. While such a slippage can be ethnographically revealing, it is nonetheless troublesome for taxonomy. A great deal of the music thus referred to—particularly the corpus of Umm Kulthum—was composed during the twentieth century and not in some more ancient period. In fact, the period of the 1880s to the 1950s was a time of self-conscious construction of an Arab national identity, and this musical corpus represents an aspect of that era's emerging nationalism. Moreover, the classical corpus of the twentieth century refers self-consciously to such heritage links, rather than manifesting them. It is worth remembering that Arab nationalism, when applied to popular music, was openly syncretic and synthetic in its outlook, and even overtly nationalist texts were often set to musical arrangements that hybridized Arabic and Western musical traditions (Massad 2005, 179).[5] As a result, I am not comfortable using the phrase *musiqa al-turath* as a technical term beyond its use as an ethnographic term.

For my purposes, at first experimentally in the field and now more systematically in this book, I have come to apply a taxonomic neologism, based upon another descriptive term used by at least a few Egyptians: *musiqa al-ṭarab* (the music of enchantment). A similar usage can be found in A. J. Racy (2003), although Racy, I should point out, does not use the term quite as taxonomically as I do. The word *ṭarab* refers to the hypnotic enchantment or state of transported engagement that falls upon people who experience something especially beautiful, such as particularly beautiful music. The word *ṭarab* is not confined to music or even to a genre of music in lexicographic terms, and has a long history as an element in discourses of religious ecstasy—compare, for example, Frishkopf's explanation (2001) of the application of the word within Sufi rituals, or Hirschkind's discussion (2001) of *intisha'* (exaltation) as an audience reaction to Islamic preaching.

Nowadays the word *ṭarab* is most often applied to contexts involving this older form of popular music. Racy illuminates this point by parsing the taxonomic implications this way: "it denotes the theoretically based, modally structured, and professionally oriented tradition of music making, a domain that Western scholars sometimes refer to as 'art music'. . . . In a more specific sense however, the word '*ṭarab*' refers to an older repertoire, which is rooted in the pre-World-War I musical practice of Egypt and the East-Mediterranean Arab world and is directly associated with emotional evocation" (Racy 2003, 5–6). There is, then, a powerful associative link between the evocation of *ṭarab* and the performance of this genre of music. Moreover, I found that most of my friends in Egypt considered the idea of other genres of Arabic pop music inspiring the feeling of *ṭarab* to be, at best, humorous. Because the link in popular imagination between the emotion of *ṭarab* and this genre of neo-classical music is so strong, I habitually used this phrase to describe the musical genre itself.

Musiqa al-ṭarab is the style of music performed by the iconic singers of Egyptian popular music in the mid-twentieth century: Layla Murad, Muḥammad ʻAbd al-Wahhab, Farid al-Aṭrash, ʻAbd al-Ḥalim Ḥafiẓ, and the most iconic of all, Umm Kulthum.[6] ʻAbd al-Ḥalim Ḥafiẓ is something of an odd man out in this grouping, since he pursued a slightly different compositional and performative aesthetic than did his predecessors. (He was several decades younger than his colleagues named here.) Some of my historically minded interlocutors told me that in the early days of ʻAbd al-Ḥalim's career he was considered a youthful, vulgar upstart by cultural mandarins accustomed to the longer songs and slower passages of the dominant style of the first half of the century. Nowadays, however, young people perceive ʻAbd al-Ḥalim as either a member of the *musiqa al-ṭarab* category, or as a bridge between *musiqa al-ṭarab* and the genres of popular music that arose in the latter half of the twentieth century, which I shall describe later.

Cairenes do not agree on how to draw the precise historical boundaries of Egypt's heyday of expressive culture. Particularly for aficionados of *musiqa al-ṭarab,* the potential divisions are filled with meaning, largely as a reflection upon the cultivation and good taste of the arbiter. Among serious lovers of Arabic music, the desire to prove one's discriminating taste—especially in comparison to one another—can lead to a kind of one-upmanship. This phenomenon is hardly limited to Cairo:[7] Jonathan Shannon describes a social encounter in Syria in which he felt pressured to fake his way through such an articulation of hyper-elevated taste, and claimed an aficionado's preference for the earlier and somewhat more obscure recordings of Umm Kulthum. His interrogator approved and commented, "Her best recordings are from the period of about 1928 to 1930. Afterwards she became too repetitive and emotionally less sincere *(mufta'ala)*" (Shannon 2006, 46). As with other musical genres and contexts, one's reputation for aesthetic discrimination in *musiqa al-ṭarab* rests partly on fluent knowledge of obscure recordings that must be actively sought out, rather than passively encountered through broadcast media.

In Cairo, an additional pressure on pretenders to cultivation is the sociopolitical resonance of their declared listening habits. A conversation about music can quickly become a referendum on national politics: this situation hinges chiefly on the respective feelings of speaker and listener about the July 23 Revolution of 1952, which ushered in a program of Arab nationalism and socialism. To say that Egyptian music of the 1940s cannot compare to that of the 1950s is to imply (unwittingly or otherwise) that the massive political and social changes wrought by the revolution affected popular culture for the better. Likewise, those fans who prefer the musical output of the 1930s and 1940s may be offering a critique of Egyptian society through the filter of nostalgic music appreciation. But this latter group is a small minority; as a rule, Cairenes will assign to the decades of the 1940s, 1950s, and 1960s the distinction of a Golden Age in which Egyptian music reached its zenith by the grace of superior lyricists, innovative composers, and supremely talented singers. In my experience, music fans who enjoy *musiqa al-ṭarab* are most inclined to grant this status to the 1950s and 1960s; relatively few such fans, especially those among the current youthful generation, are sufficiently familiar with earlier decades to form an opinion on their musical output. As Shannon's anecdote illustrates, this lack of familiarity can be troubling for devoted fans, who identify several distinct artistic periods in the career of Umm Kulthum, and would never take her late recording career as representative of her entire *oeuvre.* Despite this, most young Cairenes of my acquaintance[8] do exactly that, referring only to those songs she recorded from the early 1950s to the early 1970s, as though this were her entire recording career.

There is, however, widespread agreement that the best years came to an end in the 1970s. The exact cut-off point is a matter of idiosyncratic variation, but the general theme is so common as to be predictable in conversation: aficionados of *musiqa al-ṭarab* will say that, by the time that a number of the great musical stars died within a few years of each other in the mid-1970s, the good years were gone. This theme crosses all political lines: although Gamal Abdel Nasser's death in 1970 brought an end to the political, social, and economic policies he espoused—all of which were either blunted or reversed completely by his successor, Anwar Sadat—no one hears in this musical opinion a figurative lamentation for the era of Nasserism. Rather, one hears a literal lamentation for the great musicians who passed from this life, and thereby foreclosed on the possibility of further musical greatness.

A. J. Racy elaborates on the expectations that audiences bring to concerts of *musiqa al-ṭarab.* Regarding vocal strength, Racy quotes an anecdote from the Egyptian writer Ni'mat Aḥmad Fu'ad telling how, although Umm Kulthum had been accustomed to singing into amplifying technological devices as a necessary part of the recording process since 1926, she reacted angrily in 1932 when a microphone was placed on the stage for one of her live concerts. She soon accepted live amplification as a practical necessity, however, as she began to play to larger halls, and as composers[9] increasingly incorporated electrically amplified instruments into their arrangements and demanded larger *takht*s (Racy 2003, 63). Thus, all archived sound and video recordings are, by definition, also electrically amplified or even enhanced. Ornamentations *(ḥilyat ṣawtiyya)* that produce vibrations within or around a precise tone can take a wide variety of forms, "ranging from subtle grace-note effects to long held tremolo-like gyrations. They may also coexist with various other effects, such as the subtle portamento (or sliding between notes) and the wave-like manipulation of individual notes" (Racy 2003, 86–87). (Such ornamentations can be produced on nearly all the instruments of the classical *musiqa al-ṭarab* repertoire as well.) The expectation exists that singers will utilize "a full, somewhat throat-controlled chest voice, in contrast to the 'head,' or falsetto voice (*ṣawt musta'ar,* literally, borrowed or artificial voice)," which is considered poor form, or at least a foreign technique that contrasts awkwardly with traditional *musiqa al-ṭarab* vocal style (Racy 2003, 88–89).

Another key element of *musiqa al-ṭarab* is its compositional theory: nearly all songs in this genre are composed in accordance with Arabic music theory. In practice, this means that the scales *(maqam,* plural *maqamat)* upon which composers construct songs do not align with the even-tempered[10] scales that, for centuries, have given shape to Western musical composition. Rather, *maqamat* are based upon various possible tunings of the strings of the *'ud,* the lute that features prominently in Arabic music. Such scales and tunings, which calculate ascension through a given scale in quarter-tones, depend of necessity on monophonic unison when an ensemble performs: it is so difficult to produce euphonious harmony in this musical system as to be impossible in practice, especially if the *'ud* is used as the lead instrument. Harmony therefore features only occasionally in some more experimental and synthetic compositions,[11] and even then only when it will not conflict with the singer. Soloists, both vocalists and instrumentalists, work to produce euphonious improvisations using quarter-tones and, frequently, micro-tones as well—such finely distinguished shadings of pitch characterize the *ḥilyat ṣawtiyya* that Racy describes. Soloists also take some freedom with the rhythm of a song, and can slow down or speed up (in comparison to the ensemble) as they consider it necessary to emphasize these *ḥilyat* in their featured passages.

All of these qualities contribute to the "high modernism" of *musiqa al-ṭarab:* an especially prestigious register of *musiqa al-ṭarab* that incorporates all of those elements that musicians and aficionados consider most difficult to produce, most beautiful to hear, and most apt to evoke the ecstatic emotional state of *ṭarab.* Such high modernist musical aesthetics, as I style them, do not fully correspond historically to other aesthetic movements referred to as "high modernist," such as in literature; indeed, as noted above, the period of historical time when Egyptian music was at its height varies to some degree according to the arbiter. Still, the ongoing process of cultural memory in Cairo encourages music fans to identify the best years of Egyptian musical production with the decades of the 1950s and 1960s—a period of time chiefly associated in Egyptian history with Gamal Abdel Nasser's pan-Arab nationalism, Arab socialism, and a now-bygone sense of optimism for Egypt's political ambitions and social renewal.[12]

This high modernist *musiqa al-ṭarab* was not the only iteration of Cairo-produced popular music available to people during those twenty years; the high modernist music of Umm Kulthum and Farid al-Aṭrash coexisted with the music of 'Abd al-Ḥalim Ḥafiẓ, which Egyptian cultural mavens held in lower esteem. And in the succeeding decades, high modernist musical aesthetics have come to seem dated and historical. Since I consider it a mistake to classify contemporary Egyptian popular music as postmodern, I speak of 'Abd al-Ḥalim Ḥafiẓ's music as exemplifying a "low modernist" aesthetic, one that substantially resembles high modernism while also departing from that aesthetic in some significant ways.

A newer genre of popular music began to appear in the 1970s. This genre, which is known as *al-musiqa al-sha'bi* (literally "people's music," and idiomatically "working-class music"), derives much of its vocal style and lyric composition from the folk music tradition of the *mawwal.* The *mawwal,* technically speaking, is a variant of the *zajal* poetic form, composed in colloquial Arabic, and characterized by wordplay and an affinity for conscious violations on the composer's part of the prosodic rules usually applied to poetry in Classical Arabic. The word *mawwal* in Egypt has also come to denote a folk song genre characterized by wordplay and a high-pitched "crying" intonation in the singer's voice, often composed to comment on local issues (Salim 1999, 5–7, 15–17; Racy 2003, 160). In its urban recorded variant, such a song may be considered part of the corpus of *sha'bi.*[13]

Sha'bi singers often make use of a short phrase excerpted from the song text to serve as a vehicle for numerous high-pitched variations on the basic melody. The songs of this genre range in lyrical content from extremely simple repetitions of a single phrase to poetic texts; songwriters frequently use bawdy imagery or double entendre as stylistic devices, especially in comparison to other musical forms in Egypt. *Sha'bi* songs, like songs in every genre of Egyptian popular music, may treat the subject of romantic desire, but by common reputation, they are more often lamentations on everyday problems faced by the narrator. Khulud, a young Cairene woman who avidly followed pop music, disdained much of *sha'bi* as vulgar and whiny, particularly the lyrical emphasis on nonromantic subject matter: "It's like crying, you know? All about 'Oh, my friends did this to me, I don't have any money.'" At the same time, the underground nature of much of the genre and its cassette-based industry, the potential for bawdiness and the relative lack of focus on romance allow *sha'bi* the possibility of commenting directly on social matters in a manner to which other genres do not easily lend themselves. In addition, the genre's compositional vehicle of "ordinary street language and witty, even irreverent street attitudes in its song texts" (Marcus 2007, 161) wins it the affection of many working-class Cairenes.

Although it is highly stigmatized among the *haute bourgeoisie,* who consider the musical genre part of a low-taste culture,[14] a great many Cairenes listen to *sha'bi* at least once in a while. In recent years, different registers of *sha'bi* have articulated themselves: while some performers, notably Ḥakim, have invested their music with a great deal of professionalism and have won some respect from the cultural establishment as working musicians (Marcus 2007, 165–66),[15] others trade on the bawdier and less critically acceptable aspects of the genre. In particular, Sha'ban 'Abd al-Raḥim, whom virtually all elite music critics and aficionados loathe, practically wallows in his public image as an ignorant, untalented, and disrespectable character (Grippo 2006).[16] And even decades before such a high–low distinction could be made within *sha'bi,* cultivated music listeners in Cairo could observe (or reluctantly admit) that the *sha'bi* singer

Aḥmad 'Adawiyya's songs, while superficial and often vulgar, could also contain or convey "a touch of *ṭarab*" (Racy 1982, 401).

Walter Armbrust suggests that part of the popularity of *sha'bi* music lies in its willingness to critique social conditions and mock what he regards as a declining modernist aesthetic that reverberates in social and governmental policy (1996, 173–90). More generally, *sha'bi* seems to hold the same sort of appeal to its Egyptian fans as does American country music to its fans: that is, much of the genre revels in the "abject sublime" quality of complaining about the sheer mundanity of the narrator's problems (see Fox 2004b). Beyond reveling in its own low-class reputation, though, *sha'bi* also resembles American country music by evoking "a sense of local identity, tradition and heritage, and the aura of authenticity" (Grippo 2007, 259).

Sha'bi has a lesser visual presence than other musical genres in Egypt, for several reasons. It is less commonly seen than *musiqa al-ṭarab* because the latter, as a traditionally prestigious genre, has often been captured in filmed concert performances and television broadcasts. It is less commonly seen than *shababiyya* (the genre I shall discuss) because the latter is heavily reliant upon video clips that function as both advertising—for the artists themselves and for the various business concerns that can purchase advertising space around the broadcast videos—and saleable products in themselves. The limited amount of professionally produced *sha'bi* video clips tend to feature male singers who dance suggestively while mouthing their lyrics, and may have a setting no more complicated than a city street in which they perform the song much as they would perform on a concert stage.

The songs themselves are usually performed in a nasal voice in a high range, such that the singer is pitched just below the breaking point for his falsetto. The rhythms and vocalization patterns are shaped to facilitate dancing among the audience. Depending on their level of appreciation for the form, my interlocutors varyingly described these patterns as either hypnotically catchy or irritatingly repetitive. The instruments, whether acoustic,[17] electrified, or synthesized, often express a reediness of tone that complements the nasality of the singer's voice. Among female singers, the higher singing register is more common as well, as is nasality of timbre, although the latter quality is less prominent than among men.

In recent decades, there has grown up a genre of Arabic pop music that takes little if anything from traditional roots, as does *sha'bi;* in terms of compositional structures, modal possibilities, and melodic progressions, it is highly influenced by Western pop music. Speaking generally, the dominant song format is a love song, either upbeat or downbeat, although the genre admits a wider variety of formats and topics—including, on occasion, social critique—than does the highly formalized *musiqa al-ṭarab.* (As noted above, *sha'bi* also delves into social critique from time to time.) Because this genre—and really, it is as much a social designation as a musical genre—is strongly associated with young people, it is known in Cairo as *al-musiqa al-shababiyya* ("youth music").

Shababiyya inhabits the middle ground of prestige among Cairene musical genres, although its exact placement on the scale depends very much upon the arbiter. It does not bear the stigma of urban poverty and ignorance, as one finds with *sha'bi.* On the other hand, it is more often than not judged a form of music inferior to *musiqa al-ṭarab,* a judgment that can easily be loaded with deeper and broader implications in the hands of a culture critic. Some of its fans, though, suggested to me that there is almost a sense of relief in listening to what they acknowledge as a less exalted form of popular music: a friend commented to me that she cannot listen to "great art" for more than an hour or so before it overwhelms her and she needs to set it aside, but she can listen to *shababiyya* all night. The criticism that the genre receives from the cultural establishment tends to focus on two aspects, only one of which is musical: its brevity and simplicity compared to *musiqa al-ṭarab* compositions, and the tendency of the genre and its performers to traffic in sexuality. Perhaps unsurprisingly, some of its fans mention the same attributes to me as positive virtues.

In my experience with *shababiyya,* its popularity derives from a combination of pop aesthetics that young people described to me as culturally accessible and easily understood—far from the formal and even physically taxing concerts that Umm Kulthum famously performed—and imagery of physically desirable people: that is, sex appeal. Without at all wishing to denigrate contemporary Egyptian pop music as the death-knell of Egyptian society, I feel obliged to point to the Frankfurt School's characterization of the culture industry as "pornographic and prudish" (Adorno and Horkheimer 2002, 38); there is indeed a degree of pornographic teasing, sometimes deeply submerged and other times relatively explicit, in much pop music that derives from the tendency to eroticize and sexualize performers both male and female in a way that Umm Kulthum or Muḥammad 'Abd al-Wahhab never presented themselves. This tendency articulates itself far more obviously in music video clips than it does in the songs themselves, sometimes presenting performers—more so women than men—in unmistakably bawdy, sexualized gestures and situations.

What is more, pop music tends to make very few aesthetic demands on the listener (or indeed the spectator), in comparison to the music of the high modernist icons. One can find lyrically demanding *shababiyya,* if one looks for it—particularly since the genre has attracted performers close to or involved in various forms of social activism. This sort of enterprise, though, is dwarfed by the sheer mass of *shababiyya* that, lyrically and melodically, is easily and lightly consumed. Indeed, one of the pleasures of *shababiyya* that many young people mentioned to me was that it was well suited for background music while driving through Cairene traffic.

Because of the huge numbers of *shababiyya* songs that are recorded every year, it is somewhat difficult to speak of a single overarching aesthetic. There exists, on a general level, a set of aesthetic assumptions on which virtually every *shababiyya* composition is based. Songs are relatively short, usually less than five minutes in length. They are usually composed within a framework of Arabic music theory fused, to varying degrees, with Western even-tempered music theory, with a structural foundation that Egyptian music professionals have characterized to me as heavily influenced by Western-style pop music. Whether the song is slow or fast, romantic or not, there is always a prominent, reliable 4/4 rhythm. While a great many productions feature a variety of instruments used in traditional Arabic music, these are not a requirement of the genre.

Beyond these essential criteria, *shababiyya* songs break down into several varieties, although I have yet to hear anyone attempt to name or define them. In my observation, these varieties are distinguished primarily by tempo: they are slow or fast, and the rest of the song's character derives from this. Cairenes sometimes speak vaguely of *rumansi* (romantic) songs, and usually point to slower-tempo love ballads as examples of this, but the lyrics of these songs are hardly distinguishable from many fast-tempo pop songs. Slower songs may in fact be either romantic or, as it were, anti-romantic—that is, they may describe any point in a love affair, from first glance to the last embittered parting. Up-tempo songs, while often featuring the exact same lyrical content, tend to be received by young people not as *rumansi* but as dance pop: the quick, steady rhythm is conducive to a sense of movement, both on the dance floor and, as is often the case, in one's car while covering the miles from one part of Cairo to another. A common although not universal trait is the use of flamenco-influenced guitar lines, which is most closely associated with the Egyptian singer ʻAmr Diyab and the Lebanese singer Elissa.

Arabic-style ornamentations, the *ḥilyat ṣawtiyya* that Racy described, appear in *shababiyya* as well. Unlike the situation that obtains in *musiqa al-ṭarab,* however, *shababiyya* singers pursue such ornamentations as flourishes rather than performative obligations to the audience. And, even more distinct from other musical genres, such flourishes are inserted in songs that are not structured in any way upon Arabic music theory. (This leads aficionados of *musiqa al-ṭarab* to complain that *shababiyya* singers and listeners literally do not know or understand music, and that they are simply playing around with techniques without any overarching comprehension of how things "ought" to be performed.) The even-tempered Western theoretical foundation of these songs encourages singers to focus their vocal efforts not on the multifarious fluctuations of pitch that characterize *musiqa al-ṭarab* but rather on the ability to hit and sustain a single note without any fluctuation at all; only those singers with more formal training than most of their peers attempt the old-fashioned *ḥilyat.* In another sharp distinction from *musiqa al-ṭarab, shababiyya*'s speedier rhythms often encourage singers to cultivate the skill of enunciating words very quickly without losing the meter or falling off-key.

The visual aesthetics of *shababiyya* are, for most youthful consumers in Cairo, defined primarily by video clips, through which the songs are widely publicized. Video clips often bear scant narrative relationship to song lyrics; indeed, there is often no apparent relationship at all, the video clip having become a separate artistic and commercial creation that sells the singer more than the song. Because the music industry has grown so reliant upon video clips to make songs popular and generate interest in a singer, the physical beauty of the singer has grown far more important to *shababiyya* than it was to *musiqa al-ṭarab.* Many people, both young and old, told me confidently that *shababiyya* is in many ways more about visual than aural aesthetics. There exists not only a premium on pretty faces but attractive bodies as well: especially for female singers, there is an expectation that their video clips will feature them dancing or posing in tight-fitting outfits that eroticize them.

Why Some Artists and Not Others?

No doubt, some readers familiar with popular music of Egypt and the Arab world will be surprised to see, in this book, some artists discussed at length and others less so. Many more might wonder that I do not devote significant space to discussing a number of artists who have gained widespread fame only in the wake of the uprising that kicked off the 2011 revolution. The answers to this question of selection are twofold. First, the direction of my research was shaped partly by what my interlocutors told me mattered to them, and whom they judged an important artist in several different aspects. As fascinating as I found some lesser-known and relatively obscure artists, I felt a scholarly obligation to give priority to what my interlocutors said was important. Second, the overwhelming trend in popular music of the 2011 revolution has been "underground" musical acts known only to small fan bases in Cairo and Alexandria rising in the public consciousness outside the commercial apparatus on which *al-musiqa al-shababiyya* depends.[18] While these newly famous acts complicate musical taxonomy in interesting ways, I regard them as a fundamentally different phenomenon from the larger world of corporate-industry, mass-mediated music that I take as my subject of study in this book.

My choice to hold these newer acts separate from my larger discussion may pain some of my colleagues, since they are frequently drawn to the underground music scene in Egypt as much for long-standing aesthetic reasons as for more recently coalesced political motivations. I am sympathetic to both of these critiques but at the same time feel constrained to resist them as epistemologically seductive, much the same way as I characterize video clips as seductive. For many years now, the aesthetic preferences of scholars have articulated themselves in the scholarly record itself: the music that anthropologists and ethnomusicologists have examined at length tends to be not only what their interlocutors prefer but what the researchers themselves prefer.

From the foregoing, it should be clear to the reader that the aesthetics of pop music presentation in Egypt have changed drastically over the past sixty years. The point I wish for the reader to take from all this is that mass-mediated pop music in Egypt is fundamentally entangled with discourses and practices of gender, nation, and aesthetics. It is, in fact, a clearinghouse for all of these institutions as they relate to each other in Egypt. Part of my aim for this book is to set forth the complex social architecture that is the contemporary Arabic pop music industry as it operates in its center of production, Cairo, and how people who live there receive and consume that industry's output.

"Why would you study *shababiyya,* anyway?" This question was put to me, not by my American teachers and colleagues but by a number of Egyptian teachers, colleagues, and respondents. As mentioned above, the genre enjoys less cultural prestige than *musiqa al-ṭarab,* and the idea that a researcher would go all the way from the United States (much less Texas) to Egypt in order to devote himself to an examination of this unserious pop cultural form struck many people as ridiculous. Several different people—neither of whom had met me before—took it upon themselves to intercede in this apparent academic folly, begging me to abandon my topic as unworthy and shift my focus to the glorious corpus of the old greats. They looked plainly wounded that anyone would grant *shababiyya* serious attention, let alone a foreigner who would go home and report to his countrymen that Egyptians scorn their rich artistic heritage by listening to disposable fluff.

These incidents, while amusing and annoying in equal measure for me at the time, also reminded me that people are socially invested in their publicly known tastes, and that an ineptly staged investigatory intervention is less a matter of what I study than of who these interveners consider themselves to be. As Washburne and Derno put it,

> Anytime anyone makes a discursive judgment of "good" or "bad" this is first and foremost a positioning gesture, which serves to construct or reimagine specific modes of subjectivity or to restructure social relationships by asserting deliberate musical agency. . . . The very act of passing an aesthetic judgment assumes and bestows authority upon the judge. By explicitly disaffiliating ourselves with certain forms of music expression, we make a claim for being "in the know" about things, we demonstrate an educated perspective and activate a wide range of underlying assumptions about what is "good." (2004, 3)

On a similar note, Washburne and Derno have observed that professional scholars who ought to know better have played the role of gatekeeper in music scholarship, allowing their personal preferences to prescribe the bounds of their inquiries and contributing to the conventional wisdom in scholarly circles that certain genres of music are without value and unworthy of study (2004, 4–5).

This latter observation, I believe, helps to explain why both American and Egyptian scholars of music continue to produce voluminous books about *musiqa al-ṭarab* and its most famous performers and composers, although few of them bring forth any substantively new information—indeed, many recent Egyptian publications (ʿAbbud 2004; Hashim 2004; al-Jamiʿi 2005; Khashaba 2008) are little more than dated almanacs populated with deceased musicians. But even among the finest published research, there are found only two genres of Egyptian music in quantity: *musiqa al-ṭarab* and rural folk music from the agricultural communities of the Nile Delta and Upper Egypt, the latter a topic of particular interest to Egyptian folklorists. In the last five years, there have appeared a few early efforts at analysis of *shaʿbi,* especially the work of James Grippo (2006, 2007); of *shababiyya,* one finds even less.

What is more, the scant references to *shababiyya* are often less analytical than scornful or, at best, asides to larger (higher-prestige) musical concerns. The entire academic discussion of *shababiyya* consists of a few paragraphs of largely hostile or dismissive prose. At best, scholars have briefly mentioned the genre as background to a discussion of another genre, usually *shaʿbi* (Armbrust 1996, 181) or *musiqa al-ṭarab* (Danielson 1996, 301; Racy 2003, 223). Other scholars, generally through the reported speech of an interlocutor, have referred to the genre in more negative terms, drawing on derogatory tropes of cheapness and shoddiness (Shannon 2006, 37), fast food (Marcus 2007, 161), and pornography (LeVine 2008, 65).

To the extent that these researchers of other musical genres take note of *shababiyya,* they tend to acknowledge its presence as an inferior genre of music, competing not only with *musiqa al-ṭarab* but also, in the case of LeVine's research, with heavy metal and rap. In other words, LeVine regards *shababiyya* as inferior and "inauthentic" (his own oft-repeated term) in comparison to both traditional and contemporary commercial genres that he himself enjoys. In a rare admission among scholars of contemporary Arab music, Shannon touches upon the important point that the sheer volume of the *shababiyya* industry and its audience demands analytical attention, as well as the fact that the musical genre has its consumers even among the Syrian intellectuals who vehemently explained to him that there was no aesthetically redeeming quality to *shababiyya* (2006, 14–15).

Michael Frishkopf has recently acknowledged his own subjective position within Arab musical aesthetics as an analytical hurdle to overcome, and suggested that the over-representation of *musiqa al-ṭarab* in both Western and Arab scholarship reflects "a late Orientalist discourse of the

West adhering to a decline-theory of Arab culture and civilization" (Frishkopf 2010, 15). In blunt terms, this nostalgic obsession with older musical forms is freighted with the politics of nationalist modernity, and whatever the conscious political goals of an interlocutor who lauds the old music and decries the new, such an interlocutor also inflects himself with an Orientalist and, potentially, a neocolonial political stance. The glorious past stands in contrast to the degenerate and decrepit present, which then may be figured as beneath scholarly notice. It is this attitude that I detected years ago when embarking on my own research.[19]

Now that the "Arab Spring"[20] has presented new and explicitly political artists that Western scholars are quick to champion as "authentic" and more interesting than their commercial, mass-mediated competition, I detect the same attitude underlying the words of praise. I do not contest that these new artists are interesting and aesthetically valuable subjects of study; I am certain that such studies will soon appear. I wish for this book, however, to serve another purpose than championing the underground act: I wish for it to explain the massive commercial pop music world against which an artist can be characterized as "underground." In a larger sense, though, I hope to explain consumption of this commercial pop music in and of itself—to hold it up to serious scrutiny, rather than foregrounding some other genre.

Methodologies

My interest in contemporary Egyptian popular music began with a conversation with a colleague at the University of Texas, at a time when I was in the throes of confusion over what on earth I planned to study during my time in graduate school. I had entered the Folklore and Cultural Studies program in the Department of Anthropology knowing only that I was intrigued by the relationship between popular music and nationalism, and I had originally entertained a vague idea of building upon research I had conducted as an undergraduate that had touched upon such a relationship in the United States. I quickly discovered that my heretofore accumulated theoretical knowledge was insufficient for me to explain such a research concept satisfactorily to my fellow students, much less compose a coherent and structurally sound field research grant. The resulting angst from this crisis did not begin to clear until my colleague John Schaefer brought up the name of Umm Kulthum, the late, widely celebrated Egyptian singer, and explained to me that she had been closely tied to Gamal Abdel Nasser's anticolonial nationalist government during her lifetime. My project has proceeded from this starting point.

For reasons of ethnographic affinity as well as theoretical interest in contemporary music, my research developed a focus on the music that has succeeded or, arguably, displaced the repertory of Umm Kulthum—that is, the music to which Egyptians listen now, decades after the great singer's death in 1975. As I shall discuss at length in this chapter, this focus raised some productively provocative questions, not least because many Egyptians consider contemporary popular music of so little artistic value that they could scarcely believe that I wished to treat it as the subject of serious academic inquiry. Were I in their place, I would very likely voice similar incredulity. The great mass of contemporary Egyptian pop music is intensely formulaic, superficial, and uncomplicated; it is commercially produced, commercially driven, and distributed through commercial networks by multinational companies who compete fiercely to wring profits from a saturated market whose profitability perennially hangs in doubt. These economic factors contribute to (but do not fully explain) the superficiality and disposability of many of the pop songs that Cairenes can hear for a day, a week, or a month, until the selections on the radio and music television channels are refreshed to showcase the new flavor of the moment. Some people to whom I explained that my university and the United States government had seen fit to grant me a research fellowship in order to travel to Egypt, live among Egyptians, and study their young people's bubblegum pop plainly believed that I was either a liar or a madman.

And, lest I be mistaken for a fatuous cheerleader for "the music of the people," I will make clear that, in my professional and personal judgment, much of this music is terrible. Many songs fulfill the aesthetic charges launched by some of my interlocutors in harmony with public intellectuals against the contemporary pop music market in Egypt: charges of superficiality, meaninglessness, gratuitous resort to eroticism, and crass pandering to mass-market tastes. I do not see how it could be otherwise, given the conditions of the Arabic-language culture industry's multinational capitalist structure, which reminds me of nothing so much as the intensely corporate country music industry in the United States that operates out of Nashville. Given the Internet-borne destruction in the twenty-first century of the Egyptian music industry's old profit model of retail sales of cassettes, vinyl LPs and CDs, augmented by public concerts, Egyptian music executives are understandably frantic to record and distribute as much music as they can; to the best of my judgment, they believe that they can assess in relatively short order the most popular new releases, direct their marketing resources toward the most promising singers, and discard the market failures while grooming new possibilities. Such a mode of thinking encourages the publication and distribution of a great deal of dross as well as good music, since the only way to test an executive's recruiting instincts is to release a song (in both video and audio formats) and wait for consumers to react.

At the same time, I hold far more respect for the output of some active musicians in Cairo than many of their compatriots, and I do not subscribe to the idea, which I shall discuss at length in chapter 1, that everything produced nowadays is categorically inferior to what came before. On a purely aesthetic level, I would criticize this attitude simply for assuming the same evaluative parameters for different genres of music, when these genres not only possess but in fact require very distinct sets of evaluative criteria. And, moving beyond aesthetic matters, I will argue throughout this book that how a Cairene perceives the relative value of a song has much to do with his or her generation in Egyptian society, and thus with the particular societal concerns that are likely to weigh upon the listener.

While some very fine ethnographies examining various aspects of popular music have emerged in recent years, they have mostly concentrated their analyses on the production of music, as a mass-market phenomenon (Yano 2002; Wallach 2008; White 2008), as a smaller-scale craft industry within the larger industrial complex (Racy 2003), or even on the amateur and semiprofessional level that often intersects with but does not equal culture-industrial production (Fox 2004a). Since my interest lay chiefly not with production but with what Skinner describes as "the mutually constitutive nexus of subjectivity and expressive culture" (2009, 14), I felt obliged to depart from these more common—and, it must be said, easier—forms of ethnographic praxis in order to deal more programmatically with everyday consumption during my initial research period. Relatively few ethnographic endeavors that pursue anthropology of music or popular culture have engaged deeply with the consumption end of the spectrum; those that do, such as Marc Schade-Poulsen's work on *raï* (1999), have illustrated the difficulty of such an endeavor. In Schade-Poulsen's case, the mundane practical difficulties of long-term "deep hanging out" were unexpectedly and drastically complicated by the outbreak of a civil war in Algeria, but it is clear from his book that the work was never simple to undertake. As in any ethnographic project, it can take a great deal of time before interlocutors feel sufficiently comfortable with the researcher to discuss personal thoughts or politically sensitive issues. In addition, the ephemerality of much of popular culture and people's reactions thereto necessitate an especially sharp awareness of the moments when such ideas make themselves known—unlike, say, relatively constant concerns such as kinship relations or economic networks. Moreover, because many (although certainly not all) people rarely give any conscious, coherent thought to the nature of their engagement with popular music, directly soliciting comments on such topics often yields stilted, empty phrases that mean little to the speaker and less to the listener.

In order to focus my research on the consumption of pop music in Cairo, I chose to seek out the opinions and analyses primarily of ordinary youthful listeners throughout the city, with relatively little input from performers and industry professionals. This allowed me not only to emphasize the words of consumers whose thoughts on cultural matters are rarely heard in a public forum but also to shape my pursuit of well-known performers to follow up on the preponderance of consumers' interests and suggestions of whom was most worthy of close study. I spent many hours engaged in the classic ethnographic technique of hanging out in coffeehouses, at concerts, and on the street, engaging youthful Cairenes in conversation about the music we encountered either as conscious listeners or as passive recipients of ambient music in commercial spaces. This method led to my closest friendships and some rich sources of interlocutory data; however, this catch-as-catch-can method did not yield as deep or broad a pool of data as I desired, and once I acquired the proper intermediaries, I began to supplement hanging out with formal interviews of college students—a huge and readily available pool of youth. Later on in my doctoral research, I also collected a number of interviews with youth affiliated not with a university but with a church: as it happened, one of my academic contacts was also a member of the close-knit Protestant community of Egypt, and arranged for my access to the membership of the youth group at her local church.[21] Since it was unthinkable simply to run into well-known music professionals in an informal setting and strike up a conversation, most of my conversations with them also took the form of formal interviews.

Middle-Class Youth

The majority of the people I sought out during my doctoral research were between the ages of eighteen and thirty, which covers most of the age range that contemporary Cairenes regard as the period of "youth" that follows childhood. I have heard different numbers from various interlocutors, but most Cairenes I consulted opined that one's youth begins at the age of fourteen or fifteen. As a practical matter, the tacit consensus I gathered from conversations is that the period of youth begins approximately near the end of puberty, when one has visibly developed secondary sexual characteristics but does not look at all full-grown. "Youth" in this sense resembles the English usage of "adolescence," but with the additional implication of the time of life in which one is old enough to marry but probably has not yet done so.[22] For reasons that I shall discuss, they were considerably less certain about the end of youthfulness.

I originally theorized this classification rather thinly, as I now recognize. My initial plan was simply to focus on that segment of the population that had money and opportunity to enjoy the occasional luxury purchase—a cassette, a compact disc, or, for the wealthier ones, a concert ticket—and did not yet have pressing need to conserve their financial resources for more elemental or existential concerns. From what I had gleaned of *shababiyya* video clips and their attendant advertisements before beginning my field research, the target market was just this age range. I was more right than I realized at first, but not because the corporate music industry is so laser-focused on young people as I had imagined. Rather, Cairenes associate this age range with selfishness, immediate personal gratification, social instability, and potentially destructive sexuality—social dangers that can only be brought to heel by marrying and becoming a fully recognized adult. Such instability is inherent in any given youth—both male and female—in this perspective, but it is exacerbated by socioeconomic pressures that prevent the stabilization that marriage provides. This anxiety about the destabilizing effects of adolescence is hardly unique to Egypt, especially when a large proportion of a country's population is not only youthful but, as is the case in many Arab League states, unemployed with few prospects of acquiring gainful employment.

Similar anxieties about uncontrolled adolescents in large numbers have been documented in various parts of the Arab world (Alt and Fairfield

2008) and far beyond. Notably, Jennifer Cole has written about the ambivalent sense of admiration and anxiety that the Malagasy community of Tamatave, Madagascar, feels about such youth, mostly in terms of young men and especially in regard to the lingering uneasiness occasioned by long-term unemployment or underemployment of such men, who are raised to hope and expect that they will go to work and quickly amass the necessary capital to establish themselves as independent economic entities, rather than wage laborers. As Cole makes clear, the residents of Tamatave believe that the egotism and irresponsibility of young men will not cease until they marry, establish (ideally) a virilocal residence, and settle into a household economy. In the full Malagasy ideal, the man works outside the home and entrusts his entire income to his housebound wife, who will spend the money shrewdly (and soberly) on necessary household expenses and long-term property investments (Jennifer Cole 2005, 893–97). Similar concerns have been documented in many parts of sub-Saharan Africa as well as the Arab world, since, as in Egypt, many African societies accord social status largely on the basis of age (Chabal and Daloz 1999, 34) and, more to the point, age-related positions within a variety of economic and kinship networks (Jennifer Cole 2011, 60–61).

Although wage labor is not of itself cause for concern among Cairenes, there is a parallel expectation that a young man will somehow amass the necessary economic resources and possessions to prove himself a trustworthy marital prospect in the eyes of a prospective bride and her family. Chief among these resources is a virilocal[23] residence of his own, neither a rented property nor his parents' home; a new bride often lives in dread of her mother-in-law, and her parents are often anxious to ensure that their daughter will not be tied to either a domineering in-law or an impoverished man who cannot afford to provide for his family by himself. The youth's parents may well contribute to the acquisition of his home, however: Cairenes of all classes commonly save up for years in anticipation of this expense for their children, and many of modest means who live in "popular neighborhoods"[24] slowly build additional stories onto their apartment buildings to furnish a son with a self-contained flat of his own with the added benefit of proximity to his natal household.

The other resources to which the young man must lay claim generally depend on the socioeconomic class and attendant aspirations of each family involved in formalizing the marriage. Every Cairene I consulted on the matter averred that the bride's family usually makes or breaks these negotiations, since the bride's family frequently contributes to the household in the form of a trousseau, as well as to the substantial costs of the parties that the middle and upper classes expect to throw in celebration. Less affluent middle-class families may ask for a small residence with relatively austere household furnishings—a new refrigerator, television, and other such appliances—while wealthier families may bring extensive expectations of material wealth to the table, such as an expansive flat in a fashionable neighborhood and a car to guarantee the couple's mobility independent of Cairo's efficient but uncomfortably crowded mass transportation networks. As a matter of social prestige, everyone hopes to throw the most lavish parties that their finances can bear, not once but twice: it is now fashionable in Cairo to throw a party to celebrate the signing of the *khuṭuba* (formal engagement) as well as to celebrate the wedding ceremony itself. Among the wealthy, the *khuṭuba* party can be every bit as elaborate and ostentatious as the wedding festivities.

Even with the considerable financial assistance of both bride and groom's families, these costs frequently constitute an enormous burden on the prospective groom. Unless he comes from a truly wealthy family in which income and livelihood are not matters of concern, the young man expects to work for at least two or three years with the primary goal of putting aside the necessary funds to make such purchases. Many men, as I heard over and over during my doctoral research, resigned themselves to working toward this goal throughout their twenties and thirties, since their meager salaries would not permit them to marry any sooner.

To attempt to differentiate the inhabitants of Cairo into the classical Marxian social classes is to some degree an exercise in frustration, since the terms "working class" and "middle class" that have become commonplace in Western social science do not easily align with the sources of income, the relative cultural capital, or the political power associated with various socioeconomic positions in Cairo. Indeed, the word "poor" is itself insufficient to explain the distinctions within a large swath of the population that an outside observer from a wealthier industrialized nation of the Global North may well qualify as such, including many people employed in ostensibly white-collar professions. Cairenes of my acquaintance are generally much more inclined to make socioeconomic differentiations with a suite of terms that connote degrees of cultural capital, rather than degrees of access to wealth and power. It is important to recognize that these terms are not euphemisms for Marxian classes; rather, they cross-cut economic positions and only irregularly imply rather than describe them. The terms they employed are as follows.

Baladi

This term literally denotes someone or something from the countryside. It is also common in Cairo to use the word with the connotation of "autochthonous," in the way that my language tutor, Yaḥya, a native of Alexandria, referred to that city as his *balad.* It is deployed by Cairenes in several ways to connote qualities both positive and negative. To call a person *ibn al-balad* or *bint al-balad* is generally a term of approval, referring to his or her perceived loyalty to country or hometown, and qualities such as honesty, humility, and piety that Cairenes associate more with rural Egypt than with the capital city.[25] The derived adjective *baladi*, however, is deeply derogatory when applied to a person, connoting crassness, vulgarity, ignorance, and, counterintuitively, even low moral character.[26] In sum, this term refers to those whom Cairenes deem uneducated and culturally unsophisticated, for better and for worse. Another term often used to describe members of this social class without the same derogatory flavor is the Egyptian Colloquial Arabic (ECA) word *ma'allim/a* (el-Messiri 1982, 526). This word, whose Modern Standard Arabic (MSA) variant means "teacher," is used in ECA to connote men but especially women who wear traditional dress and work at various menial trades or as street vendors, and whose language and comportment could be described less charitably as *baladi.*

Sha'bi

This term literally means "of the people," and therefore can have positive connotations of "something for everyone." However, in regard to music, as noted above, this term refers to a genre of music that, although it is indeed listening fare for a broad cross-class swath of Cairenes, carries resonances of low education and the cultural environment of the menial laboring poor. (And it is from this class that most performers in the genre appear to come.) More by vocal inflection than by any firm meaning of the word, Cairenes sometimes use this word as a term of derogation toward behavior or expressive culture that they regard as a sign of poor education, coarse manners, and a near-opposite of *muthaqqaf*. In essence, although

Cairenes with a political investment in the masses—such as Muḥammad Munir or politicians playing to the crowd—valorize the *sha'b* (the people) in various ways, most Cairenes of my acquaintance are just as likely to use the word in a dismissive, condescending way.

Mutawasiṭ

Literally, "middle," and the only term I heard with any frequency that specifically indexes economic standing rather than cultural capital. Depending on the speaker, this designation can encompass a wide range of Cairo's economic strata, and may be applied to anyone from the impoverished ranks of state bureaucratic functionaries as well as to people in possession of the economic means associated in Western social science with the middle classes.[27] To be *mutawasiṭ* is not quite as anxious a social position as the Western middle class / bourgeoisie, since only some of the middle classes have a real chance to rise in status, but anxieties certainly remain in regard to falling in status either economically or socially. Virtually all Cairenes with some investment in being or becoming *mutawasiṭ* anxiously examine their own behavior for traces of *baladi* or *sha'bi* qualities. This is often less a question of rising in social rank within a single generation than of cultivating a future rise through an advantageous marriage of one's children.

Muthaqqaf

This term, which literally means "cultured," speaks plainly to the desire for cultural literacy and social sophistication. While sometimes used to refer broadly to the upper classes, who have access to both good formal education and elite socialization environments, it is more often used to refer to anyone perceived to demonstrate profound formal education, sophistication, cultural capital, or fine interpersonal manners. Cairenes frequently seize upon the English word "polite" when searching for an equivalent to the ECA term—likely because of the implicit relationship between being *muthaqqaf* and being *mu'addab* (possessing fine manners). In the common parlance of Cairenes, all of these qualities are interlinked, and therefore evidence of one such quality is taken to imply the presence of the others as well. While Cairenes assume that members of the upper classes will be *muthaqqaf* in affect, it is not only possible but strongly encouraged for members of the middle classes as well. I have yet to hear the word applied to anyone from the lower classes of Cairo; *muthaqqaf* is, in Cairene cultural understanding, the diametric opposite of *baladi.*

Every *mutawasiṭ* Cairene of my acquaintance strove to be *muthaqqaf,* but they generally took care to avoid overdoing the overt display of their cultural sophistication. To be *mutawasiṭ* with fine manners and advanced education is highly desirable; however, to be a member of the middle classes who flaunts knowledge of foreign languages among other Egyptians of lesser status or goes out of one's way to showcase one's personal acquaintance with foreign customs and cosmopolitan cultural knowledge is crass.[28] A common way of committing such a *faux pas* is to claim, gratuitously or not, that one cannot recall a particular word in Arabic, having grown accustomed to using its equivalent in English or French; in both real life and in cinematic depictions thereof, such behavior is a perennial cause for scorn.

Although I spoke with and interviewed a number of people on various rungs of Cairo's socioeconomic hierarchy, my research can be fairly characterized as focusing on the middle classes of the city, and perhaps leaning toward the more financially secure and socially aspirant segment of that broad designation—the *mutawasiṭin* and the *muthaqqafin* (the plural form in each case). Few of the people with whom I came into contact came from wealthy families, and those who did were generally students at the American University in Cairo; my research affiliation with the university library and my language lessons with a tutor who worked in the university's adult education division guaranteed that I became acquainted with a number of AUC students and faculty. The largest single group of my interlocutors were students enrolled at the Faculty of Music Education at Helwan University, and these students appeared to range considerably in socioeconomic status.[29] Indeed, I was puzzled by the attraction of a career in music education or performance—hardly a growth industry, much less a stable source of employment—to students of modest means when the unemployment rate for Egyptians aged 15–29 hovered at 27 percent (Alt and Fairfield 2008). I wondered aloud to the dean of the faculty why students worried about earning a living would opt for such a career track, and she compared it to the tens of thousands majoring in commerce at any given moment in Egypt's public universities who did not seriously expect to find employment after graduation. "It's free. What good would it do them to just sit at home all day? Nothing comes from nothing." Better to obtain a state-subsidized degree in *something,* she reasoned, than to take one's chances on the labor market with no higher education.

Revolutionary Serendipity

My second research period took a significantly different form from the first. I had been awarded a postdoctoral research fellowship to go back to Cairo, and the grant imposed the condition that all of my research had to be archival in nature: ethnographic research was strictly prohibited.[30] Ethnography is a complex and multifarious intellectual endeavor, one whose nuances the average authoritarian governmental censor is ill-equipped to comprehend. It became apparent that "ethnography," as the Ministry of the Interior understood the matter, primarily meant the distribution of survey questionnaires. Behind the prohibition, of course, lay the fear of a foreign national in some way stirring up or giving voice to political opposition or in some way demeaning or criticizing the state too directly.

I was not happy with this situation, since I strongly suspected (and eventually confirmed) that there was no significant material of any interest to me in any archived form. I chafed under this restriction—I had hoped to win a less constrained form of research grant—but as a matter of professional ethics, I felt constrained to obey the rule to the letter, if not the spirit. Ethnography, after all, includes all manner of informal interviews, and in a sense every interpersonal interaction is part of this enterprise. It would have been madness to insist that anyone, foreign national or not, spend eight months living in Cairo without speaking with anyone. More formal ethnographic interviews were not a practical option: if it were to come to the attention of the Ministry of the Interior that I were conducting anything it recognized as ethnography, the consequences I would have faced would have been trivial in comparison to those faced by my Egyptian interlocutors. I resolved to treat the fellowship primarily as a writing grant, and supplement that with whatever music-related conversations came my way in the course of my daily activities.

Three months into my fellowship, the 2011 Egyptian revolution began, and threw my research into upheaval, much as it did everything else in Cairo. A week into the uprising, I began to worry seriously that the city would degenerate into an urban war zone, as the masses grew increasingly vocal and angry, and the regime responded with increasing violence and outright threats of mass destruction of its own populace.

Due to a combination of the potential for large-scale political violence and the realization that I would be entirely cut off from contacting my friends and family back home if anything catastrophic occurred, I reluctantly decided to evacuate temporarily. I took a flight from Cairo to the Republic of Cyprus, ostensibly a "vacation" on the customs forms, and spent a month in Nicosia, monitoring the situation via Internet, telephone, and television.

A month after I left Cairo, I flew back to resume my research in a very different political and social landscape. Hosni Mubarak had been deposed by his own military establishment, which was now charged (or had charged itself) with organizing a post-Mubarak governmental structure. Egyptians, who had developed a stereotyped reputation even among scholars as being so tolerant and accepting of structural misery that they would never revolt against a leader, had demonstrated that this was untrue, and that they could and would rebel *en masse* against their ruler if they considered the regime fundamentally unjust. The atmosphere was a mixture of optimism, fear, and anger: Egyptians in my experience have always been optimistic people, so what stood out to me was the degree to which they now felt comfortable expressing their fear and anger aloud to a curious foreigner with a notebook. I had heard such things before, but usually from close friends, and always spoken in hushed tones. Cairenes suddenly felt free to say out loud what they thought.

I took stock of the situation, and decided that, although I forced myself to obey the letter of the law before the revolution, it would not be reasonable to do so now.[31] Practically speaking, almost the entirety of the highest echelon of the government that had imposed those restrictions on my fellowship by then sat in jail awaiting trial. The structure of the security state at large was in tatters, and there were so many immediate concerns to address that, I felt certain, no one would be interested in the doings of an anthropologist studying popular music. Moreover, upon making some discreet inquiries, I discovered that my colleagues and acquaintances were, for the most part, eager to speak with me. Their polite reticence, and reluctance to speak at length about sensitive topics with the foreign researcher, had vanished, and in its place I now found a powerful desire to speak openly about politics and social thought—no matter what the putative topic of conversation might be. People wanted to speak on record, to be heard and recorded, to give voice to everything that they had earlier feared to say. It was a heady change of pace for an ethnographer accustomed to gingerly and slowly drawing out complex thoughts from people who preferred to speak in polite vagaries. I concluded that the revolutionary context demanded more active ethnography than I had sought before, and proceeded on this basis throughout the rest of my fellowship.

The chapters of this book each focus on a major component of how the contemporary youth generation of Cairo comes to its engagement with the popular music industry, primarily its *shababiyya* output. This requires a broad-based approach to encompass the fundamentals of some elements that may strike some readers as disparate and unrelated; other readers more immersed in the specifics of these elements may judge this approach dilettantish. I have made such editorial decisions as I felt necessary to cover the essentials of the discussion without getting the reader bogged down in excessive detail. I do not apologize for my choice, but I recognize readily that there are other approaches that one might take. I have done my best to alert the reader to these alternative approaches and to the authors who have pursued them.

Chapter 1 tracks the parallel histories of the Egyptian state and the Egyptian culture industry, particularly since 1952 when a nationalist military junta overthrew King Farouk and established the republic. This history provides the necessary background to explain the ways in which the musical icons of Egyptian national modernity have aged poorly in the eyes of contemporary youth. The only *musiqa al-ṭarab* singer who seems to have maintained an active fan base among the current youth generation is 'Abd al-Ḥalim Ḥafiẓ and, as I discuss in this chapter, 'Abd al-Ḥalim can be credited (or blamed) for a decades-long trend in Egyptian popular music toward a more directly seductive form of emotional engagement with the listener, predicated on the ever-increasing use of technological mediation in the music industry. Such reliance on technological mediation has contributed to an increasing suspicion of artifice among older music listeners, even as it has contributed to an increasing assumption of authenticity among younger listeners.

Chapter 2 is devoted to an examination of the archetypal ideas of sexuality and race that shape Cairene perspectives on musical talent and ethnicity. The identity complex of Egyptianness is shot through with self-consciousness about proper gendered behavior just as much as it is infused with racial or quasi-racial ideas of difference between the inhabitants of the Nile Valley and other peoples of the Arabic-speaking world. Moreover, Egyptians often point to musical acumen as an inherently Egyptian quality;

this perception seems to have held more constantly through the last few centuries than Egyptian beauty standards, which have shifted radically over the last hundred years. The result of this cocktail of influences, as I describe, is a racialized and gendered understanding of who and what qualifies as a good Egyptian, and as a good singer of pop music.

Chapter 3 examines the taxonomies that Cairenes apply, however haphazardly and inconsistently, to the aesthetic components of their own identities in concert with the aesthetics of popular music. Taxonomic systems present difficulties to researchers who place too much faith in their objective reality, and I have accordingly striven to demonstrate how these taxonomies operate while creating inconsistencies of their own. An examination of these taxonomies and their aesthetic criteria, however slippery, reveals a gradual change over decades of the kinds of political rhetoric that can appeal successfully to the contemporary youth generation of Cairo, since the aesthetic criteria in each field overlap each other.

Chapter 4 applies the ideas discussed in these earlier chapters to the output of the commercial music industry up until the January 25 revolution, and the ways in which consumers reacted to such productions. I begin with an anecdote that illustrates the morose atmosphere of Cairo in early January 2011, and underscores the way that Cairenes, and perhaps especially Cairene youth, tend to express political sentiments in aesthetic terms. I proceed to explain the music created by both major commercial recording artists and lower-profile musical acts popular primarily within Cairo in response to the protests and, eventually, to Mubarak's ouster. As I discuss, the large commercial acts tended to focus upon memorializing the people killed during the initial uprising; this focus created an aesthetic incoherence that audiences soon found unsatisfying. But even the more explicitly pro-revolutionary musical acts tended to focus upon the actions and paraphernalia of the protests themselves, rather than the larger political grievances that brought people out into the streets.

Chapter 4 is the last chapter based primarily on my field research, but of course much has happened since then that readers may expect me to integrate into my work. Following that chapter, I have included an epilogue dealing with events following 2011, up to August 2013. I have tried insofar as I feel professionally able to explain these more recent events in terms of my field research and analysis. Accordingly, I have dealt with such events at a nationwide level, rather than the localized view of a field researcher in Cairo, and I acknowledge a degree of speculation in my conclusions.

1

"My Patience Is Short"

Youth Talk about Grandpa's Music

Historical Background

Egyptian political movements and philosophies over the past hundred years are weighty subjects in their own right, and have been widely analyzed. It would be foolhardy to tackle them in their entirety here. It is necessary, however, to gloss several major developments of the last half-century in order to elucidate how politics and popular culture have moved along somewhat parallel tracks.

In 1952, amid rising public discontent with the corruption and ineffectual governance of King Farouk, Egypt's monarchy was overthrown in a coup orchestrated by a group of dissident junior officers known as the Free Officers. The Free Officers set up a military junta called the Command Council of the Revolution (CCR); this council was at first informally guided and then, as of 1954, headed entirely by Gamal Abdel Nasser. Nasser promulgated a number of sweeping social and economic changes based on his interpretation of socialism, such as nationalization of foreign-owned businesses up to and including the Suez Canal, redistribution of agricultural lands to disempower the *ancien régime* aristocracy and alleviate the poverty of the peasantry, and reorganization of higher education as free and open to all, rather than a privileged elite. He maintained broad popularity with his socialist reworking of national economic policy, as well as his image as an anti-imperialist leader who successfully stood up to the great Western powers of Europe and the United States, and an Arab nationalist who led the Arab world in challenging the State of Israel. It was during this period of Nasser's rule that the Egyptian culture industry produced many of the songs and films now fondly remembered by the old and seldom recalled by the young: songs and films performed and headlined, respectively, by such newcomers to the scene as 'Abd al-Ḥalim Ḥafiẓ, Shadiyya, and Su'ad Ḥusni, as well as established artists such as Umm Kulthum and Muḥammad 'Abd al-Wahhab.

The one major loss that Nasser suffered in his political career was Egypt's defeat in the 1967 War,[1] which he famously euphemized as *al-naksa,* "the setback." In 1967, after months of escalating tensions and saber-rattling between Israel and its Arab neighbors, Israel attacked Egypt, Syria, and Jordan, all of which had massed armies along their borders with Israel, including expeditionary troops from many other Arab countries. Egypt led the Arab military coalition, amid boastful claims from Nasser before the fighting began that they would destroy Israel and reclaim Palestine in a matter of days. Instead, Israel surprised the coalition by swiftly destroying Egypt's air force on the ground, and then pushing back the Arab armies on all fronts as Israel occupied Syria's Golan Heights, the Palestinian-dominated West Bank territory (under Jordanian administration at that time), and Egypt's Sinai Peninsula. The outcome was such a serious blow to Egyptian military and diplomatic power that the government did not at first permit full reports of the severity of the defeat to reach the public (Vatikiotis 1991, 409). Despite this nationally humiliating loss, Nasser continued to rule as a military dictator until his death in 1970.

The Nasser era represents to contemporary students of history the zenith of pan-Arab nationalism, the time when the governments (and, no less importantly, the populations) of Arabic-speaking countries seemed most inclined to cooperate on economic and political issues. The 1967 War, by many people's reckonings, sounded the death knell for this political philosophy, but this perception is as much myth as analysis, in ways both positive and negative. While the combined Arab armies' defeat in 1967 exposed their weakness relative to the Israeli Defense Forces, it did not scatter all thoughts of Arab collaboration to the winds. Egyptian historiographers frequently prefer to view 1967 through the lens of the 1973 War, when another combined Arab military force led by Egypt—this time led by Nasser's successor, Anwar Sadat—confronted Israel and made some temporary gains, most notably the crossing of the Bar-Lev defensive line into the Sinai Peninsula.

The progress of the 1973 War is one of those historical incidents that have come to mean very different things, depending upon whom one consults. For Egyptians, 1973 is an unmitigated victory, a demonstration that Arab unity and careful preparation could achieve military success and glory; Cairo boasts a museum entirely dedicated to representing the planning and execution of "the miracle of the crossing." For Westerners who visit this museum, however, the claims of victory can sound, to say the least, unrealistic: the museum's curators devote no space to acknowledging how the war ended. Westerners tend to recall the 1973 War as yet another Israeli victory over Arab forces, since, by the time an armistice was declared, Israel had again pushed back the armies on all fronts, and an Israeli cavalry division had advanced perilously close to Cairo itself. In fact, both stages of the 1973 War were heavily influenced by Cold War politics: the Soviet Union had furnished Egypt with much of its military matériel, and when Israel called for help in response to the initial Arab push, the United States quickly sent its own military supplies (Hourani 1991, 418). Neither Arabs nor Israelis wish to discuss their sources of military aid; such acknowledgments might dampen each side's nationalist narrative of postcolonial "go it alone" autonomy and ethnicized battlefield skill. The authenticity of postcolonial modernity does not reconcile with serving as a geopolitical client state.

The crossing of the Bar-Lev line on the first day of the war is the significant part of the story to Egyptian nationalist historiographers, which confounds Western observers who tend to analyze the meaning of the war in terms of its end results. But Western visitors often miss the point that, by 1973, Egyptians had begun to believe that their military forces were capable of nothing except abject failure. The loss of the Sinai in 1967 had stung badly; 1973's temporary victory was far more palatable to national remembrance than 1967's unrelieved parade of losses. Moreover, since historiographers commonly ascribe Egyptian president Anwar Sadat's political capital, which enabled him to negotiate final peace terms with Israeli prime minister Menachem Begin, to his measured success in planning Egypt's participation in the 1973 War, Egyptians do, in a manner of speaking, read the war in terms of its end results; in Egyptian nationalist historiography, the outcome of the 1973 War is neither the crossing nor the Israeli counterattack, but the Camp David Accords and the return of the Sinai to Egypt.

On the other hand, a glance at the political spectrum of the Arab world before 1967 hardly looks like political unity: it was an assortment of monarchies, dictatorships, and democratic republics with drastically different economic needs and political aims. Nasser, the architect of postcolonial Arab nationalism as national policy, did not mean for these disparate Arab governments simply to shake hands and declare a vague sense of common purpose; he also meant for them to follow Egypt's lead—literally so, in the case of the short-lived merger of Egypt and Syria in the United Arab Republic (Jankowski 2001, 115–36)—by overthrowing the monarchies and replacing them with "Arab socialist" republics dedicated to a program of industrial modernization (Hourani 1991, 405–12). And, whether by intent or simply as a matter of pragmatism, the Arab nationalist regimes with which Nasser maintained the warmest relations were run by military dictatorships or military oligarchies.

Even decades before the 1952 revolution that put a military junta in power, the Egyptian Armed Forces occupied a special place in the minds of Egyptian historiographers and the socioeconomic elite that tended to produce them. This historiographic tendency emerged in the early twentieth century, when Egyptian nationalist historians and intellectuals began to fix upon the nineteenth-century ruler Muḥammad ʻAli as the progenitor of Egyptian national modernity. These historians generally sought to justify and even glorify Muḥammad ʻAli's infrastructural modernization projects and especially his founding of a tightly disciplined military as fundamental steps toward Egypt's eventual destiny as an independent nation-state. Nearly all of these historians regard every industrial, social, and political reform as stemming from the creation of Muḥammad ʻAli's personal army, all in support of the nationalist goal of making Egypt an independent and prosperous political entity.[2]

One such historian, Mohammed Rifaat, acknowledged the incongruity of a conservative, hierarchical instrument of state power serving to advance progress and reform, but judged it a necessary expedient in a state of incomplete civilization—meaning, apparently, industrialization and bureaucratic centralization. Rifaat wrote: "It is understandable that in modern civilised states many reforms should emanate from the people and for the people. But in semi-civilised states, progress cannot emanate from the masses. They have to be tutored" (Rifaat 1947, 47). The military, as the most "modern" institution in a country whose ruler sought to emulate European modernity, seemed the natural engine for further modernization. Several decades later, another generation of historians tended to perceive Gamal Abdel Nasser as following in the footsteps of Muḥammad ʻAli, for good and for ill. These historians also tend to perceive the military as the master symbol of Egyptian modernity, the thing that personifies and defines national modernity (Gilman 2005, 72–77).

This understanding of history echoes in public discourse about the military's role in politics to this day. Hosni Mubarak rose to power through his affiliation with the military regime[3] created by Nasser, and maintained his power partly through a dense network of military and security personnel who shared not only his political vision but also the spoils of corruption that have become commonplace for the upper echelons of the Egyptian armed forces (Sayigh 2012, 4–7). Despite this fact, Egyptians of my acquaintance were inclined to fault Mubarak personally as the proverbial bad apple, rather than blame the system that spawned Mubarak. In similar fashion, people were elated when, following Mubarak's ouster, the Supreme Council of the Armed Forces (SCAF) convened to rule the country as a transitional authority, citing the military's concern for Egypt's welfare as its paramount motivation.

The idea that the membership of SCAF held views about governance fundamentally identical to Mubarak's own was rarely mentioned aloud in the early months of SCAF's rule; much as I had only heard critiques of Mubarak before the revolution as whispered jokes in taxis or private rooms, I only heard grumblings about the continuity between Mubarak and SCAF in the same circumstances. It was not until after I left Egypt in the middle of 2011 that people began to fault SCAF openly for mismanaging the transition. Even then, the critiques generally focused upon SCAF's authoritarianism[4] and willingness to resort to violence to maintain order, rather than on the conflict of interest inherent in a group of military-industrial oligarchs overseeing a transition to democracy and (as supporters of the revolution hoped) greater political transparency. When the military seized power once again in July 2013, the majority of Egyptians at least tacitly supported its efforts to suppress the Muslim Brotherhood, often citing the idea of the military as the ultimate guarantor of the country's general welfare.

The disjuncture between what Nasser had envisioned and what came to pass—even by the time of his death, let alone in the subsequent decades—is so vast that the Egyptian novelist Ahdaf Soueif has played upon it to imagine the leader in his last years as a tragic figure, "suspecting, maybe, but refusing to believe that his glorious dream had been aborted, that what he had thought of as a prelude was really all there was to be" (Soueif 1992, 357). It would perhaps, then, come as dolorous but not totally shocking to Nasser's ghost to know that contemporary youth in Cairo (and elsewhere in Egypt) are often strongly critical of his regime and its associated political philosophy, when they privilege in discourse the perceived rise of divisive sectarianism. A few of them declared themselves to me as actual monarchists—albeit, in this context, more nostalgic fantasists than reactionary political agitators. Sami and Ragab, two highly educated and by no means conservative young men[5] whom I knew through my association with the American University in Cairo, once explained to me over lunch that, in their view, Egypt as a whole was in better shape under King Farouk than under the military junta that deposed him. Sami in particular waxed nostalgic while describing the elegant, cosmopolitan, late-colonial world that he sees in this historical era; his emphasis fell primarily upon his impression of that era's economic opportunity and stability, and upon his impression that the prerevolutionary period marked the last gasp of a happily multireligious Egyptian civil society. Ragab spoke in more measured, qualified terms than did Sami in his estimation of Farouk's era—Ragab is a student of postcolonial theory who reads history more critically than does his friend—but he essentially echoed much of Sami's critiques of the succeeding republic over our plates of *shakshuka* and Alexandrian-style liver.

The monarchist or quasi-monarchist critique that Sami and Ragab mounted against the postrevolutionary Egyptian state is a minority point of view, to be sure, but I consider it significant that such people—educated young men from the nonaristocratic contemporary middle classes of Cairo—would offer such a critique in 2007. By contrast, the disenfranchised and disinherited aristocracy of Egypt, which saw its power and wealth sharply diminished by the CCR's policies, has never made a secret of its contempt for Nasser. But, as Joel Gordon (2000, 167) has mentioned, even those persecuted and jailed by Gamal Abdel Nasser's regime later recalled his era with a degree of nostalgia, or at least affection; Nasser has been associated more closely with Arab nationalism and a general sense of national renewal than with socialist economic policy, in Egyptian historiography. The historiographers most critical of Nasser had to tread lightly in their commentaries, since an overly harsh critique could indict his successors' regimes as well; the playwright and public intellectual Tawfiq al-Ḥakim managed to write a scathing analysis (al-Ḥakim 1985) of the Nasser regime's disastrous military overconfidence without once criticizing Nasser by name.

It is difficult to imagine, even ten years before this conversation took place, that educated youth could read the Nasser era so negatively that they declared the disgraced and deposed monarch as the superior ruler of Egypt. But Sami and Ragab do not stand as spokesmen for their entire generation. The two young men critiqued Nasser and his rule from a very particular historical vantage point that privileged two forms of nostalgic fantasy for the late colonial era: the idea that all inhabitants of Cairo lived a graceful lifestyle under King Farouk, and the twinned idea that sectarianism in Egyptian society emerged subsequent to and in reaction to Nasser's social and economic policies. In their view, the worst problems that had come to trouble their country stemmed from policies that Nasser put into effect in sharp distinction to what had come before. This attitude contrasts jarringly with the renewed nostalgia for Nasser and his political ideology that I saw increasingly since the January 25 uprising, to say nothing of its intensification among the political opposition under Muḥammad Mursi's Islamist administration. Since a larger treatment of Nasser and his still-evolving political legacy is beyond the scope of this book, I will observe in passing that Egyptians deploy Nasser's memory in complex ways, depending on the context and their focus on economic policy, anticolonialism, state secularism, military involvement in politics, and myriad other issues. At the time of my conversation with Sami and Ragab, Nasser nostalgia in general was at a relatively low point, unlike the situation that obtained four years later.

If Cairenes are divided in terms of their engagement with Egyptian political history, then they are much more fragmented on the subject of the larger Arab world, and how their country ought to relate to other members thereof. Paralleling the current youth generation's apparent willingness to criticize some of Gamal Abdel Nasser's philosophical principles—and sometimes even his entire governmental program—is the current youth generation's vexed relationship to the concept of Arab nationalism. This principle, one of the fundamental assumptions of Nasser's program, is called into question every day in ways overt and implicit in the words and deeds of young Cairenes.

Just as Cairenes' view of the "Arab nation" has fragmented along national lines, the Arab world has itself indeed fragmented along national lines: although the Arab League now boasts twenty-two member states, there is no longer any pretense that the entire membership shares any consequential political or economic goals.[6] In 2008, regional powers such as Egypt and Saudi Arabia freely snubbed Arab League–sponsored summits when they perceived a potential threat to their national policies;[7] nominally secular regimes such as Egypt and Tunisia distrusted the pan-Islamist and deeply conservative *salafi* missionary work (and its attendant political implications) that Saudi Arabia underwrote; neighboring states with multireligious populations such as Syria and Lebanon or Iraq had to negotiate constant shifting tensions based on which confessional community seemed strongest and most politically influential at any given time; the cash-strapped North African states craved the financial assistance of the oil-rich Gulf states while hoping to dodge the attendant political obligations. The fragmentations within the Arab world that Nasser sought to bridge or mend through Arab nationalism had not only endured into the twenty-first century but in some ways seemed wider than ever.

Young Cairenes recognized the Arab League's posturing for the political theater it was (and is), but it could be a painful process for them to admit how much Egypt's political capital had diminished in recent decades. Their concerns about Egypt's engagement with other Arab states often revolved around the fact that Egypt was neither financially nor politically capable of setting the agenda for the entire Arab world in the way it once had done—indeed, many youths fretted to me that while Mubarak's regime insisted on trying to direct regional politics, it appeared too incompetent or too corrupt to look after domestic matters that struck them as more needful and, at any rate, the government's first responsibility. In terms of political priorities, these young people tend to be far more nationally focused than elder generations: the latter group tended to comment to me about what Egypt ought to do to manage regional political affairs, and rarely acknowledged political, social, or economic problems specific to the state. Young Cairenes' political cynicism toward Arab nationalist sentiment therefore could take their parents' generation as an object as well.

Such generational conflicts extended beyond political concerns, and expressed themselves in economic terms as well. A taxi driver in his fifties picked me up one day when I needed to get from the northwestern tip of Zamalik to my apartment in the neighborhood of Tahrir Square. The route required crawling through dense inner-city traffic, particularly the constantly overcrowded road that abuts the Corniche, the wide pedestrian promenade that runs along much of the Nile as it flows through Cairo. The snarled traffic gave us time to chat, and the view of numerous teenagers hanging out on the Corniche provided him with an anchoring topic of conversation. He pointed to the kids goofing off, strolling around, and checking each other out, and scoffed to me at what he regarded as the shiftlessness of the current youth generation. As a contrast, he described his own youthful bootstrapping. "Long hours, little sleep, I saved my money. I worked hard, you know? I *struggled.* And then I got married. And now I have grown children, and I sent them to college. Sure, it is hard to earn a living nowadays, but so what? You cannot find a job that pays you enough? So take a second job! Life is not easy!" He was convinced, despite my polite advocacy on behalf of Egyptians my own age, that laziness was a worse problem for youth than economic deprivation.

I discussed such economic issues with many people but with no one more than with Yaḥya. As happens often with nonnative ethnographers, the first interlocutor I came to know was my tutor in Egyptian Colloquial Arabic, the thirty-year-old Yaḥya. Yaḥya came from a family of recently urbanized peasants in Alexandria, and thus from neither wealth nor cultural capital; but if his family origins could be described in Cairene terms as *baladi,* then he was rapidly working his way into being *muthaqqaf.* A fine student and a pious Muslim, Yaḥya had excelled in school and earned a place in al-Azhar University, the Islamic institute of higher learning that has drawn religiously minded students to Cairo for over 1,100 years to study the Arabic language. After he graduated, Yaḥya found a position teaching English in the adult education division of the American University in Cairo, and supplemented his salary by tutoring foreigners in Arabic. In his spare time, he was preparing a textbook on teaching English to native Arabic speakers. He had married a few years before but the match had not worked out, and his wife had asked for a divorce. He worked long hours each day, as must a great many Cairenes, but his labor was paying off more than for many others: he was quickly amassing for the second time the requisite funds to put himself forward as a serious candidate for marriage.

Yaḥya was perhaps the best example I came to know of someone rising surefootedly in socioeconomic status—an increasingly rare phenomenon during the years I was in Cairo. Unlike many of his compatriots and age peers, for Yaḥya this was no pipe dream: he managed to save a great deal of money by teaching Arabic to foreigners and English to Egyptians. The latter in particular was so lucrative—I heard fees quoted of LE100 ($17.85) per hour in 2008—that some people I met considered me foolish to spend my time in Egypt on research when I could have been giving English lessons to rich people. Yaḥya's trajectory was founded upon his expertise in the Arabic and English languages, and his devoted practice of Islam, since both are necessary to matriculate to al-Azhar. Al-Azhar is essentially free to Egyptian nationals as a public university, but the entrance requirements are relatively stringent and prospective students must demonstrate facility in various aspects of the deep and difficult Classical Arabic as well as Qur'anic exegesis and other theological topics. Yaḥya is a *ḥafiẓ* (one who has memorized the Qur'an in its entirety) as well a good student of language, and thus acquired a more prestigious public education than most Egyptians can claim. Consequently, he was well positioned to work at another prestigious institution, and to charge relatively high fees for his private tutoring services.

While many of the young working-class and middle-class people I know would like to believe in such ideas, they generally told me that the time when the taxi driver's words rang true has passed, and that even their friends who maintain two jobs to save up marriage money barely keep themselves afloat. "A doctor at a state hospital earns less than LE200[8] a month," lamented a recent graduate of a Faculty of Commerce who was working as a tourism fixer, an omnibus occupation of guide-cum-facilitator common in the Egyptian tourism industry. "Why should he care if you're sick? Unless he ignores his official work and sees private patients on the side for high fees, how will he ever marry?" It is difficult for me to gauge the degree to which class factors into these calculations, since one must consider both the financial means of the prospective marital partners and the socially influenced extravagance of the planned wedding festivities, but the impression that every young person seemed to have of his or her own circumstances—unless they were scions of the oligarchic class—was that even formerly prestigious occupations like medicine and engineering could no longer offer wages commensurate with their social prestige.[9] As the fixer suggested glumly to me, even professionals in these fields had to corrupt the ostensible social mission of their work by servicing the upper class disproportionately, if they wished to earn anything above starvation wages.

Yaḥya was as attentive to his acquisition of cultural capital as he was to his accumulation of marital finances. In tandem with his formal education, he cultivated a fondness for *musiqa al-ṭarab,* especially performances on the *'ud.* His befuddlement at my interest in *al-musiqa al-shababiyya* occasionally shaded into condescension early on in our relationship, although he eventually helped me to comprehend the nuances of particular vocal techniques as well as lyric texts. I often suspected him of overplaying his lack of interest in *shababiyya* to emphasize his rising status, although I did not doubt his love for the *'ud.* He was also well attuned to the fact that he would have to go to some trouble and expense to give his children the best possible education, which he perceived more in terms of socialization to the elite habitus and its attendant taste culture acquisition than of the institutional curriculum.

Yaḥya often discussed with me his plans of getting married and raising a rising middle-class family. When I asked him what professions he hoped his children might enter, he smiled and explained that it truly did not matter, provided that he arranged for them to go to prestigious private schools at which they would be socialized into the economic elite, and develop friendships with children who would grow up to become points of contact in the elite social networks. Although Yaḥya seemed to regard this state of affairs as natural, he also seemed ambivalent about the idea that his own profession commanded little respect in contemporary Egypt; he plainly loved teaching, and savored quoting to me from *Qif li-l-mu'allim,* the Aḥmad Shawqi poem likening a teacher to a prophet. Like other talented and ambitious young men, however, Yaḥya has had to discard the achievement ideology taught to him in childhood, recognizing that economic success and social status would be won more surely by *wasṭa* (connections or influence) than by the virtues of hard work espoused by my taxi driver.

This generational divide in terms of economic optimism and pessimism has now articulated itself in a deeply resonant way: the 2011 revolution that toppled the Mubarak regime, and which was, famously, instigated by the youth of Egypt, rather than by their seniors. Young people marched into the streets and confronted the regime, organized around broad issues of political corruption, poor economic conditions, and lack of political freedom; notably, there was an apparent lack of political ideology uniting these protesters, who included Islamists, leftists, secularists, and every other political stripe. While there was an obvious generational divide between the youthful protesters and the octogenarian Hosni Mubarak, there was also a widespread sense that the established opposition parties and movements—both the powerful Muslim Brotherhood and toothless parties like Tagammu'—were left to catch up with the prosecutors of the revolution.[10] All of my youthful Cairene friends were supportive of the revolution—indeed, some of them participated quite actively, camping out in Tahrir Square and coordinating some protest activity—and nearly every older Cairene with whom I discussed the matter was considerably more ambivalent about challenging the regime directly, if not actually counterrevolutionary. The difference in political outlook was as stark as the difference in musical aesthetics.

Egyptians have sung about politics for decades but public reception of political songs—almost all of which are essentially nationalist paeans—appears ephemeral and dependent on a song's political moment. Umm Kulthum is now remembered as a great Arab nationalist, but few people seem to have much time nowadays for the songs she sang about the Arab nation. The most political song among her evergreen repertory that still commands public attention is in fact a love song, *al-Aṭlal* ("The ruins"), whose lyrical plea, "remove my chains," has been interpreted as a political comment on various situations in the Arab world at different historical moments—anything from a pro-Palestinian song directed against American imperialism to an antirepression song directed against Gamal Abdel Nasser's government (Danielson 1997, 168, 180). Although ʻAbd al-Ḥalim Ḥafiẓ built much of his early career by singing Egyptian nationalist songs commissioned after the 1952 revolution, young people never mention them to me now, and appreciate him strictly as a fine singer of love songs. The *musiqa al-ṭarab* singer most closely associated with Egyptian[11] nationalist songs, Shadiyya, was virtually unknown to my youthful interlocutors, and seems to be forgotten by all except a few old die-hard devotees.[12]

And all of that pertains strictly to *musiqa al-ṭarab*. Within the domain of *shababiyya*, the number of compositions with any political content or implication is statistically insignificant in comparison to the great mass of apolitical pop music. The pop music industry has an obvious and compelling reason to avoid political sentiments in its product: articulating a political stance can alienate as well as attract customers, and the industry wishes to sell its product to as many people in as many forms as possible. Production heads within the *shababiyya* industry constitute a deeply risk-averse group, and usually prefer to repeat a successful formula *ad nauseum* rather than experiment with something untried (Frishkopf 2010, 17–18). In addition, government censorship throughout the Arab world means that a political song, if it seems somehow opposed to the aims of a particular regime, may be banned from the airwaves before it even has a chance to alienate listeners. Of course, a singer or company intent upon publicizing a banned song could simply upload it to an Internet web site, but this maneuver would serve only for publicity purposes, without involving the extensively interlinked revenue streams that music companies have developed to capitalize on the broadcasting of video clips on satellite television channels (Abdel Aziz 2010, 87).

Political expression in *shababiyya* is therefore limited in scope and scale, and more noticeable on the local level than on the transnational level. Muḥammad Munir and Wusṭ al-Balad, both of whom are based in Cairo, can be seen on the satellite channels that broadcast across the Arab world, but their more politically sensitive songs are not to be found there, even (or especially) within Cairo. To hear such songs, one must purchase an album or attend a concert. On an ordinary day, one would be hard-pressed to divine from the songs of such artists featured on the satellite channels that they had any coherent political stance on anything. In ordinary—nonrevolutionary—times, the only clear political stances one might encounter in mass-marketed *shababiyya* are opposition to the American invasion of Iraq (particularly several songs recorded by the Iraqi-born artist Kaẓim al-Sahir), and opposition to Israel's occupation of Palestinian land, about which pop singers occasionally record commissioned songs that seem noticeably different from their usual *oeuvre* in musical style, and tend to feature inferior art direction. In less heady political times, young Egyptians indicated to me that they mostly ignored political pop songs, and regarded the nationalist works of the Golden Age as curios of the past. Indeed, those songs often came across as stilted and unmoving to youth, who felt alienated not only from the musical aesthetics but also from the historical time period that generated such compositions.

The 2011 revolution turned this usual state of affairs on its ear. During the street protests of early February of that year, 'Abd al-Ḥalim's patriotic songs reemerged briefly among the protesters assembled in Tahrir Square, although this did not appear to signal a larger trend. On the radio, a steady stream of patriotic songs played with little regard for time period, segue, or even the nationality of the singer: an old song by Warda al-Jaza'iriyya followed one by Umm Kulthum, and was in turn followed by the *sha'bi* singer Baha' Sulṭan, which was followed by a song newly composed for the revolution. There seemed little pattern or reason to the mix, other than a frantic desire to keep the nationalist content flowing.

The trend intensified once Hosni Mubarak was deposed. On the satellite channels Mazzika and Mazzika Zoom, video clips of apolitical romantic songs were programmed cheek-by-jowl with Egyptian nationalist songs—not only anodyne patriotic odes but songs written for and about the 2011 revolution itself. Videos were bookended by innumerable patriotic intertitles proclaiming statements such as "The people's revolution" and "Long live Egypt," no matter the content of the song that preceded or followed. These videos included both the most exhortatory, like Muḥammad Munir's angry, accusatory song *Izzay* ("How"), and more commercially contrived efforts, like Tamir Ḥusni's baldly pandering song *Shuhada' 25* ("The martyrs of 25"). For a month following Mubarak's fall, the newfound zeal for video clips glorifying Egypt even pushed video programmers to broadcast videos that seemed awkwardly inappropriate, such as a Hayfa' Wahbi video clip about Egypt that concluded with a parade of portraits of famous Egyptians shown alongside the credits—first and foremost, Hosni and Suzanne Mubarak.

Origins of Egypt's Culture Industry

Egypt has dominated the world of Arabic-language popular music and cinema almost since commercial recording media were invented. Through the entrepreneurial efforts of British and German phonograph companies, by 1907 Egyptian shops already were advertising the latest recordings of popular Egyptian singers, produced on the newest available technology: flat discs that would supersede the older cylindrical model of phonographic record (Racy 1976, 25). By the mid-1920s, British Gramophone and its Egyptian counterpart Baidaphon were in competition with each other to record rising stars of Arab music, most of them Egyptians: Umm Kulthum (Figure 1), Muḥammad 'Abd al-Wahhab (Figure 2), Munira al-Mahdiyya, and others (Racy 1976, 42–43). Following closely after the development of the music industry, Egyptian artists began to produce motion pictures in 1909; in 1934, Bank Misr, under the direction of its founder, the Egyptian nationalist financier Ṭal'at Ḥarb, established the first Egyptian film company, Studio Misr (Shafik 1998, 11–12).

The Egyptian culture industries benefited from a number of positive circumstances that made the nascent state fertile ground for the business of entertaining people. First, in comparison to the less densely populated North African states to the west and the geographically compact Levantine and Gulf states to the east, Egypt has a very large population, with an accordingly large pool of native talent upon which to draw. Second, Cairo in the early twentieth century was a multiethnic, religiously diverse city, and a destination for artists and intellectuals from all over the world, many of whom considered themselves Egyptian of foreign derivation. The capi-

FIGURE 1. Umm Kulthum singing in the film *Dananir* (Badrakhan 1940).

tal accordingly had access to a wealth of artistic traditions of expressive culture, synthesized through local practice. Third, theater, and particularly musical theater, was already well established and popular in Egypt, drawing instrumentalists, singers, actors, composers, and playwrights from across the Arab world and the former Ottoman Empire as well as native Egyptians. When motion picture technology arrived, the artists associated with musical theater generally transitioned easily to the new medium (Shafik 1998, 13).

Just as important, though, were political and economic factors in Egyptian society that made Cairo an attractive destination for film and musical artists. First, in the pre-independence period (prior to 1922), the British colonial authorities tended to exercise salutary neglect of popular culture created by the colonized populace;[13] this was not at all the situation in French-colonized lands such as Syria or Algeria, where the colonial authorities did their best to inhibit indigenous popular culture—with its concomitant popular sentiments—from having any voice at all. This laissez-faire attitude toward popular culture gave Egyptian artists a relatively free hand to create music, theater, and film that articulated popular opinions and spoke to local issues and tastes. Second, after independence,

FIGURE 2. Muḥammad ʻAbd al-Wahhab at work in the film *The Flirtation of Girls* (Wagdi 1949), holding a Turkish *cümbüş* which, despite its Western banjo-like appearance, more closely resembles the Eastern *ʻud* in its sound.

as mentioned above, Ṭal'at Ḥarb spearheaded the establishment of Studio Misr; this was no altruistic gift to the nation but a canny act of nationalism-informed investment capitalism—Ḥarb and his associates had examined the industry in other countries, and had concluded that a motion picture studio would make a good investment, in the context of the recently independent state. This meant that, in contrast to other Arab states, there could be a cinema not only filmed and produced but also bankrolled under local auspices, making foreign capital unnecessary to bring Egyptian films to the screen. This factor was strengthened by the opening of another seven movie studios in Egypt in the decade following the founding of Studio Misr. And third, once Egypt became independent, the nationalist government promulgated a thorough policy of Egyptianization of all industries, giving native Egyptians the chance to write, direct, and act in plays and films at a time when, if other Arab lands had a cinema industry at all, they were essentially forbidden from creating anything that resonated familiarly and positively with the local population (Shafik 1998, 12–15).

In a sense, the subsequent history of the popular culture industry in Egypt, as compared to the rest of the Arab world, may be summed up as "they got there first." No other Arab country has anything like the well-developed music and cinema industries that flourish in Egypt, largely for the reasons given earlier for the birth of those industries. Those lands dominated by French colonial authority were, in practical terms, unable to produce anything resembling a distinct indigenous cinema until independence, and those countries beyond France's control generally came to cinema at a much later date than did Egypt. When they had the opportunity to make films free of French oversight, most countries lacked the economic backing necessary to underwrite such an enterprise; the relative handful of films that come out of North African and Eastern Arab countries had to be filmed on a shoestring, with foreign capital, or both, and in either case there has been very little infrastructural support for the endeavor.

In terms of music, the situation is not quite so sparse: in recent years, Lebanon has become a major producer of Arabic pop music. Indeed, Lebanon now produces so much pop music in a distinctive style of rhythm, melody, and, as important as the music itself, visual presentation through its music video clips shown on satellite television, that Egyptians now speak of "the Lebanese singers" to connote the image rather than the nationality. In addition, although it does not command the same international market share or number of fans that Egyptian and perhaps Lebanese pop does, the Algerian pop music genre of *raï* has developed a high profile as indigenous popular music of the Arab world (see Schade-Poulsen 1999).

The Revolution's Nightingale

'Abd al-Ḥalim Isma'il Shabana, known by his stage name of 'Abd al-Ḥalim Ḥafiẓ, belonged to the generation that followed Umm Kulthum's; when he was born, in 1929, the Lady already had been recording under contract for three years. 'Abd al-Ḥalim grew up during the period of Umm Kulthum's early, prerevolutionary successes, and when he began to perform professionally as both a concert singer and cinema actor, he quickly tapped into the same vein of nationalist-inflected popular culture that the older singer was herself learning to mine. The cinematic quality of 'Abd al-Ḥalim Ḥafiẓ's public image is reflected in his nickname, "the Dark Nightingale" *(al-'andalib al-asmar)*; unlike most big musical stars, his persona was marked by a particularly visible, physical quality as well as a vocal style. And indeed, the iconic image of 'Abd al-Ḥalim Ḥafiẓ in performance is not, as with many stars, on a stage but on a screen: the singer starred in a number of films in the 1950s and 1960s. Much like Elvis Presley, 'Abd al-Ḥalim presented many of his romantic songs within the context of his filmic performances, singing them in character, often to a physically present addressee. And, again like Elvis, 'Abd al-Ḥalim maintains his musical and sensual hold over his fans decades after his death.

'Abd al-Ḥalim Ḥafiẓ built his musical and cinematic career at the same time that Nasser and the CCR were reshaping Egyptian state and society, and the singer gladly participated in the new nationalist project. Culture critics of the time, however, were perturbed by 'Abd al-Ḥalim's approach to emotional evocation in music, a seductively direct approach that put him at odds with the older preferred aesthetic technique of more oblique hints of emotionality. As with Elvis, 'Abd al-Ḥalim starred in a number of films produced as vehicles for his singing and, although the Egyptian never approached the hip-shaking, intense eroticism of his American counterpart, sensuality was as much part of his on-screen affect as his class-inflected, self-effacing modesty. The cinematic performance of his song *Ahwak* ("I love you") in a scene from the 1957 Henry Barakat film *Banat al-yawm* (*The Girls of Today*) is exemplary of both 'Abd al-Ḥalim's aesthetic sensibility and his suavely erotic persona. The young singer, neatly dressed in a suit, sits down at a baby grand piano in the drawing room of a beautifully

FIGURE 3. 'Abd al-Ḥalim Ḥafiẓ serenading Magda in *The Girls of Today.*

appointed European-style apartment home—the family home of his character's love interest, played by the actress Magda (Figure 3). He begins to "play" the instrumental introduction to the song; 'Abd al-Ḥalim in fact is not playing the piano at all, judging from the lack of synchronization between the movements of his hands over the keyboard and the sound on the audio track.[14]

After the brief piano solo, the *takht* begins to play through the soundtrack, and after several bars, 'Abd al-Ḥalim begins to sing, "I love you, and I wish that if I forget you / I forget my soul along with you / And if it remains lost, then it's just as well if you forget me / So I forget you, and forget all about your coldness / But I long for my torment with you / And I find that my tears remember you, and so I return again." By the time he has sung these first two verses, Magda has been captivated by his voice while setting a tea service in the drawing room; her bodily reaction to 'Abd al-Ḥalim's rich voice crooning the sentimental lyrics is so intense that she appears on the point of swooning. As 'Abd al-Ḥalim continues with his song, the little sister of Magda's character enters the scene, also entranced by his voice. Unlike her older sister, who attempts to maintain her composure in the face of erotic and romantic temptation, the little girl walks right up to the piano, which she leans on while staring dreamily at the singer. Magda continues to watch the performance, at first from a safer distance, half-concealed by the support columns that separate the drawing room from the kitchen area.

As 'Abd al-Ḥalim transitions to the bridge[15] of the song, Magda wheels the tea service near the piano bench, and unsteadily takes a seat on a chair; she appears completely fixed upon the man, breathing heavily through parted lips. He sings longingly of a dream, "I find you preoccupied," and then turns around on the bench to address Magda as he continues, "and I preoccupied by you / And my eyes meet your eyes." Magda frantically grasps the back of the chair for support as she finds herself addressed directly, and politely casts her eyes downward while smiling weakly. But before the next line, 'Abd al-Ḥalim turns his head back toward the camera, now apparently addressing no one in particular, "and their words are written on you, though you try to hide them." Magda's fascination appears intensified by this flirtatious performing style, and she magnifies her bodily gestures of desire accordingly. He repeats this tactic on the next refrain of the bridge, addressing directly to Magda the same lines , before turning away again at the same point. When the bridge ends, 'Abd al-Ḥalim pivots slightly on the bench to resume the conceit of piano player, pantomiming the striking of the keys as he sings the final repetition of the three opening verses.

When the lyrics have ended, the *takht* continues to play for another half a minute over the soundtrack. His singing finished, 'Abd al-Ḥalim sheds the character of the smooth, confident performer, and takes up again the character he plays in the film. He turns around on the bench, and gazes into Magda's eyes, but this gaze is not the powerful instrument of seduction seen during his song. Instead, he looks anxious and overawed, frowning in confusion as he looks up at her—Barakat has seated Magda on a chair higher than the piano bench, giving her a haughty angle in profile as she returns the gaze—before he turns away, casting his head down in a look of sorrow and defeat before resuming the pantomime of playing the piano. As the last note is played, the little sister, who has not stirred from her post at the side of the piano, applauds the performance, gives 'Abd al-Ḥalim a kiss on the cheek, and hugs him before running off.

This scene represents a common theme in many of 'Abd al-Ḥalim's films: the poor but honorable boy who seeks the heart of the beautiful upper-class girl. Such a plot line played very well with Egyptian audiences in the 1950s and 1960s—both with the masses and with the government that oversaw and, as it found necessary, censored the film industry. Gamal Abdel Nasser's government, in fact, encouraged Egyptian studios to produce such films, since the romantic plot line echoed Nasser's ideas of Arab nationalism and socialism. The good guy could triumph over the bad guy (generally, a distasteful rival for the girl's affections); the poor boy could prove himself to the rich girl and her family; and, although this last point was more subtextual than the others, the dark-skinned boy could ascend in social class by marrying the light-skinned girl.

While 'Abd al-Ḥalim was not as phenotypically dark-skinned as many other Egyptians, especially those from Upper Egypt, he was still considered, in Egypt's racialized discourse of skin color, *asmar* or *asmarani*. These terms literally mean "brown" in the sense of "copper-colored skin," but, because black skin is disfavored by Cairenes, such words are often used euphemistically to refer to black-skinned Egyptians as well (Badawi and Hinds 1986, 429). The only leading man in Egyptian cinema darker than 'Abd al-Ḥalim was, in fact, the actor who later portrayed him, Aḥmad Zaki. Zaki, whose public image mirrored 'Abd al-Ḥalim's in its "poor boy makes good" narrative, not only portrayed the singer in his final screen role but five years earlier had played the leading role in a biopic of another Egyptian poor boy who made good: Gamal Abdel Nasser himself.[16] Long before Nasser gained a cinematic avatar, however, he was a patron of 'Abd al-Ḥalim Ḥafiẓ, whose public image was fashioned as a synecdoche of the new Egypt that would emerge through Nasserism: a country in which talented people from humble social backgrounds could rise to their rightful positions despite the obstacles represented by the old class structure and its attendant political regime.

The adulation of 'Abd al-Ḥalim Ḥafiẓ that I heard from virtually all Cairene music fans does not reflect a constant public discourse of his aesthetic value. At the time of 'Abd al-Ḥalim's early success in show business, culture critics and music aficionados sneered at his singing style as vulgar "crooning" *(ghina' 'aṭifi)*, a cheap and sentimental variety of popular song that reflected Western-inspired aesthetic debasement and a loss of "authentic" Arab culture. It was only many years after his death that public critical discourse came to vindicate him as a late-stage "propagator of the older musical aesthetics" (Shannon 2006, 15). This scornful criticism of 'Abd al-Ḥalim as a crooner depends upon an understanding of his vocal and spectacular aesthetic effect as a direct assault upon emotions, rather than the emotional evocation inspired by well-performed *musiqa al-ṭarab*. In comparison to contemporary musicians in *al-musiqa al-shababiyya,* ʻAbd al-Ḥalim now seems far more old-fashioned and "classical" than such dated criticisms might suggest to contemporary readers. The difference, especially for listeners who hear him long after his lifetime, lies in the details of song composition, vocal production, and personal presentation, which I shall address at greater length in the following chapter.

Hibabiyya

Of all the people I came to know in Cairo who preferred *musiqa al-ṭarab* to *al-musiqa al-shababiyya,* none was as steadfast in his devotion nor so vitriolic in his distaste as the retired journalist and culture critic Manṣur. I met with Manṣur at his apartment in the Duqqi district of Cairo,[17] on a block that may once have been posh but was now down-at-heel. The building and the apartment were also run-down: the bathroom, built decades ago with all the usual conveniences of modern plumbing, now lacked running water, and all ablutions had to be performed with the aid of a large jerrycan that Manṣur had installed in the shower stall. Manṣur's affective environment appeared to have aged alongside his household fixtures: virtually all of the art, books, and paraphernalia to be seen on the shelves and the walls indexed the Egyptian politics and artistic landscape of the late 1950s and early 1960s.

Manṣur held two particular figures in high and intense esteem. One of them was Gamal Abdel Nasser, the president of Egypt from 1954 to 1970. Manṣur was an unreconstructed Nasserist and Arab nationalist who had never come to terms with Anwar Sadat's economic or foreign policies, nor with the subsequent intensified neoliberalism of the Mubarak regime. Every mention of Nasser's name brought forth a reverently murmured *raḥḥimahu allah* from Manṣur's lips, in exactly the same fashion that many self-consciously pious Muslims will murmur a benediction following the name of the prophet Muḥammad—even on those rare occasions when Manṣur expressed an opinion critical of some of Nasser's actions. His bookshelves were crammed with biographies and analyses of the former president, as well as cassette recordings of, it appeared to me, nearly every speech that Nasser had given during his rule. This cassette collection also indexed Manṣur's investment in Arab nationalism as a kind of secular religion: as scholars have noted at length, cassette recordings of Qur'anic scholars' sermons, to say nothing of Qur'anic recitations themselves, circulate widely throughout Egypt (Hirschkind 2006) and the Arab world at large (Miller 2007). A collection of spoken-word cassette recordings about anything other than Islam is as notable for what it is not as for what it is.

The other key icon in Manṣur's worldview was Shadiyya, the retired singer and actress who had been a major star during the 1950s and 1960s. He was even more ardent in his devotion to Shadiyya than he was to Nasser: he recommended her music to me with all the sincerity and seriousness of purpose of a preacher exhorting the faithless to see the light. Manṣur's cassette collection of Nasser's speeches was dwarfed by his collection of Shadiyya's studio and concert recordings on vinyl, eight-track, cassette, and compact disc.[18] The paintings and photographs of Nasser that hung in one corner of the living room were overshadowed by the far larger number of framed photographs of the entertainer throughout the house: Shadiyya in concert, in film stills, and, in one soul-stirring moment for a young Manṣur, giving him an interview. He was almost frantic to explain her greatness to me, after I told him that I had never heard of her before; the fact that I declared myself a researcher of *al-musiqa al-shababiyya* only added to his agitation. He played one recording after another for me, rifling through his records and CDs for favorite pieces, while simultaneously pressing upon me CDs to copy into my computer, which I had brought with me. In a tone approaching moral panic, Manṣur repeatedly insisted to me, "Once you listen to Shadiyya, you will realize that all of *shababiyya* is nothing but *hibabiyya* (smuttiness)!"

Manṣur was making a play on words that I had heard before: a neologistic pun that turns upon the rhyme between youth *(shabab)* and smut *(hibab)*. The context of this remark—spoken by a man in his seventies in his living room dedicated to the world in which he lived during his twenties—suggests how fraught these terms can become. For Manṣur, everything in Egyptian culture that had come to pass since the mid-1960s was a downward spiral with little to recommend it. The politics, the economics, and the expressive culture that had succeeded the high-water mark of Nasserism and its associated phenomena in Egypt were, in his mind, increasingly corrupt and grotesque—musical aesthetics no less than national economic and foreign policy.

Indeed, from Manṣur's point of view, Shadiyya not only symbolized but personified his vision of Egyptian cultural modernity. She was a highly talented singer who opted to sing both light pop tunes of the time and a number of heavy, bombastic nationalist anthems in Egyptian Colloquial Arabic (ECA), which had the effect of hailing Egyptians as a discrete group. Manṣur contrasted this linguistic practice with that of Umm Kulthum, who, he claimed with a hint of polite disdain, usually sang in Classical Arabic and associated herself with pan-Arabism rather than Egyptian nationalism. In fact, Manṣur was making a highly debatable claim in this regard: Umm Kulthum often recorded love songs in ECA, including many of her more beloved pieces that one still hears today on Egyptian radio. And, it is worth noting, Manṣur was the only person I ever met in Egypt who suggested that Umm Kulthum was more invested in pan-Arab nationalism than in Egyptian nationalism.[19]

But Manṣur may be correct in associating Shadiyya with a particularly Egypt-focused public persona, perhaps to a greater degree than other music and cinema stars of the era.[20] Shadiyya also was a beautiful woman, and like many other such singers of her time, tried acting in films: unlike most of them, however, she proved good at it, and earned a reputation as a respected actress in comedies and dramas as well as a singer (Gordon 2002, 97–98). She, alongside a few contemporaries such as Su'ad Ḥusni and Huda Sulṭan, embodied the classic "triple threat" of entertainment: beauty, acting talent, and singing talent[21]—all qualities associated with a sense of Egyptianness that my own interlocutors frequently cited to me, and which in former days contributed to Egypt's glamorous image throughout the Arab world.

In reflecting upon my encounter with Manṣur, days after the fact, I was struck by its similarity to another researcher's interview of a different elderly Egyptian. Joel Gordon describes a lugubrious meeting with Galal Mu'awaḍ, a former radio announcer from the Nasser era—and Nasserist devotee—who was forced into retirement shortly after Sadat succeeded Nasser as president. Gordon explains that Mu'awaḍ was difficult and morose, and seemed on his guard against questions the answers to which Gordon was not entitled to hear. "I sensed I was hearing an oft-recited script and only later realized its intrinsic value. The underlying theme was loss, of close friends in broadcast and music, pioneers, giants. Abd al-Halim, Umm Kulthum, Farid al-Atrash (Figure 4), Muhammad Abd al-Wahhab, Nasser. And, although not clearly stated, of an Egypt that no longer exists. 'We've lost a lot,' Mu'awaḍ sighed" (Gordon 2002, 2–3).

FIGURE 4. Farid al-Aṭrash performing alongside Samiyya Gamal in the film *Love of My Life* (Barakat 1947).

No doubt Mu'awaḍ's voice introduced many of the speeches that sat on Manṣur's shelves. The two men were products of the same era, and they experienced the loss of their idealized moment of Egyptian culture as personal and exquisitely painful. Manṣur did not express this sense of loss directly; instead, he persistently indexed it in his home décor and his listening preferences; the word "loss" never even came up in the four hours we spent talking in his apartment.

"Umm Kulthum Was of Her Time, Not Ours"

Umm Kulthum, like most other singers of the Golden Age of *musiqa al-ṭarab*, is distinctly unpopular among young people in Cairo today. For most of my interlocutors, she holds little appeal, and they associate her music with memories of being forced to listen to her as children, while their parents and grandparents sat enraptured. Even for the few youth who speak knowledgeably and approvingly of the quality of her voice or her song selections, she represents an aesthetic standard that they can enjoy only on a cultivated, intellectual level—she does not touch their emotions in the way that she did (and still does) those of older generations. Some of these youth complained to me that her songs are simply too long to endure, particularly when they must engage the music on such a conscious, strenuous level. Others failed to appreciate the necessary aesthetic engagement in the first place, having grown up with *shababiyya*-trained ears that do not easily catch the sense of *kulthumiyyat.*[22] Nearly all of them commented to me at some point that, for them, Umm Kulthum is situated in a historical period to which they have no emotional access: this place is described variously as "a time of war," "the period of nationalism," "Nasser's era," or simply "a long time ago (*zaman*)."

Alice exemplifies this attitude in her analysis of her own distaste for Umm Kulthum. "Umm Kulthum was of her time," she explained to me as we sat in the youth meeting room of her church. "She is not ours, she is not of our time, precisely because we as youth like everything fast! I mean: fast Internet, fast music, and fast words! Umm Kulthum, for example, a song of hers was written with a five-minute introduction, [instrumental] music only, before the words get going!" She could have added that young people often have no choice about the pace of their lives: particularly for those bent upon building careers for themselves and maintaining or raising their economic status, speeding through the day is a fact of life. Alice, in fact, was nursing a cold that day, and suffered through a sore throat as she spoke with me for several hours: she had raced over to the church immediately after taking a final exam in her faculty at 'Ayn Shams University, for which she had just spent the last several days cramming frantically. I felt guilty when I met her at the church that day and found her under the weather, but she insisted that we could sit and talk as we had arranged. When I asked her if she wanted to go home and rest after this, she assented, but then observed that she had another exam for which she had to start cramming, so rest would be limited.

Alice was one of a number of university students whom I met not through their school but through their church youth group. Alice belongs to Egypt's small and tightly knit indigenous Protestant community, a church known by its adherents as the Evangelical Presbyterian Church (*al-Kanisa al-Ingiliyya al-Mashikhiyya*) and much less formally by nonadherents as the Coptic Evangelical Church.[23] One of the more important mediating figures in my doctoral research happened to be an Evangelical, and when her efforts to facilitate my research within 'Ayn Shams University met with failure, she suggested that I pursue interlocutors through the large and active youth group of her home church in Heliopolis. Alice proved to be the most thoughtful and articulate of these youth.

Alice's family were clearly situated among the *muthaqqafin* of Cairo, although Alice's own economic prospects had been somewhat compromised by the untimely death of her father. She and her mother often socialized with her maternal aunt and her family, who lived in a richly furnished flat in an expensive and exclusive gated compound in the eastern suburbs of Cairo called Rehab City,[24] to which I was invited on several occasions. Alice's family spoke among themselves in English as often as in Arabic: all of the adults spoke English competently, albeit with noticeable Egyptian accents, and Alice's younger cousins attended a private "language school"—Cairene parlance for a school in which a language other than Arabic was used for instruction in nearly all subjects besides Arabic itself—which endowed them with perfect American accents.

The most telling socioeconomic detail here is the nature of Rehab City. The development is one of a number of gated communities—satellite cities, in fact—that have been built in the last two decades along the outskirts of the Cairo metropolitan area for the exclusive use of the elite (Denis 2006, 48–50). These self-contained suburbs are uncannily similar to their Western counterparts, which at the time made for a disorienting experience after driving out of Cairo proper. Upon passing the gates of Rehab City after driving through a series of poor neighborhoods that have grown up along the Cairo-Suez Desert Road, one enters a compound of gleaming white apartment blocks, neatly manicured lawns fringed with palm trees, and all the comforts of a wealthy suburb: private schools for resident children, private police force, expensive restaurants and coffee shops that cater to cosmopolitan elite tastes,[25] and so on. Such accoutrements require not only large amounts of cash but also an intensely unequal distribution of natural resources: these satellite cities built by and for the elite must pump water from the already overtaxed Nile out to their desert locales, following an intensifying pattern dating at least to the late 1930s of the state expropriating and commodifying public resources—especially the water of the Nile—for the use and enrichment of the elite (Mitchell 2002, 31–79).

As Alice's frantic pace suggests, speed is, in fact, a major trope in the discourse of *al-musiqa al-shababiyya.*[26] As a commercial product, *shababiyya* is often likened to fast food (Marcus 2007, 37) in its speed, its mass production, and its disposability. Less judgmentally, people often observed to me that they find *shababiyya* most appropriate listening for driving around Cairo, jockeying through hectic traffic as they crawl over the choked highways or wend their way through tight side streets from one side of the city to another. It is not the ideal music by which to sit still for an hour at a time, doing nothing but relaxing; it is, rather, a music of activity and movement, which adds to its association with (hyperactive) young people.

Young Cairenes, even if they admit some enjoyment of the old *musiqa al-ṭarab* repertory, rarely evaluate the music in terms of the precise aesthetic standards that Danielson and Racy have outlined. Those few youthful interlocutors who declared their appreciation for Umm Kulthum spoke less of her musicological qualities than of her social and affective benefits: chiefly, the pleasure of sitting for a while after work and relaxing by absorbing one of her long recordings. Such listeners identified this behavior as distinctly un-youth-like, and explained to me that they had had to grow into this musical appreciation. "When I was a kid," Khulud offered, "I used to complain when my father put those records on. 'It's too long and boring!' I told him. I needed to grow up and gain the maturity to listen to her." Yaḥya, my language instructor and an immense fan of *musiqa al-ṭarab,* told me a similar story: "When I was much younger, I preferred faster stuff. But when I was around fifteen, I began to enjoy the old, slow songs. It depends upon the age of the person."

It may also depend partly upon immersion in the cultural context in which this evolution of taste can occur: the late Palestinian-born, Cairo-raised, and U.S.-trained academic and music critic Edward Said confessed in several writings that he never learned to love Umm Kulthum as virtually every other Arab he knew did. "Having been fed a diet of her music at far too young an age," he wrote, "I found her forty-plus minute songs insufferable and never developed the taste for her. . . . But for those who like and believe in such cultural typing she also stood for something quintessentially Arab and Muslim . . . which I could sometimes find pleasure in but never quite came to terms with. Her secret power has eluded me, but among Arabs I seem to be quite alone in this feeling" (Said 2001, 230). In a more musicological venue, Said described a late-in-life epiphany that allowed him to appreciate if not love the sort of leisurely, relaxing listening that my interlocutors cite. "The point of the performance, I later realized, was not to get to the end of a carefully constructed logical structure—working through it—but to luxuriate in all sorts of byways, to linger over details and changes in text, to digress and then digress from the digression" (Said 1991, 98).

Said was a self-described anomaly in this situation, as someone born in the Arab world in the 1930s and at least partly raised there, yet unable to grasp on an affective level the pull of the music that led to the ecstatic emotional state of *ṭarab.* It is worth noting that Said began to attend school in the United States when he was fifteen years old—the approximate lower end of the age range known to Cairenes as "youth." It is around this time in a young person's life, as I have experienced first-hand in the U.S. and observed as an ethnographer in Cairo, that he will begin to articulate his own tastes in music. It is possible, although strictly a matter of conjecture, that Said's physical separation from the Arab world at this point in his life prevented him from developing the affective skill of experiencing *ṭarab* in response to Umm Kulthum and her colleagues' performances.[27]

Studio Session

In late January 2011, I accepted an invitation from Murad, a studio producer in the *shababiyya* music industry, to observe a recording session. In the early evening, I took a taxi out to Giza, deep into the entertainment district centered along Pyramids Road. This district is known first and foremost for its stock of seedy and down-at-heel nightclubs and cabarets that cater to Gulf Arab tourists (Wynn 2007, 129–30), but music insiders also know it as the location of a great many recording studios, usually located a few blocks off Pyramids Road, the main drag in that area of Cairo. The first to arrive were Murad himself and his recording partner, Dawud, and they immediately started setting up their gear, giving me time to take stock of the beautifully appointed studio. They had an extensive arrangement of digital recording equipment, operated through a big iMac. The studio had a separate sound room with acoustic panels that could be moved around to accommodate various sizes of instrument set-ups and numbers of performers.

As Dawud got himself situated in the studio, he unpacked a small shopping bag with some Egyptian perfume, a bottle of water, a little ceramic bowl and votive candle, and a hypodermic needle. I was unsettled to see something cooking in the little bowl with the needle sitting next to it, and I noticed that others were, too. Everyone, upon catching sight of the paraphernalia, asked the same question: "Heroin?" Eventually, it became clear that the needle did not relate to drugs at all: Dawud was just an eccentric dude who used the needle to spritz small amounts of water into the bowl of perfume to dilute it without pouring in too much at once. I was relieved to understand that this was Dawud's eccentricity and not his addiction; I had been steeling myself to face the prospect that doing ethnographic research among music industry people would require being unflappable when confronted with the use of hard drugs.

In the course of the set-up, Murad produced an external hard drive from his bag, and I inadvertently offended him by asking if he did as I had heard 'Amr Diyab does: wiping studio hard drives of all session work after downloading it to his personal drive. Murad and Dawud explained to me gently that they trust each other, and they have a trusting relationship with this studio in general, and they would not do something like that. From their reactions, I realized that I had accidentally implied that they might suspect each other of stealing material from each other, and I was terribly embarrassed. Since I had no understanding of who owned what or who was a frequent collaborator with whom, it never crossed my mind that the question could be offensive. Also, I had not absorbed the full implication of 'Amr Diyab's reputed paranoia in the recording studio: his behavior suggested that he expected someone within his own circle of close musical collaborators to rip off his work and sell it elsewhere. I immediately apologized, and they recognized that I was fulfilling one of the classic roles of the ethnographer: a dunce who needed to catch up with what everyone else already knew.

Soon, the first of the session musicians arrived: the bassist, Sayf. I managed to make him ill at ease at first, as well: I was not introduced to him until after he saw me scribbling in my little black notebook, while looking over the shoulders of the producers from time to time. After speaking with Murad and Dawud for a bit, Sayf gestured toward me warily, and he asked me in an uncertain, joking tone, "Are you writing for State Security?" When I realized what I must look like to him, I remembered to produce my business cards and announce myself properly. It would not be until several months after this encounter that I comprehended the extent to which State Security—that is, the secret police of the intelligence services—imposed itself in all sorts of contexts that held no detectable security threat (Stack and MacFarquhar 2011), including pop music studios. At the time, I believe I overestimated the degree to which Sayf had been joking.

I asked Dawud and Murad if the song were already created or still in process, and they explained that it was indeed written, although the lyrics might change soon: the lyricists had been swapped out, so there might be some revision. This led to general conversation about how production operates. Murad corrected my impression that everyone now creates a framework (*shakl*) for a song, and only then brings in artistically handcuffed composers and lyricists to shoehorn something into the prearranged framework: Murad himself, as he claimed, only did things "the traditional way," arranging a song that had already been written—albeit in basic form—by the composer and lyricist. This means that he gets a song that one can actually sing, but it has, as yet, no harmony or full instrumentation. He did, however, affirm that the other, super-Fordist way is particular to *shababiyya* and unknown in what he refers to as *musiqa al-turath.*[28]

Once Sayf was set up, the two producers and he collaborated on creating the bass line. Instead of sitting in the sound room, he sat next to them, and plugged his bass guitar into one of their machines that fed into the computer system, so that they recorded the licks as he played them. This gave me the chance to chat with him a bit between takes, which he was quite happy to do after confirming that I was not some shadowy State Security figure. Knowing this question could be offensive, I very carefully broached the subject with Sayf: why hire a bass player when the computer could automatically generate a digital bass line? He took my point without offense, and he explained that it was in fact possible to do exactly that. However, getting all the little flourishes and touches of a good, funky bass line on the computer would "take a hell of a lot of time" to program, and he noted, with a touch of pride in his voice, that it would lack the sense of "craft—the sound of the fingers hitting the strings, the ghost notes,[29] it won't be there. And even if you did it all on the computer, it would still sound artificial."

While they worked out the bass line, Gibril the percussionist, a hip chain-smoking dude in a leather jacket and Kangol cap, arrived, and soon after him came the singer himself, with his manager in tow. The singer, a goofily cute Moroccan who goes by the name Garini,[30] arrived just after Sayf left. He was dressed in a trendily mismatched ensemble featuring a suit vest worn over a T-shirt, canvas shoes with the laces missing and, his trademark, a gigantic head of puffy, curly hair. He looked somewhat like Lenny Kravitz after a cheeseburger binge.

I noticed during Gibril's recording stint that Murad and Dawud fiddled with the speed (and, epiphenomenally or not, the key transposition) of the song, making it faster, and then slower than their intended natural speed. When I asked Murad about it, he said that this was a temporary change just to aid Gibril's audition of the song, so he could hit the various rhythms and accents crisply. This is another example of contemporary technological mediation in music recording that reflects the lack of direct exchange between musicians: in the Golden Age, when studio musicians recorded as an ensemble, they were forced to adjust their ears and their performances to each other as they went along. Murad's recording technique conflicts not only with its predecessor technique but with the intersubjective emotional concept of *ṭarab* itself, in which musicians must interact with and play off each other as well as their audience in order to achieve an emotionally resonant performance.

Still, as Murad, Dawud, and Sayf all indicated to me, sophisticated digital technology has its limits for recording euphonious music. I could hear clearly that there was a striking difference between the robotically generated and real-life *'ud.* I would think that it would be even harder to make a pleasant-sounding digital approximation of an *'ud,* with its many microtones and subtle shadings, than of a bass, as Sayf commented. One must listen closely to notice that a bass line is digitally generated; a digitally generated *'ud* line, though, is painfully and jarringly apparent. Alongside the undeniable technological mediation of the recording process, there was also real effort by all the musicians whom I observed to play beautifully, and, as far as the music allowed, creatively.

A little before midnight, the *mizmar* player, a tall and broad-built man, came in. He was dressed impeccably in the formal *ṣa'idi* (Upper Egyptian) attire of a *gallabiyya,* a turban, black slip-on oxfords, a scarf folded symmetrically around his neck, and a scrupulously groomed handlebar mustache; his ensemble inspired jokingly admiring comments from his fellow musicians, all of whom were Cairenes who lived in jeans and T-shirts. Almost all the *mizmar* licks in the song were identical, so the *ṣa'idi* had little to play; once he played the main lick correctly, Murad and Dawud could replicate it infinitely in the computer. Getting to this point, however, proved something of a challenge. They tried having him play in unison with the *'ud* during the dance break, and then playing accents and rhythmic hits underneath the *'ud.* He had trouble getting the rhythm right, due to his learned instinct to add little ornamentations to the line. Eventually, Murad had to tell him beseechingly, "*Mafish ḥilyat* (There are no ornamentations)!"

While fiddling with their instrument panels, Murad and Dawud chuckled quietly to see this huge, physically imposing man play such a tiny instrument. They also expressed their amusement about how much the *mizmar* sounded like a child's toy, and they were absolutely right: the *mizmar* is a high-pitched double-reeded instrument, much like an oboe but with more limited range and control, and it indeed sounds unnervingly like a plastic toy horn. The timbre of the *mizmar* is so resistant to blending into accompanying instruments that Murad and Dawud opened their Autotune program for the only time that evening in a failed attempt to force the *mizmar* to be a bit more in tune with everything else. As even I with my amateur's ear could distinguish, when they tried to adjust the sounds slightly for perfect pitch, it no longer really sounded like a *mizmar* but a robotic thing—very much like the fake *'ud*. After hearing what Autotune could do with it, they agreed to undo the attempt and leave the *mizmar* as it was. When I commented, "That's sort of the nature of the beast, isn't it," Dawud laughingly agreed with me.

After the *mizmar* player finished, the *nay* (end-blown flute) player stepped into the recording booth. I found the low sound of the *nay* haunting and elegant, in comparison to the laughter-inducing honk of the *mizmar*. The *nay*, much like the *'ud*, is an essential instrument of the old *musiqa al-ṭarab* ensemble, and in the hands of a skilled player can produce the quarter-tones and inflectional subtleties that characterize Arabic music. This contrasts with other instruments commonly used in Egypt, including the *mizmar*, which are structurally incapable of producing such tonal qualities, and are therefore regarded as more suitable for lower-prestige musical forms, particularly the folk tradition called *sha'biyya*. Murad and Dawud were combining elements of higher and lower prestige in this recording, in order to strike just the right balance of skilled craftsmanship and playful informality in their *shababiyya* song.

At 1:30 a.m., still at the recording session that seemed on track to go on all night, I was almost dead on my feet, and I was aware that it could take some time to get home. Regretfully, I packed it in for the night and bid everyone thanks and good-bye. The *mizmar* player even exchanged business cards with me, hoping that I might have work for him. I walked a few blocks past the studio, and hailed a cab. I was surprised that the driver knew exactly where I had been when I explained that I had been at work in a music studio, since I was not even on the same street as the building, but the lack of other points of interest near that street made the answer obvious to him. He asked if I were a musician, and I explained, no, I was an

American researcher, and I studied the pop music industry. He asked me which musicians I had encountered in my work, and I named Muḥammad Munir and Wusṭ el-Balad, and mentioned that I had just met Garini. The taxi driver knew the name better than I did, commenting, "Sure, he has a bunch of songs out." Since he knew I was American, the taxi driver thought to honor me by switching the music on his MP3 player, which he had hooked into the car stereo, to Eminem songs. After a whole evening of listening to *shababiyya* in process, I ended the evening cruising down the Cairo Autostrade, the stereo blasting "Ass Like That."

Mediating Technology of Production and Consumption

It is an understatement to say that sound recording technology has had an impact on the way music is produced for commercial consumption in the Arab world, as it has elsewhere. Once the technology used in recording the human voice in the studio is applied to the practice of amplifying the human voice in concert performance, the entire endeavor begins to shift in reaction. The most obvious manifestation of this shift is that recording and amplification technology created an opportunity for a person with a relatively weak singing voice to become a star: machinery could substitute in some measure for a powerful, diaphragm-driven voice. Such a move was not universal, of course: opera, for example, still places a premium on a strong, supple voice, and microphones cannot compensate for an operatic voice that cannot fill the concert hall. In general, however, the industry centered on Arabic song began to give ground to the new aesthetic possibilities, albeit slowly and grudgingly.

In the case of *musiqa al-ṭarab,* high modernism engaged with recording technology much as opera did: technology became an essential tool to record albums, but its amplifying and isolating possibilities were held at stiff arm's length. Umm Kulthum reacted angrily when first presented with the onstage microphone because its mere presence suggested that her vocal powers were not sufficient to reach throughout the performance space. To an artist whose professional training included constant engagement with audiences without benefit of any such technological devices, the microphone seemed a blatant insult. In studio recordings, the singer and the *takht* were able to engage with each other directly, and to play off each other's improvisations and elaborations within the basic text and melody of a song, although they lacked the engagement of a live audience whose role was not to perform but to encourage and to demand of the singer particular varieties of vocal acrobatics. As concerts became larger affairs in larger performance spaces, even high modernist *musiqa al-ṭarab* acceded to the practicality of a minimal amount of amplification technology. (Such technology could also double as recording technology for broadcasting purposes.)

This meant, however, that studio recordings of *musiqa al-ṭarab* artists had to be consumed by the public not as the full flower of the art but only as a basic and abbreviated form thereof. *Musiqa al-ṭarab* is heavily dependent on the interaction between performers and audience members, and thus a song recorded in a studio could only serve as a hint of what the artist could do in person—broadly if imperfectly analogous to a two-minute trailer for a two-hour film. (The analogy runs into difficulty due to the necessarily live and personal interactions through which *ṭarab* is evoked, in classical terms.) This also explains why, in the years since the great voices of high modernist *musiqa al-ṭarab* have died, people are far more likely to listen to their concert recordings than studio recordings. To listen to an eight-minute studio recording of Umm Kulthum when one could choose the hour-long concert recording, in which one can hear audience interventions as well as the performers themselves, would be to miss the point altogether.

Late modernist *musiqa al-ṭarab,* however, makes more extensive use of technological mediation, with numerous implications for the consumers. In particular, ʻAbd al-Ḥalim Ḥafiẓ structured much of his concert singing style around a microphone that had no other purpose than to amplify his voice, which was not strong enough to carry over the *takht.* In ʻAbd al-Ḥalim's case, the microphone was no longer an intrusion or innovation in a musical performance that could do without it, but an essential element in the performance itself.

Martin Stokes approaches this topic by critiquing the distinctly hierarchical standpoint so often heard from Egyptian culture critics, in which ʻAbd al-Ḥalim's rise represents the end of the good old days. Stokes writes that such a critique thereby inappropriately forces the discourse to "constantly return to early twentieth-century modernism and turn away from the supposed moment of decline with embarrassment. The case of ʻAbd al-Halim Hafiz, with his collaborations with the major artistic and literary figures of his day, suggests we draw these lines too quickly; specifically those that separate twentieth-century modernism from sentimentalism"

(Stokes 2009, 73). At the same time, it is hard to miss the keenly felt ambivalence that Stokes's own interlocutors—many of them friends and admiring colleagues of the late singer—express about what 'Abd al-Ḥalim hath wrought. 'Abd al-Ḥalim's career established a new professional model for singers, one in which a voice that had some pleasing qualities but insufficient strength to project to a room could be bolstered by a microphone. Similarly, 'Abd al-Ḥalim's reliance on amplifying technology changed the nature of the interaction between singer and audience: his performances, which in the minds of listeners may feel personally directed toward them, were in fact directed toward no one but the microphone. The technology he utilized has the uncanny ability to inspire a sense of intimate, even secret communication between singer and listener, despite the fact that, by its nature, it *mediates:* it stands between singer and listener, and allows the singer to detach himself from the immediacy of something like a *musiqa al-ṭarab* audience that might attempt to influence how and what he sings.

This new model has since become widespread, almost universal, in the field of contemporary popular music in Egypt. Whether this development is a blessing or a curse depends on the perspective of the listener, on an unconscious level: if one poses the question outright, Cairenes generally hear the question as an accusation or derogation, and will instinctively try to position themselves on the "correct" side of the argument. If one simply asks Cairenes, however, especially youth, whom they like to listen to and what they like about those singers, then one will hear some unintentional defenses of this increased technological mediation. 'Abd al-Ḥalim was (and still is) loved partly for the romantic nuance of his phrasing, the quivers and shadings of his voice which communicated a variety of emotions. Part of his talent lay in singing such shadings in much the same way that people would speak them: that is, not at the high operatic volume and loft that Umm Kulthum often used but at a more conversational volume and timbre that, in the context of a song with backing orchestra, could only be achieved through the use of a microphone. Listeners respond to this sort of singing very positively, in my experience; it is part of the reason that young women famously swooned at his shows, and why Cairene youth young enough to be his great-grandchildren still sigh happily when they contemplate his auditory virtues.

The painful truth for many discriminating music fans, though, is that the model that 'Abd al-Ḥalim brought forth created an opportunity for people with poor voices to pursue musical careers. He is, in this regard, the beginning of the proverbial slippery slope: his voice sounds beautiful "up close" (that is, mediated through amplification technology) and he at least occasionally demonstrated thorough knowledge of the vocal techniques of *musiqa al-ṭarab,* but his example led to people with much worse voices and more limited training than his to attempt the same thing. The obvious solution for someone with limited vocal strength and limited vocal sweetness is to seek larger degrees of technological mediation in order to compensate—a process that inevitably pushes the would-be singer ever further from the classical *musiqa al-ṭarab* scenario of a singer communicating with and responding to both the instrumentalists and the audience.[31]

Technological mediation as a solution for errors and inaptly sung passages—to wit, post-production editing—has long existed within the Arabic music industry, and did not always convey weakness or inferiority. Even Umm Kulthum concerned herself with splicing together the best moments of several concert performances in order to create an ideal concert recording for commercial distribution (Danielson 1997, 132). After the fact of the concert itself, as it appears, such technological recuperation was fair play. Nowadays, such recuperative editing has gone to a new level, not only through the old technique of splicing together several pieces of audiotape but through a much newer and, according to almost all who have written about it to date, very troubling device. Autotune, a software program that digitally alters audio recordings in a number of ways, is particularly known for its ability to correct off-key vocal passages by adjusting them higher or lower in pitch to match what an errant singer intended to sing. By this method, a sound engineer can create a recording that includes notes that the singer never sang in the first place.[32] This scandalizes anyone with a personal investment in authenticity as a desirable quality in popular music.

Complaints about such technological wizardry in *shababiyya* remain at the informal conversational level, as far as I have encountered, with some fans aware of the nature of the device through hearing its more egregious usages[33] and others more vaguely suspicious of poor-voiced singers and their ability to launch careers. The suspicion is well founded: according to Murad, the use of Autotune to improve singers' voices after the fact is essentially universal in *shababiyya.* In critiquing the song *Mush ḥatiqdar* by the notoriously undertalented singer Ruby, Murad acknowledged with a bit of surprise that she did not sing the song so badly. *Mush ḥatiqdar* is not the standard *shababiyya* song but a piece in the old *musiqa al-ṭarab* style, composed in the difficult *maqam bayati.* It is, to say the least, an unexpected choice for a singer lambasted by critics and even by some of her fans for lacking vocal talent. But Murad thought it a worthwhile effort, and judged her voice "about seventy percent on target" for singing with the appropriate aesthetics of vocal production in *musiqa al-ṭarab.* I asked him if he were not being lulled by the judicious use of Autotune on the song, and he shook his head, saying, "Of course they are using Autotune, but she has got about seventy percent of it." I asked him how he could know that they were using Autotune, and he simply broke up laughing. "All singers use Autotune!" he chuckled. "It is a rule. It is not even an option, but *obligatory!*" When I asked him why this should be, he answered, "People do not practice [their vocal technique] as much as they should, or as much as people used to, like Umm Kulthum. Singers nowadays need the help, because they are not constantly practicing to keep their voices in shape."

In fact, the only commercial genre in which Autotune and its uncanniness have become explicit topics of debate is American country music. As Fox (2004a, 318–19) has demonstrated, Nashville's country music recording industry, no matter how deeply it may have commodified itself, retains its fans among ordinary people partly by its ability to speak to a sense of authenticity. The knowledge that country singers are literally not singing those notes has led to some public lamentations by commentators on the Nashville music scene as well as self-promoting disavowals of Autotune by a few singers (McCall 2004; Braddock 2007). The use of Autotune by sound engineers in the genre of Western pop music is a much different matter. Critics have complained there, too, of the corrosive effect such technology has on an audience's ability to distinguish authentic talent from studio concoction, but the pop music world, particularly the subgenre of dance pop music, hardly seems to care. In the acerbic estimation of music critic Neil McCormick (2004), this apathy is based on the sheer preponderance of technological mediation that, for him, defines contemporary popular music:

> Pop is about looks, ideas and attitude. As for musical ability and vocal skill, well, as they say in recording studios: "Don't worry. We can fix it in the mix."

> There was a time when singers could sing. You could say it was a prerequisite of the trade. You had to be able to deliver live because that was the main selling point of the music business.
>
> But since the 1960s, when recorded music became preeminent, the quality of vocals has deteriorated in almost direct correlation to advances in studio technology.
>
> In multi-track studios, you can endlessly re-record vocals until even the most average of vocalists can achieve technical perfection. Probably the majority of modern recordings are made up of what is known as "comps", a composition vocal in which every phrase has been taken from a separate take and stitched together into a flawless whole, then doubled up with a matching backing vocal just slightly out of synch, which gives it a kind of sensual echo.
>
> But there is one particularly sinister invention that has been putting extra shine on pop vocals since the 1990s. It is a piece of software called Autotune. Essentially, it takes a poorly sung note and transposes it, placing it dead centre of where it was meant to be. . . .
>
> Autotune, however, works by adjusting a pre-recorded vocal—which isn't much use live.[34] Hence lip-synching remains a popular fallback position for today's vocally challenged pop star.

There is little in McCormick's sardonic analysis that one might not hear from the mouth of an Egyptian sound engineer or music critic of a certain age.

Lip-synching, in my observation, remains uncommon in *shababiyya* concerts: rather, weaker voices will attempt to avoid singing too much by letting their back-up singers cover passages for them, or by encouraging the audience to sing entire verses for them, pointing the microphone at the crowd. When they do sing, such singers generally reveal their limitations in surprisingly honest ways. I recall being somewhat impressed with one such Lebanese *shababiyya* singer, Myriam Faris, at a concert held in a private sports club at what was, at the time, the furthest reaches of New Cairo. Although it was clear that she could not have projected adequately to the soccer pitch full of fans without her microphone, she also sang in a better voice than I had heard on her recordings: lower in pitch and richer in nuance, albeit strong enough to sing only with amplification technology.

In this regard, she resembled ʿAbd al-Ḥalim Ḥafiẓ, the forefather of contemporary *shababiyya,* more than Madonna, at whom Neil McCormick took especial aim in his lamentation. The trade-off that I could distinguish between Myriam Faris's concert voice and her studio voice was that she occasionally missed notes in live performance that she never missed on her records, but her studio voice was on the whole higher-pitched, thinner, and indicative of significant "fixing in the mix."

Technological mediation at the production level begins, in fact, long before the singer enters the process. A number of *shababiyya* recordings now originate not as poems that might be set to music (as in much of *musiqa al-ṭarab*) nor as collaboration between a professional lyricist and professional composer (as in the United States' Tin Pan Alley industry) but as a series of digital impulses manipulated by a producer. It is a simple matter to devise an elementary framework *(shakl)* for a song consisting of, at a minimum, a chord progression and beats. In lower-end production, once the producer is satisfied with the framework, he invites a composer to come up with a melody that fits. The composer's job is thus minimized: he has authorial control over neither the meter nor the basis of the melody.

The deep level on which *shababiyya* is a product of technology rather than human creativity invokes Adorno's critique of the American culture industry.[35] It seems even a step beyond what Adorno saw, in that the music is not only created for avowedly commercial purposes in the most standardized fashion possible, but it can in fact be created without musicians in the first place, and in a way that actually prevents musicians from exercising more than cursory influence on the sound of the song. I found it hard to avoid a sense of disillusionment while watching one such small-time producer, alone in a small, dark, cavelike studio, press a few toggles with his mouse to set up some convenient rhythms and chords, click to confirm, and say half to himself and half to me, "There, it is done."[36]

Still, even in the *shababiyya* industry, there remains the assumption that more prestigious and higher-quality recordings must be based upon the more traditional model of a composed melody and a suitable lyric text, which is then presented to a producer to arrange and embellish with a combination of studio gadgetry and live musicians. Many studio producers, in fact, prefer to call themselves "arrangers" when translating their occupation into English, to emphasize their trained musical judgment and aesthetic sensibility over the associations with machinery and commerce. The professional producer (*muwazziʿ*) has at his or her disposal enormously sophisticated computer programs and peripheral hardware devices that can simulate—with varying degrees of verisimilitude—any instrument needed, both Arabic and Western. Nevertheless, in many cases, a thoroughgoing *muwazzi'* with sufficient funds on which to draw will prefer to hire session instrumentalists and record them as comp tracks. This preference explains why Murad and Dawud went to the trouble and expense to hire Sayf to record their bass line. As he commented to me, even the best studio technology available still sounds artificial in comparison to a physical instrument.

It is worth pointing out here that, as much as *shababiyya* sounds heavily Westernized to many Cairene aesthetes' ears, the form maintains a thin undergirding of Arabic musical theory. As a *muwazzi'* observed to me, all of the bare-bones demo recordings he receives for consideration are composed in traditional monophonic *maqamat:* it is easier to distinguish the *maqam,* he explained, when one listens to the composer singing the melody while accompanying himself on an *'ud* or guitar. It is not until the song is in the hands of the producer that it acquires an overlay of Western instrumentation and musical architecture.[37] Even then, a competent listener trained in Arab musical theory can distinguish the *maqam,* which will usually be one of the set of *maqamat* that lend themselves to such studio elaborations: the majority of *shababiyya* songs are composed in *kurd, nahawand,* or *ḥigaz,* all three of which can be combined euphoniously with Western-style production by a skillful *muwazzi'*. Less common, oddly enough, is *maqam 'agam,* which corresponds to the natural major scale of Western musical theory, and would thus be ideal for such productions. On rare occasions, one even hears a song performed by a *shababiyya* singer composed in *bayati* or *rast,* both of which *maqamat* are considered so irreconcilable to polyphony[38] and other Western pop aesthetics that such songs are inevitably arranged in imitation of *musiqa al-ṭarab* recordings, complete with the old-fashioned *takht* ensemble and the singer performing the song in his or her best approximation of *musiqa al-ṭarab* vocal aesthetic standards.

1977 and the End of an Era

'Abd al-Ḥalim Ḥafiẓ, despite his relative youth, died in 1977, a mere two years after the passing of Umm Kulthum: he had suffered from schistosomiasis, a parasitic disease borne by snails that live in the stagnant water at the edges of the Nile.[39] That same year, Egypt convulsed with antigovernment demonstrations the likes of which it had not seen since before the 1952 revolution. As part of the shift in economic policy engineered by Anwar Sadat—the set of free-market, investment-courting policies known collectively in Arabic as *al-infitaḥ* ("openness")—governmental subsidies on essential goods, especially bread, were reduced. In response, masses of Egyptians participated in bread riots, demanding that the government restore the subsidies that allowed poor people to survive (Hourani 1991, 423). Many intellectuals as well as ordinary people also demanded the end of *al-infitaḥ,* which they read as the reinstatement of the old prerevolutionary class structure and its attendant differentiated access to wealth and power—this disparity between Egyptians had been a prime target of Nasser's domestic political and economic policies.

Eight months after 'Abd al-Ḥalim Ḥafiẓ's death, Sadat committed himself to another policy that rocked Egypt as well as the larger Arab world: in November 1977, he flew to Jerusalem and delivered an address to the Knesset, beginning a unilateral[40] peace process that culminated a year later in the Camp David Accords. This policy shift resulted, at least for the ten years immediately following, in the sharp decrease in Egypt's political capital among Arab and Muslim-majority states:[41] most obviously, in the expulsion of Egypt from the Arab League for eight years, subsequent to the signing of the Egyptian-Israeli Peace Treaty (Hourani 1991, 420–21). After Egypt was readmitted to the Arab League, the Mubarak government was no longer the leader of pan-Arab resistance to Western hegemony but instead now found itself in the position of uncomfortable interlocutor between Israel and the Arab world—a role that many Egyptians considered neither appropriate nor effective.

The commercial music recording industry was about to change drastically in 1977 as well. For decades, the only media by which Egyptians could consume recorded music in their homes were radio, vinyl records, and, for the wealthier people, television broadcasts. This began to change in the late 1960s, when production labels experimented with issuing recordings on the newer medium of cassette tapes; the early experiments performed well on the market, and by 1977, there were no less than eight corporations that produced cassettes for the general listening public (el-Shawan 1980, 112). This new medium was cheaper, more durable, and more portable for consumers than vinyl records, and cassette sales became profitable business for such corporate entities; until at least the mid-1980s, such companies could earn dependable profits from sales of their cassette recordings (el-Shawan Castelo-Branco 1987).

Moreover, as Peter Manuel (1993) has investigated famously in the case of Indian popular music, cassettes were also more conducive to low-cost recording and unofficial reproduction of underground music, as well as pirated reproduction of copyrighted material. Although Egypt did not experience the same increase in musical styles as Manuel describes in India, cassette culture clearly contributed to the development of at least one major new genre: *sha'bi.* As Walter Armbrust (1996) has described in detail, by the early 1990s Cairenes were avidly passing around cassettes—many of them, technically, pirated second- or third-generation copies—of various *sha'bi* singers in a manner that simply did not occur on the same scale with either *musiqa al-ṭarab* or Western pop.[42] This unofficial and uncontrolled flow of popular culture through the new medium began around the time of 'Abd al-Ḥalim's death, when the urban musical genre of *sha'bi* began to take shape and new singers turned to cassette culture as a practical solution for low-cost distribution and promotion.[43]

All of this is to say that 'Abd al-Ḥalim's death coincided with a critical point in Egypt's history; the cultural world in which he as well as Umm Kulthum and most of the stars of the Golden Age had lived was dying along with them. Farid al-Aṭrash died in 1974, Umm Kulthum in 1975, and, in 1977, 'Abd al-Ḥalim followed them. As the old world of the Egyptian culture industry was dying or retreating, a new one was emerging. It is to this new world that we will now turn.

2

"Oh, My Brown-Skinned Darling"

Sex, Music, and Egyptianness

As in a great many nationalist contexts studied by anthropologists, Cairene understandings of Egyptian nationalism are shot through with intertwined notions of sex and race. This imbrication is so thoroughgoing that the three phenomena, as they operate in Cairo, are fundamentally inseparable and, when regarded separately, incomprehensible. This fact remains true even when Cairenes are loath to acknowledge their own racialized thinking; race, unlike nationalism and sexuality, is a relatively difficult topic for Cairenes to broach outright and forthrightly. (Although there is, as one may expect, a good deal of reluctance to engage in frank discussions of sexuality, Cairenes of my acquaintance are largely untroubled about discussing at least the normative and putatively desirable qualities of properly controlled sexuality, both by itself and as part of their nationalist thinking.)

The hesitation I encountered among Cairenes to speak frankly of the racial thinking that partially structured their understanding of various cultural phenomena resembles the reported discomfort surrounding Mary Weismantel's work on Andean mythic archetypes, which are a tangle of race, sex, class, and nationalism. This tangle only became more difficult to unravel in the context of several preceding decades of social science research that, for particular reasons of self-reflexive anxiety on the part of the researchers, tended to elide, misconstrue, or pointedly ignore the prominent role of race in these mythic constructs (Weismantel 2001, xxvi–xl). In somewhat analogous fashion, I found Cairenes occasionally reluctant to recognize the racializations at work in their own thinking, even among critically minded thinkers. The elision seems all the larger for the crucial place that race holds in their thinking, while simultaneously remaining invisible—invisible, at least, to the unmarked population of Cairo.

Although I speak primarily of musical aesthetics in this book, it is impossible to avoid the salience of visual aesthetics in the commercial propagation of *al-musiqa al-shababiyya,* due to its heavy dependence upon music video clips distributed on satellite television channels to attract consumers and popularize songs and singers. Even so, I might have tried to set aside the topic of visual aesthetics, had not a critical mass of my ethnographic interlocutors insistently directed my attention to it: on a number of occasions, when the conversation transitioned from *musiqa al-ṭarab* to *shababiyya,* people would say something like, "Well, now we are no longer talking about listening to singers but about watching them." There simply is no avoiding the importance of the commercial video clip as a key form of technological mediation in the *shababiyya* industry, especially because music consumers in Cairo receive a wealth of messages and cues that touch upon their attitudes toward nationalism, sexuality, and race. Let us examine, then, a particularly elaborate video clip as a point of entry to this topic.

"Calling Something Cheap Dear"

Naṣr Maḥrus's video clip (2002) of Shirin 'Abd al-Wahhab's song *Garḥ tani* ["Another wound"] opens with a close-up shot of Shirin's face wearing a look of bitter hurt, her pale-lipsticked mouth twisted into a frown (Figure 5). Her jet-black hair is cut short to frame her face, which appears faintly olive-toned in the bright lighting. Her dark eyes and eyelashes are thickly enhanced with kohl, and above them her precisely trimmed and penciled eyebrows match the color of her hair and eyes. As this shot comes into focus, the viewer hears the first strains of the song—a strongly *musiqa al-ṭarab*–influenced instrumental introduction featuring a string section, timpani, and *nay*. As the orchestra plays the introduction in *tempo rubato,* Shirin runs out of an expensive-looking manse, hops into a late-model Jaguar sedan parked outside, and motors away. As she flees the house, we see that she is wearing a long-sleeved, form-fitting silk blouse, a dark scarf thrown around her shoulders, a loose skirt that extends to just below her knees, and knee-high black leather high-heeled boots. A brief montage informs us that she has driven all through the night[1] to the seaside of Alexandria, where she stops the car, alights from the driver's seat, and leans against the sedan as she begins to sing,[2] expressively, "Another wound, and my heart was still recovering from the first . . ."

The video clip proceeds in similar fashion, with Naṣr Maḥrus cutting between the action of a romantic infidelity discovered and Shirin's passionate mourning of the resulting heartbreak. She acts out the role of a woman

FIGURE 5. Shirin 'Abd al-Wahhab in the video clip of *Garḥ tani.*

discovering that her "beloved"[3]—she wears no ring on either hand—is entertaining another woman at his home; the mansion itself appears to embody the singer's wounded reaction in the numerous framed portraits of Shirin that sit on tabletops or hang on walls throughout the living room and mock the man as their flesh-and-blood subject storms out. Alone on the beach, Shirin laments to herself, "I made the mistake once of calling something cheap dear," shaking her head in performance of someone making this statement, rather than someone singing it—such a physical gesture would not aid a singer. Likewise, although she frequently adopts the performative attitude of someone singing directly to the camera, opening her mouth wide as in the manner of a musical performer, she simultaneously adopts the physical attitude of the character who narrates the song, complete with hand gestures associated in Egyptian conversational style with sorrow and lamentation (a rolling extension of the arm beginning with the hand by the mouth) and argument and defiance (a vigorous head-shake that dips the shoulders, gesturally shooing away the unfaithful lover). It is doubtful that Shirin would employ such vigorous gestures in a live performance, since they could only constrict or disrupt her airflow and thus weaken or choke off her voice; it is similarly impossible that she would employ them in the studio while recording the voice that we actually hear while watching the action of the video clip. These gestures do not—cannot—aid a vocal performance; they are instead intended to aid the performance of a narrative character, one who indicates through her physicality as well as her language and appearance that she is a strongly localized Egyptian woman.

Among many other qualities for which she was known, Umm Kulthum was known for being physically unattractive—or, rather, she was considered physically unattractive for a woman who held so many in her thrall. When Egyptians comment on Umm Kulthum's plain looks, they tacitly finish the statement with, "But how fascinating she was!" An Egyptian-American writer, in describing her playboy father's rumored affair with the singer, notes that it was "surprising, that a connoisseur of female beauty who didn't even deign to look at a woman unless she met his exacting standards would have a liaison with someone who, despite her opulent wardrobe and finery, was rather a plain Jane. Her talent was the ultimate aphrodisiac" (Lagnado 2007, 16–17).

More than simple physical judgment lurks in such statements by contemporary Egyptians. Collective memory of Umm Kulthum recalls not just the singer and her era but the values associated with them. People draw on this cultural nostalgia when they fondly recall how plain the great singer was, as a means of emphasizing that, in the good old days, even a remarkably unattractive woman of humble background could rise to the top of the music industry by virtue of her vocal talent. As my friend Alice commented to me, "She was no *qamura* (cutie-pie), but she could sing." This story fits cozily into the narrative of nationalist modernity that held sway after the 1952 revolution, and which Umm Kulthum herself carefully promulgated in her cannily managed dealings with the press (Danielson 1998, 116–19). Since nostalgia rarely manifests itself without commenting critically on the present, it is possible to mine still more commentary from this judgment: those who recall the talent-driven rise of Umm Kulthum also implicitly indict the contemporary pop music industry for its obsessive attention to female physical beauty.

Although no one ever said so to me explicitly, it seems clear that today, if a female singer of Umm Kulthum's unadmired looks were to attempt to build a music career for herself, she would have no luck. It is not simply a matter of increased visibility through video clips. Although Umm

Kulthum's primary broadcasting medium was radio, she performed numerous live concerts in halls and in private homes. To those with sufficient discretionary income to purchase a vinyl recording or a concert ticket—to say nothing of those with wealth and prestige enough to arrange for a private house concert or to seek the lady's romantic favors—her face was familiar. The difficulty would instead lie in the fact that, as so many Egyptians ruefully remarked to me, the physical desirability of a female singer is now paramount, and vocal talent can appear an afterthought.

"It's all about commerce (*tigara*), not talent." This was one of the more commonly expressed opinions that I heard from Cairenes on the subject of *al-musiqa al-shababiyya.* As with other pronouncements about the relatively low cultural prestige of the genre, this statement is meant to express several ideas at once. Among these is the notion that *shababiyya* is more commercial in nature than *musiqa al-ṭarab,* although both genres are well represented in the commercial recording industry, and the great stars of Egyptian high modernism were as concerned with their sales figures and public images as with their musical craft. Another is that *shababiyya* recording labels—and, perhaps more significantly, their consumers—are only modestly interested in the musical talent of their artists. What the speakers do not always state explicitly is that the quality most valued in female *shababiyya* performers often appears to be physical sexual allure.

Egyptians and I tend to disagree about the relative physical beauty of pop stars. I was constantly surprised to hear that Shirin 'Abd al-Wahhab was generally not considered beautiful, since she appeared so to me. But Egyptians of both sexes and all ages bluntly informed me that Shirin is ugly *(wiḥsha)* in comparison to almost anyone else in the music industry. The Arabic term sounded extremely harsh to me—the word is also used commonly to denote a bad or evil person—and it shocked me to hear her looks disparaged so. I was further confused to hear many young men speak admiringly of the beauty of other pop stars many years Shirin's senior, some of whom have had numerous plastic surgeries to achieve their current appearances.[4] Surely young men would orient toward younger rather than older women, I thought. But no: Shirin has dark brown skin (a complexion that Cairenes refer to as *samra*) and a full, rounded face and figure (Figure 6); thus, to many Cairenes who bear her no malice, Shirin must be described as *wiḥsha.* As I slowly learned, youth and (relatively) natural beauty are generally trumped by plastic surgery and white skin.

Due to the paucity of young Egyptian women on the contemporary

Arabic pop music scene, I was limited in the comparisons I could draw. A felicitous comparison, though, presented itself in the physical differences between Shirin and Angham, the former's senior by eight years. Angham's appearance, by the time of my research, inclined strongly toward the Lebanese standard: petite frame, well-articulated cheekbones, and, most important, pale skin (Figure 7). Shirin, by contrast, does not conform to this ideal in any way. For a short period of time, her figure was comparable to Angham's, but this is visible mostly in a batch of music video clips produced around the same time; as a general rule, her shape is rounder and fuller than Angham's—indeed, rounder than practically any other high-profile female *shababiyya* singer in Egypt. Most consistently noticeable, however, is that Shirin is far darker-skinned than most singers, and certainly much more so than Angham.

As my friend Marwa and I spoke in a café one day, the television set mounted in a corner showed Angham's latest video clip, *Kul ma niqarrab* ("Whenever we get closer") (al-Mahdi 2007), and this provided a handy point of reference for our conversation. I assumed that Angham's physical appearance had always been part of her physical appeal, especially since she has made a genre transition over time: originally, she worked as a performer of *musiqa al-ṭarab,* much of it written by her father, a noted composer. I gestured at the television and raised the question with Marwa of how Angham managed to succeed at such a transition. I had surmised that Angham's more admired physical traits, along with some cosmetic improvements—she famously wore braces as an adult to fix an uneven set of teeth—helped her move into *shababiyya* territory, where looks tend to assume greater importance than in the older musical genre. I was, however, very much mistaken.

Marwa Rakha is the only interlocutor of mine outside the music industry whom I identify by her actual name, and, as with the professional musicians I name, I do so partly because she is a figure of minor celebrity in Cairo: during the time of my doctoral research, Marwa had published a book on romantic relationships (Rakha 2008) and was establishing herself as a pop expert on romantic and sexual matters. I contacted her originally to discuss female role models in contemporary Egypt, and our friendship grew from that point. Marwa comes from a wealthy *ṭabaqa mutawasiṭa* family, and studied English at 'Ayn Shams University. A committed feminist, Marwa is also something of a firebrand, bucking convention by moving out of her parents' home into her own apartment as a young single

FIGURE 6. Shirin 'Abd al-Wahhab, posed as the cover story for the January 23, 2008 issue of *For Her* magazine.

woman, and arguing that other young Egyptian women should follow her lead.[5] In addition to promulgating her ideas through her book, she periodically hosted a radio show and, at the time of writing, publishes an advice column aimed at young women.

When I attempted to compare the physical attributes of Angham and

FIGURE 7. Angham's post-makeover image, in a still from her video clip *Kul ma niqarrab.*

Shirin in conversation with Marwa, who remembered the beginnings of Angham's career, she vehemently disputed the idea that Angham was, in fact, light-skinned: "No, she's never had fair skin! No, no, no! When she first began singing, she did not wear braces yet at the time, and her skin was dark. It's make-up and lighting. And she looked very different. I'm looking at her now—no, that's not the girl I saw fifteen years ago, no!" Angham's cosmetic touch-ups, then, include an ongoing effort to appear more light-skinned than she naturally is, as well as various plastic surgeries and cosmetic dentistry. In other words, she is working hard to achieve, or at least approach, the vaunted New Look standard of beauty promulgated by the Lebanese singers. It is difficult to trace precisely how the phrase "New Look"[6] came into currency in Egypt to describe a particular image of female beauty. No one to whom I spoke knew its exact provenance, but they almost infallibly identified the Lebanese singer Nancy 'Ajram as its prototype (Figure 8).

Nancy 'Ajram's first (in)famous pop hit and video clip was the song *Akhaṣmak ah* ("Yes, I quarrel with you") (Labaki 2003),[7] in which she appears dressed in a style reminiscent of 1940s Egyptian cinema actresses. Framed by her dark hair and clothes, and further set off by the video clip's color palette, 'Ajram's skin appears almost blazingly white. Her figure in the cocktail dress is very slim—especially in comparison to the figures of the actresses who actually featured in 1940s Egyptian cinema—but also features a large bust, relative to her frame. Her face is defined not only by high cheekbones but also by rounded cheeks, plump lips, and a very small nose. It is, altogether, rather an artificial look that hints at the extensive plastic surgery that 'Ajram underwent in preparation for her debut as an adult pop musician.[8] Cairenes who object to such an image and its implications of surgical artifice derisively refer to this collective cosmetic ideal as "inflated" (*manfukha*), referring to the exaggerated and fetishized plumpness of the lips and cheeks. My interlocutors consider 'Ajram's appearance in this video clip as foundational to the New Look that has become closely identified in Egyptian minds with Lebanese pop music. This video clip is worth examining at length, in order to draw out the web of associations that Egyptians have with both the New Look and the term "Lebanese singers" itself.

Nadine Labaki's art direction designed the video clip's mise-en-scène to present a kind of Lebanese fantasy of Egypt, a set of noirish visual references to Egyptian films of the 1940s. The action takes place primarily

FIGURE 8. Nancy 'Ajram, in a publicity still from the mid-2000s.

in a smoky *qahwa al-qazaz,* a French-influenced glassed-in café-cum-nightclub filled with men drinking coffee, gambling, and watching the floor show: 'Ajram herself. 'Ajram appears in a slinky, low-cut, form-fitting black cocktail dress and matching high-heeled slingbacks, with long dark hair coiffed in something close to a Veronica Lake peekaboo style. As several cinematically literate interlocutors explained to me,

'Ajram's appearance in this setting evokes images of the old Egyptian film star Hind Rustum, who frequently played the *femme fatale* or the tough but sexy urban working-class woman, who might manage the nightclub as well as dance in its floor show. (To heighten this effect, Labaki intercuts shots of 'Ajram brewing tea and washing the floor—in her high heels—with shots of 'Ajram dancing for the customers.)

Labaki's shots create a hazy montage suggesting a voyeuristic equivalence between watching 'Ajram gyrate on the dance floor and watching her mop that same empty floor: in either case, the camera is positioned to focus upon the singer's physical attributes, rather than the larger context of her actions. In a close-up shot, 'Ajram draws the viewer's attention to her breasts as she dances by angling her hands to point toward her décolletage, which seems about to pop out of the top of her dress. When 'Ajram pours a bucket of water on the floor before swabbing it, Labaki films the act through an extreme close-up of 'Ajram's splayed lower legs.

Following the archetype of the sexy café manager, 'Ajram makes the rounds of the tables, flirting with the (entirely male) clientele and occasionally participating in their pastimes. She sits in on a card game and handily defeats the handsome young man wearing a woolen flat cap, a button-down shirt, and suspenders, and then coquettishly pantomimes the boastful gestures of a graceless winner, while mouthing the rapidly enunciated words, "*Da inta ḥabibi wa-munaya illi dawibni / Wa-inta illi ba'duh 'an hawaya byita'ibni* (You are my beloved and my desire that has dissolved[9] me / You are the one after whom my love has exhausted me)." After flirting with a few more card players, she sits to observe an arm-wrestling match between two muscle-bound men, one of them anachronistically accoutered in a short goatee, a conical knit wool cap, and an elaborate tattoo that snakes up his left arm. 'Ajram appears to cheer in the latter's support, cupping her hands around her mouth to direct at him the mouthed lyrics, "The world after you is impossible, and night by night my affection increases." Apparently panicked at her favored contestant's chances, 'Ajram puts her hands over his and forces a win for him. His defeated opponent, objecting to the technical violation, begins a fistfight that appears to engulf everyone in the coffeehouse. As the entire clientele descends into a brawl, 'Ajram, who appears to have removed her shoes in order to run more effectively, laughingly flees the scene as the clip ends.

The meter of the song is a fast, driving 4/4 beat, accented by ornamental percussion work on hand drums—what Egyptian music professionals refer to as the "rhythm" (*iqa'*), as opposed to a simple beat. The entire melody and bridge occurs across a small musical interval: in Western musical notation, the song is confined to the range of D up to B, and most of the words are actually sung at E or F. While such an architecture easily fits into traditional Arabic musical theory, it is characteristic only of *shababiyya,* among the musical genres popular in Cairo, to devote so much time in a song to hitting or holding particular notes in this fashion without using them as an anchoring point for melisma or other microtonal techniques. 'Ajram occasionally gestures toward such melisma, especially in her descent from G to E at the end of each melody line; in general, though, she seeks to hit these notes in the center, as one might expect of a Western-trained singer. She also sings at a fast clip, a technique associated with both *shababiyya* and *sha'bi:* she enunciates the lines "*Da inta ḥabibi wa-munaya illi dawibni / Wa-inta illi ba'duh 'an hawaya byita'ibni*" in a mere seven seconds—an unthinkably speedy rate for a singer in the age of high modernist *musiqa al-ṭarab.*

The standards by which Egyptians judge a woman's beauty have changed significantly in the past century. A hundred years ago, the favored body type inclined toward voluptuous abundance to a degree that, in comparison to contemporary preferences, seems like obesity.[10] In *Palace Walk,* the famed Egyptian writer Naguib Mahfouz describes a highly desirable courtesan in 1917 Cairo as follows:

> A carriage stopped at the entrance to the store then. . . . He saw the vehicle tip toward the store under the weight of a prodigious woman who began to alight from it very slowly, hampered by her folds of flesh and fat. A black maid had gotten down first and held a hand out for her to lean on while she descended. The woman paused for a moment, sighing as though seeking some relief from the arduous descent. Then, like the ceremonial camel litter that each year was a traditional highlight of the procession of pilgrims setting off for Mecca, she made her way into the store, swaying and trembling. (Mahfouz 1991, 87)

Those folds of flesh and fat that enraptured Mahfouz's protagonist would not stack up well today against the women who populate the video clips of *shababiyya* songs. Compare the massively proportioned courtesan to such contemporary figures as Nancy 'Ajram, and the change is evident.

Even so, Egyptians still seem to prefer a slightly fuller female figure than do, for example, Americans. One of my friends in Cairo, Huda, had studied at a university in the United States for several years, and she showed me photographs of herself from that time, in which her face and curves were more rounded than after her return to Egypt. Her standard shape in Cairo, by comparison, was rail-thin, although she generally had a good appetite and her parents put square meals on the table. Whereas an American girl[11] might long for Huda's slender Cairene shape—and, it should be noted, Huda was hardly a large girl even at her heaviest—Huda rhapsodized to me about the weight she had gained from eating the heavy, starchy food served in the college dining hall. "Oh Daniel," she sighed, regarding a photograph, "back then I was really a beauty queen!" The attention from men that Huda enjoyed in the United States had no comparison when she returned to Cairo. According to her, at least, the kind of very slender body that she possessed was not admired by her countrymen; she fretted sometimes that she would be unable to attract the eye of a man on account of her skinniness.

Among highly regarded male Egyptian singers, very few are phenotypically white enough to fit the trend; perhaps only Hani Shakir, among the most vocally talented, qualifies as such, but he is nearly sixty and thus somewhat beyond the age to attract the eyes of youthful music fans. 'Amr Diyab, atypically, was often cited to me as handsome by girls, even though he is reasonably *asmarani;*[12] as one interlocutor explained to me, he not only has a gym devotee's worked-out body, but attractive facial features and—unusual for an Egyptian—hazel-green eyes (Figure 9). Tamir Ḥusni, who struck me as a handsome man who would be a huge sex symbol in the United States, was ignored altogether by Egyptian girls thinking of good-looking singers; although his cheekbones and muscles rival Diyab's, his eyes are black and his complexion is darker than Diyab's (Figure 10). The fact that he was greatly admired as a *rumansi* singer within the *shababiyya* genre did little to raise his erotic status with Egyptians.[13]

Hayfa Wahbi and the Lebanese Other

Nancy 'Ajram, as mentioned above, is one of the foundational icons of the New Look and its associations with slickly produced *shababiyya* songs and video clips. In terms of sexual scandal and boundary-pushing, however, she is hardly foremost among the Lebanese singers who now

FIGURE 9. 'Amr Diyab, in a publicity still from 2007.

populate the radio broadcasts and satellite channels that entertain Cairenes. For sheer, overwhelmingly eroticized persona and disreputable fame, the greatest Lebanese icon is the fashion model-turned-singer Hayfa Wahbi. Hayfa, more than any other performer in *shababiyya,* embodies the role of the vamp, not only in her appearance and her behavior but in her biography and her music itself.

While biographical data of all *shababiyya* performers can be elusive, Hayfa's life history is frustratingly difficult to ascertain with any kind of rigor. The general consensus among Cairene pop music fans is that she

FIGURE 10. Tamir Ḥusni, in a publicity still from the mid-2000s.

is a good deal older than she claims to be—according to the scant promotional material that I tracked down, she was supposedly born in 1976. However, she seems to have had an active fashion modeling career by the late 1980s, and according to the better-informed gossip hounds among my acquaintances she had a daughter approximately eighteen years of age in 2008. In truth, virtually all details I have gathered on Hayfa's biography remain in the realm of unsubstantiated rumor and gossip, although some seem more credible than others. The wildest gossip, oddly enough, strikes me as potentially credible, partly because I came by the information thanks to a colleague raised in Beirut, and partly because it explains some questions that Egyptians are otherwise hard-pressed to answer, particularly why Hayfa was suddenly so prominent after entering the field of pop music comparatively late in her life, and why she has always carried an air of sexual scandal beyond that of her fellow Lebanese singers. Here is what I was told:

Hayfa had been working as a professional fashion model for years when she was caught up in a wide-ranging sex scandal in the mid-1990s. The Beirut police caught wind of an invitation-only orgy in progress at a residence in a wealthy neighborhood, and raided the house. They found and arrested over fifty attendees and booked them on a variety of charges relating to illicit sexual relations and drug possession. Hayfa, alone among all of those arrested in the raid, publicly protested her innocence of the charges, which did not sway public opinion concerning her involvement. Indeed, her intention was not to convince people of her innocence but to make the best of an embarrassing incident by playing up her newly created (or perhaps imposed) persona of the wanton sexual creature. After a few years of crafting her public image in Lebanon as a woman who stood outside of the ordinary rules of sexual comportment, all the while winkingly claiming otherwise, Hayfa began to record songs and perform in video clips that built upon this persona for the wider Arabic-language market.

Hayfa's voice falls well short of classical grandeur. She lacks the diaphragmatic strength and chest resonance that are hallmarks of most critically praised female singers. Indeed, her voice is so weak that rather than singing most notes she uses a *Sprechgesang* style, in which the singer half-sings, half-speaks the lyrics, and which depends upon breathily accented words and a staccato nasality.[14] In both her vocal technique and her on-screen persona, Hayfa seeks to imitate the flirtatious affect of a teenage girl; the total effect is comparable to the musical performance style of Marilyn Monroe. Her video clips focus a great deal of attention on her various physical attributes, particularly her heavily made-up eyes, her breasts, and her legs, accentuated by her clothing choices and her dancing. The only complimentary remark I have heard about her voice came from, of all sources, my *musiqa al-ṭarab*–loving language tutor Yaḥya, who once observed to me with a sheepish look, that Hayfa is particularly good[15] at rendering long lyric lines in a single breath with clear diction. As Danielson has noted, aficionados of Umm Kulthum often point out her crisp diction and breath control as contributing factors of her skill (1997, 92–93); in this technique alone, Yaḥya was comparing Hayfa to Umm Kulthum, and even that limited comparison felt discordant enough that he blushed while doing so.

In looks (Figure 11), recording output, and behavior, Hayfa conforms closely to the cultural archetype of the vamp, in much the same way as old film stars such as Pola Negri. Diane Negra's observations about the Hollywood-era Pola Negri as a prototypical vamp carry over reasonably well to the Lebanese singer: "a woman whose origins are unknown or obscure," who threatens to seduce men away from their socially appropriate partners. "The vamp's tendency to posture and her inclination to wear distinctive, vivid makeup combine to render her an excessively produced body. In some sense, she threatens to be out of bounds at any moment, and her body seems always to be in danger of showing" (Negra 2001, 76–77).

Hayfa represents the vamp to Egyptians in the same way as Negri did to Americans in the silent film era. She is a foreign and ultimately unassimilable quantity to Cairenes but is at the same time the focus of intense fascination in part because of this foreignness and markedness. The ethnic difference that operates in the scenario under discussion is Egyptian versus Lebanese—or, one may just as easily say, Egyptian versus non-Egyptian.[16] As with Negri's American reception, Hayfa is a figure of suspicion to many Cairene women partly because she represents temptation away from them—that is, from the kinds of aesthetic charms they possess and the social values they would have people associate with them—toward the Lebanese vamp, a highly inappropriate partner for a middle-class Cairene man. The obscurity of at least some of her origins; the "excessively produced body" that she flaunts in concerts, video clips and interviews; and her clear attention to maintaining herself primarily as an object and, following Negra's argument, a subject of sexual allure as a

FIGURE 11. Hayfa Wahbi, the archetypal vamp, in a publicity still from the mid-2000s.

professional goal are read by most (if not all) of my interlocutors as threatening what they describe as Arab, Muslim, or Egyptian cultural values.

Hayfa herself is, of course, Arab, and at least as a matter of genealogy, Muslim as well: she comes from a Shi'i Muslim family[17] in the south of Lebanon. Many of her critics allege that, given her image and comportment, she cannot be considered a "true Muslim," a tactic of derogation often directed at Muslims in the public eye accused of acting in ways that violate their inherited faith. Due to her vampiness and suggestive dancing in her video clips, Cairenes also perceive Hayfa's Arab credentials as shaky, but this is due in part to a broader sociological distinction; as my friend Khulud explained to me, "It's okay for them [the Lebanese women] to do this, because for us the Lebanese are like foreigners." When I asked her if she meant "foreigners" as in non-Egyptians or non-Arabs, she replied, "Not like Arabs at all."[18]

Although I did not yet have the ethnographic presence of mind to follow up on this comment when Khulud uttered it, I can surmise what she meant by this characterization by referring to what other interlocutors have told me. The distinction between "Egyptian" and "Lebanese" encapsulates a particular implication of cultural values and sexual mores that resonates among Cairenes. In addition, it is well to note that Lebanese people themselves often express sentiments of ethnic and cultural identity that do not align simply with Arabness; many of them, especially Maronite Christians, seem to feel some affinity with the strain of Lebanese territorial nationalism that emphasizes Phoenician, rather than Arab origins (Kraidy 2005, 128–39). Moreover, that Egyptian-Lebanese comparison was constantly thrust in the faces of my Cairene interlocutors, due to the increasing cultural hegemony of Lebanon in Arab mass media (Kraidy 2010, 80).

Bint al-Balad and the Ethnicization of Egyptians

But what of Shirin, then? For that matter, what of almost any Egyptian girl, in terms of her potential for physical admiration? If this pale-skinned standard is so dominant, then how could any dark-skinned Egyptian woman measure up? It seems clear, in that sense, why Shirin's looks should be described so disparagingly, even by people who admire her musicianship. But again, Marwa saw things differently. "Men like Shirin, but not because of her music or her voice; she's cute and she's hot and she's sexy." When I told her of the tendency of my young male interlocutors to dismiss Shirin's looks in comparison to her talent, she cut me off and said, "In consumer behavior, they teach you that not everything the consumer says is what they mean. Now, in Egypt, the beauty standards have been raised to a par that the more Lebanese you look, the more acceptable you are. But Shirin does not look Lebanese, and she does not act Lebanese. So the socially accepted beauty format would be the Lebanese looks, with their skin color and the way their eyes are and the lips and what-have-you . . . and Shirin does not have that. So for those men that you have interviewed, to be cool and to be socially acceptable, they cannot say that they like the way Shirin looks."

Marwa may well have a point about the *déclassé* status of dark-skinned Egyptian beauty, although I am struck by her phrasing of "socially accepted beauty." Whose acceptance? Shirin, who is now a major international star in the Arabic pop music world, appears to have achieved a fairly high level of acceptance from fans. Marwa's remark about the males who disparage Shirin's looks reveals the nature of this acceptability: it is the men who betray anxiety by speaking of ugliness. In fact, not just males, but fans in general—especially fans in the more self-conscious segment of the *mutawasiṭin,* the middle classes of Cairo—betray such anxiety.

Marwa, for her part, admired Shirin's music, considering the singer a notch above the average Egyptian or Lebanese *shababiyya* artist in terms of talent. But, she explained, Shirin's background in Cairo presented some difficulties for socially self-conscious *mutawasiṭ* Cairenes who wished to champion their compatriot while maintaining *muthaqqaf* status—and therefore avoiding the derogatory labels *sha'bi* and *baladi.* "She comes from *zawiya al-ḥamra* or *al-qal'a,* some place that is very local,"[19] Marwa stated succinctly. She was referring here to Shirin's family origins in her native neighborhood—in Cairene parlance, her *balad*—of Cairo, *zawiya al-qal'a* (the Citadel district). *Zawiya al-qal'a* carries positive resonances of local history and heritage as part of Fatimid Cairo, one of the medieval neighborhoods that comprised the original city of Cairo founded by the Fatimid Caliphate nearly one thousand years ago. At the same time, it carries negative associations to Cairenes through its implication of low social and economic status, as such historic neighborhoods have seen much of their traditional economic elite flee to more spacious and prestigious living quarters on the outskirts of the city. Indeed, the medieval neighborhoods of Cairo are subject to a constant state of brain drain dating back decades, as relatively few natives of such districts who complete their higher educations and enter more prestigious and lucrative professions choose to remain in the medieval neighborhoods (el-Messiri 1978, 73).

Marwa personifies the kind of syncretic Egyptian intellectual whom some nationalists on both the left and the right scorn, due to her conviction that Egyptian women and feminists in particular could profit by pushing their discourse at least slightly toward the dominant American model. Although Marwa does not come from high aristocratic origins, she certainly comes from money, and she gives an impression of elite social attitudes in her willingness to consider openly Western approaches to questions of family law and personal status: such a philosophical position has been a convenient target for conservative Egyptian nationalists to attack for well over a hundred years (Juan Cole 1981; Baron 1994, 116–17). Indeed, Marwa *is* elite, not only in terms of her economic status but also in terms of her general readership: she writes primarily in English rather than Arabic, and her advice column is featured in the magazine *Identity*, which takes the wealthy, cosmopolitan-educated elite of Cairo as its target readership. As she explained to me, the choice to write in English to Egyptian readers serves a dual purpose: it allows her to raise unsettling and possibly incendiary ideas in a limited forum without scandalizing the wider Egyptian public, and it suits her compositional strengths, which she has honed far more in English than in Classical Arabic. Unlike the young people she was speaking about, Marwa is sufficiently high in socioeconomic status that class anxiety does not afflict her.

"So," continued Marwa, "if you have an A-class girl, the *crème de la crème* or what-have-you, they wouldn't be proud to say 'we support Shirin' . . . although she has very nice songs, a very good voice and she is Egyptian! But they're ashamed of her." In other words, the class-based distinctions of cultural capital are somewhat harsher toward Shirin and her looks than toward Angham and hers. This judgment is of course not merely class-based but explicitly about class as well: the singer did not grow up in a prestigious neighborhood, is in fact from a district that most *mutawasiṭ* Cairenes would describe as *baladi,* and thereby takes on both the positive and the negative cultural associations of the district. This phenomenon is, of course, nothing new, neither in Egypt nor in other locales; Walter Armbrust demonstrates this by transcribing a conversation between himself and several Egyptian friends who remark upon fans of the "vulgar" singer Aḥmad 'Adawiyya who disclaim any preference for his music, pretending that they listen only to Umm Kulthum if asked (1996, 190). And, on the broader level, the phenomenon has been described systematically and at length in terms of French art and music taste cultures (Bourdieu 1984), French and U.S. upper-class taste cultures (Lamont 1992), and U.S. expressive taste cultures (Gans 1999). But in this scenario, it is additionally meaningful to Cairenes that Shirin not only sounds and perhaps acts slightly *baladi*—some youth from more privileged backgrounds snickered to me that Shirin used uneducated slang expressions in televised interviews—but also bodily manifests *baladi*-ness.

Shirin's success as a professional singer has hardly been harmed by the widespread perception that she is not a great beauty. It would be a mistake, however, to assume that for Shirin, looks simply do not matter in comparison to talent. In fact, many of my interlocutors observed that part of their admiration for Shirin derives from her physical appearance. (And none of them, I should point out, echoed Marwa's assertion that in fact Shirin represented a sexually desirable image of femininity.) Many of them really saw, in their view, a relatively unattractive young woman. The same physical features that they disdained as an aesthetic model, however, were lauded as an index of Shirin's Egyptian identity in ways that track closely with the multivalent meanings of *baladi.*

Alice, who was more generous than most of my interlocutors, allowed that Shirin is not necessarily unattractive in an absolute sense, but rather in comparison to sexier singers, notably Ruby. Her appraisal of Shirin included a revealing bit of identification with the singer: "Her face is a very familiar one: when you see her, you feel something that you know very well. You feel nothing strange about her that you have never encountered at all; and in the lyrics, perhaps, there is something you love, something with which you associate closely (*ta'ashir*) . . . I think she's beautiful, but she's not very beautiful. She's not Miss Egypt, but she's beautiful. Her facial features are proportional (*mashi ma'bad*). She's not a big fat woman, or really skinny. And her face and my face go together; they are so similar as to fade one into the other (*mutalaṣiq awi*)." This comment mirrors Alice's reception of Shirin's musical performances, which Alice finds evocative of Egyptian identity: "I think she's very Egyptian; I feel her to be a *bint al-balad* (girl of the country)! The words of her songs, the composition itself, the composition that the composer himself does is very Egyptian, I think. It returns to the past, and it reminds me of the old-fashioned *[musiqa al-]ṭarab.*"

It is difficult to parse fully the richly nuanced expression *bint al-balad,* which, as Sawsan el-Messiri (1978) has shown in detail, can carry a wide variety of meanings and implications depending on context. It is perhaps easier to quote from another respondent than to hazard my own explanation of the particular usage that my interlocutors employed. My friend Huda, in the course of telling me her own highly complimentary thoughts on Shirin, ended up explaining the term. "I think Shirin is a *bint al-balad.* From the way she talks, I feel you can depend on her when you fall, you know? You can depend on her, she is *bint al-balad,* she is *gad'a* (noble, honorable)! She is very light and humorous. Her songs reflect this light sense of humor the Egyptians have. Ruby, with her songs, does not reflect the same sense. Ruby reflects the naughty girl, that's it. Shirin's songs reflect that she is naughty, she is courageous, she is a survivor. Even the way she dresses! So this is what a lot of women like about her: her songs are very empowering."

U.S. scholars have written about the ethnicization of beauty, particularly that of female stars—Diane Negra, notably, has deconstructed the ethnicization of various actresses in American cinema in terms of their respective cultural moments and the qualities that their publicists and critics saw in them. Her analysis of the early cinematic career of Marisa Tomei comments on the increasingly positive stereotyped associations of ethnicized women over the course of the twentieth century, taking the Italian-American Tomei as an example of this tendency. As Negra observes, critics tended to attribute Tomei's physical expressivity to her Italian ethnicity, which they associated as well with an aura of naturalness and bodily authenticity, and linked it to "a romanticized ethnic past, epitomized by her connection to a 'neighborhood'" (Negra 2001, 146).

The manner in which my interlocutors tend to speak of Shirin reflects a comparable level of attention to the singer's localized (and thereby ethnic) origins and her regionally influenced speech patterns and comportment. Indeed, in my research, Shirin's fans consistently associated her not merely with a country and city of origin but could usually pinpoint the exact neighborhood of her birth. The specificity is arguably even stronger than in the case of Marisa Tomei, whose early publicity associated her with Flatbush in Brooklyn—a neighborhood far larger in square mileage than the compact *zawiya al-qal'a.* In a mirror-image of Marisa Tomei, however, whose naturalness and authenticity are characterized as part of her physical charms, Shirin's naturalness and authenticity are characterized as standing alongside her physical *un*attractiveness as indices of her Egyptian ethnicity. The other notable difference between the two women here is that, while Tomei is regarded in her press as an ethnic woman who is close to standard American (white) ethnicity but somehow marked, Shirin is regarded by my interlocutors as an "ethnic" woman[20] who aligns perfectly with the dominant ethnicity of Cairo. It therefore seems remarkable that she is so strongly *marked*—after all, why would Cairenes so strenuously and consistently mark another Cairene as such?

The perceptions that Alice and Huda note in regard to Shirin's face actually impart positive associations to her apparent physical ordinariness. If Shirin is a *bint al-balad,* just a girl from the neighborhood like any other, then that status depends as much upon her *samra* complexion, her unremarkable facial features and her relatively modest clothing[21] as upon her song texts, her Cairene-accented native speech, and her comportment in interviews. In a way that many other singers, especially the Lebanese women who fit the New Look, cannot hope to achieve, Shirin convincingly fills the role of the local girl who made good. In order to pull off this role successfully in the eyes of her fans, Shirin could not be too beautiful: an excess of physical beauty would impugn the purity of her vocal talent and her resulting career. Umm Kulthum, in this sense, looms large as a role model: the physically humdrum woman with the spellbinding voice. The fact that Shirin is, according to Egyptian beauty standards, far more beautiful than her illustrious predecessor ever was does not intrude upon this narrative of "talent trumps looks"; this narrative is less reported truth than origin myth, and the people who enthusiastically repeated it to me are invested in it for a number of reasons.

First, as Marwa suggested, there is a middle-class anxiety associated with overtly admiring Shirin as a good-looking woman. It is far easier for those Cairenes anxious about their social status and the stories their tastes tell about them to sublimate their physical admiration into an aesthetic appreciation of good music. Second, if Umm Kulthum is indeed the gold standard of Egyptian female singers, then it would only stand to reason that various aspects of her biography take on the aura of legendary example for future generations of entertainers. Third, this narrative functions not only as a comment on Shirin's critical and commercial successes but as a nationalist-inflected justification of the Egyptian woman's prominent position in a recording industry in which Lebanese and not Egyptian women dominate.

Ruby and Domesticized Disreputable Fame

There are two Egyptian female *shababiyya* singers who present useful comparisons to Shirin, in terms of beauty and talent. The first, as I have discussed above, is Angham; this comparison is useful not only because of the stark phenotypic differences between the two women but also because they are regarded as vocally talented singers who have sufficient natural gifts and formal training to tackle aesthetically demanding *musiqa al-ṭarab* compositions. The second, whom I have already mentioned in passing, is Ruby (real name Ranya Ḥusayn). Ruby, a notorious *shababiyya* singer, was born in the Upper Egyptian city of Aṣyuṭ—or perhaps she was actually born in Bani Suwayf, or possibly even in Cairo itself. True to the vamp prerequisites, it is difficult to pin down her precise origins within Egypt, and I have heard all three birthplaces attributed to her from one source or another. Ruby inhabits a singularly disreputable position among

FIGURE 12. Ruby, in a publicity still from the early 2000s.

Egyptian *shababiyya* performers: Cairenes of my acquaintance generally consider Ruby to have no skills of any sort, other than natural beauty (Figure 12) and what they regard as a complete lack of shame. And shame, according to them, is exactly what any other Egyptian woman would feel if she were to emulate Ruby. Her voice is commonly accounted almost unlistenably poor: she has a highly limited range (in Western musical terms, approximately one octave), can sing only in her basic modal voice[22] at weak volume, and has a tendency to slide out of tune.

Ruby's act, however, is oriented more toward her body than her voice: Ruby's video clips almost invariably show her dancing in a particularly bawdy, hip-swinging fashion while wearing skimpy outfits that reveal more skin than most Egyptian women would feel comfortable displaying in public. Sharif Ṣabri, the music industry impresario who, for five years, not only managed Ruby[23] but produced her albums and directed her video clips as well, often focuses his camera on close-up shots of her breasts, midriff, hips, and buttocks as she dances with what has always struck me as near-total incompetence. In a city long famous for its female singers and dancers, Ruby stands out not only as a poor singer but as an inferior belly-dancer as well.

In terms of physical attractiveness, Ruby conforms to New Look standards in all ways but one: her complexion. She has the same *samra* complexion as has Shirin, which would seem a hindrance to her acceptance as a sexual icon. Her facial features, her body, and her erotically charged public image, however, make Ruby exactly that: a sexual icon. In terms of music, no one in Cairo takes her seriously; in terms of sexuality and eroticism, people take her very seriously indeed. As Huda told me, even very proper middle-class girls who deride Ruby in conversation as a whore regard her as a kind of role model for certain social circumstances: "I remember when Ruby first came out with the song *Layh biyidari kida* ("Why is he so secretive?") . . . I was in my first or second year of college, we all went out . . . on a one-day trip to Suez. And there was a DJ playing songs, and they played this song. And literally *all* the girls would imitate Ruby, the way she dances! They have a sense of both respect and disdain for her—love and disdain."

I had become acquainted with Huda when I arrived in Cairo to begin my doctoral research. At the time, she was finishing up an internship at the Fulbright Commission, the agency that oversaw my fellowship, and we began chatting as I sat in the office waiting for one bureaucratic procedure or other to take its course.[24] Several years prior, Huda had won a scholarship to study in the United States, interrupting her course work at 'Ayn Shams University to attend and eventually graduate from a small liberal arts college in America. Huda was talented at languages, and two years in the U.S. had added a polished American accent to her English. It also burnished her résumé, since a college degree from the U.S. carries a great deal of prestige in Egypt. Her parents devoted much attention and care to the education of their only child, and they were deeply proud of her achievements—such study abroad would have been a financial burden out of all consideration for them without the scholarship.

As I quickly learned, Huda regarded her educational background as her meal ticket. She came from a very small *ṭabaqa mutawasiṭa* family: that is, she had few living close kin, beyond her parents, her grandmother, and a smaller number of uncles, aunts, and cousins than is common in Egyptian families. Huda's father, Gawhar, was a retired army officer who subsequently worked for several petroleum companies who had invested in the Sinai oil reserves. She and her parents lived in a small but neatly appointed flat in the Masakin al-Sheraton neighborhood located on the outskirts of Heliopolis, near the international airport.[25] I went to their home as a dinner guest on multiple occasions, and had the opportunity to wonder at length why a retired military officer and petroleum employee—two professions associated in Egypt with significant lucre, and often with outright corruption—lived so modestly.

I soon learned from speaking with both Huda and Gawhar that corruption had driven him out of the military. Gawhar had entered professional military service in the 1960s, and had fought in three wars with Israel: the 1967 War, the War of Attrition, and the 1973 War. He had risen to the rank of colonel but noticed as he did so that the talented officers did not receive promotions as quickly as did the less scrupulous and more ambitious. He described seeing both honest, dedicated officers and corrupt sycophants who would quite literally stoop to carry a superior officer's bags for him. He said that, when he was very new in the service, he saw this phenomenon as instruction and began to follow suit, but a senior officer stopped him and warned him, "Don't go around kissing up to people like that! Just do your job well and be a leader of your men." Gawhar took this advice seriously and considers it to have made him both a better military officer and unsuitable to rise into the highest ranks, which were reserved for the people who, in his view, consistently sought to tell their superiors what they wanted to hear. When it became clear that he would never be promoted to general without becoming part of this system of sycophancy and incompetence, he chose to resign his commission and entered the private sector.

Huda had grown up hearing these stories, and associated them with her own disillusionment about incompetence in Egyptian institutions. She had ambitions to attend graduate school to train as a teacher of English as a foreign language, after finishing her degree. When she returned to Egypt with her bachelor's degree from the United States, she found that she could not convince the administrators at ‘Ayn Shams University—employees of the state—to accept her as a college graduate. On one pretext or another, the functionaries she encountered refused to give bureaucratic recognition to her American degree, and Huda found herself forced to spend another two years in school at ‘Ayn Shams to earn a superfluous degree, so that she could acquire credentials that no one except the Egyptian state considered necessary. She and her father were equally outraged that her hard work at an elite college was dismissed out of hand by the state, seemingly because it did not reconcile conveniently with the bureaucratic forms already associated with her file. By the time the January 25 revolution began, Huda was determined to acquire a job in the United States, in the conviction that she had no hopeful economic future in her native country; her experiences had given her a distinctly sarcastic and cynical perspective on the Egyptian state and its various claims to cultural as well as political authority.

Huda, in fact, is one of the few Cairenes I know who will admit openly to any feelings toward Ruby other than disdain. Significantly, she frames her admiration for Ruby (such as it is) in terms of competition with the Lebanese women in *shababiyya.* When I asked her why she liked Ruby at all, in comparison to most of her compatriots, she explained, “I see her as the only Egyptian woman who can compete with [the Lebanese] . . . She’s Egyptian, her features are Egyptian . . . She’s dark-skinned, *samra,* and she can really belly-dance and everything, so she stands out, anywhere in the world, as an Egyptian woman.” Although I was at a loss to explain why Huda sees any kind of redeeming skill in Ruby’s jerky, spasmodic attempts at belly-dancing, she soon clarified the matter herself by invoking the Lebanese women again. “If the Lebanese women are attacking, then we should also attack! If all the world is totally messed up, then let’s show our women!”

Ruby represents a peculiar twist on the vamp archetype, precisely because Cairenes readily acknowledge her Egyptian nationality and ethnicity. Or, rather, they admit that she is from Egypt, but they will often heartily contest the notion that she truly is *of* Egypt. This contestation of identity is particularly meaningful to producers and consumers of *shababiyya,* if their responses to my questions are any yardstick. Over and over, people minimized Ruby’s Egyptian identity, suggesting that they wished to distance themselves from her. One such producer, the singer Adham Sa‘id of the band Wusṭ al-Balad, said there was little difference between Ruby and the Lebanese women: “Her complexion is Egyptian, and nothing else!" (Adham Sa'id 2007). Likewise, a consumer, Firas, claimed to me, "Ruby isn't very Egyptian; she uses her body in her video clips. On her last album, she tried to be original. She failed, because she just used her body."

Strikingly, the album that Firas referenced, *Mashit wara iḥsasi* ("I followed my feeling"), featured a number of pop songs that plainly drew upon the *musiqa al-ṭarab* toolkit, especially in regard to orchestral arrangements and older rhythms and melodic progressions. For the title track's video clip (Ṣabri 2007a), Ruby follows her usual methodology of erotically suggestive dancing in revealing outfits. And, in a slap in the face to those who would minimize her connection to Egyptian ethnicity, Sharif Ṣabri positions her in front of the Great Pyramids and Sphinx of Giza as she does so. The video clip seems almost calculated to offend those who associate Egyptian female musicianship with traditional decorum, sexual modesty, or vocal talent.

Ṣabri and Ruby take a different tack, however, in the video clip for another single from the album, *Mush ḥatiqdar* ["You won't be able"] (Ṣabri 2007b). The piece begins with a *musiqa al-ṭarab*–style instrumental introduction, played by a *takht,* the *musiqa al-ṭarab* orchestral ensemble heard in virtually all of the Golden Age recordings. Ruby walks onto the orchestra stage and takes a seat on a high stool in front of the *takht,* mimicking the style of older singers; significantly, she is dressed in an outfit that, while too form-fitting to qualify as modest in the eyes of most Cairenes, still covers far more of her than is common in her video clips. Although she appears unable to restrain herself from making a few slinky dance-like gestures with her arms and upper body, Ruby does not stray from the stool for the duration of the song—as a point of comparison, the Golden Age female singers never danced in the course of their performances, and the women would never even hint at such overt physical sensuality in their body language.[26] In musical content, if not in lyrical content,[27] the song is a reasonable facsimile of an old-fashioned composition from the 1960s. Yet, as Firas suggests, Ruby fails in her attempt to "do something original"—his gloss for the concept of performing original pieces written in the classic compositional style. Her voice is breathy and soft; to anyone with even a casual familiarity with *musiqa al-ṭarab,* such a style sounds completely inappropriate and, in this case, the product of a fatally weak singing voice unable to produce notes in tune at high volume with any reliability. Not only in terms of her perceived tendency toward inappropriate gendered behavior, but in terms of her feeble singing voice as well, Ruby fails my interlocutors' acid test for a "real" Egyptian singer.

But if Ruby is inescapably a poor excuse for an "Egyptian voice,"[28] she is, as Huda suggests, a fine nationalism-inflected competitor against her Lebanese rivals. Huda's mild admiration for Ruby is testament to this fact—indeed, particularly so, given that Huda is a pious *muḥaggaba*[29] who would not dream of imitating Ruby in any way other than the occasional coordinated arm-hip gesture at a party. The kind of value that Cairenes like Huda might perceive—although admittedly, Huda is clearly in a minority here—in Ruby as an Egyptian singer is that she is capable of doing what the Lebanese singers do, and of doing so to a further degree. An Egyptian colleague made a similar observation about the singer to me: "Egyptian women think that, for thousands of years, we have been the most attractive women in the Middle East. If the Lebanese women are going to steal the light from us, then we're going to take it back!"

By comparison, Egyptian men appear to have all but ceded the field to their Lebanese counterparts in terms of beauty and desirability. Much as I have described for Egyptian women, Egyptian men in *shababiyya* do not draw the same degree of physical admiration as do Lebanese, and for substantially similar reasons: *asmarani* looks do not qualify as New Look in the music industry, which discounts most Egyptian performers. There are even hints that the male exemplars of the New Look are marketed to female consumers in the same way as are their female colleagues, albeit to a far lesser extent. Wa'il Kafuri, who seems to be the most physically admired Lebanese man working in *shababiyya*,[30] appears in video clips and glamour photography sessions that accentuate his chiseled facial features and heavily muscled body just as his female colleagues are photographed to accentuate their faces and bodies. The video clip for Kafuri's song *Qarrab liyya* ("Come near me"), in which he often reclines on a chaise longue in a sleeveless T-shirt while singing emotively, is the closest thing I have seen to a female-targeted analogue to the seductive video clips aimed at male viewers.

Within contemporary consumers' discourse of *shababiyya,* it is practically taken for granted that there exists an inverse relationship between the beauty of a female singer's face and body and the quality of her voice. Such an inverse relationship appears never to have held sway for men: among the stars of both *musiqa al-ṭarab* and *shababiyya,* some of the best-regarded singers are also the most admired for their looks. In the old days, Farid al-Aṭrash and ʻAbd al-Ḥalim Ḥafiẓ were musical and cinematic heartthrobs; nowadays, ʻAmr Diyab and Wa'il Kafuri are admired as much for their handsome faces as for their singing. There is, however, one aspect of public acclaim in which men and women both participate: the relationship of a good singing voice to Egyptian national identity.

I have never found any archival materials that indicate the degree to which this received wisdom existed during the Golden Age, so it is difficult to draw comparisons with the likes of Umm Kulthum, Asmahan, or Layla Murad; however, it is worth observing that the latter two were considered beautiful women, and Layla Murad starred in a number of Egyptian films. To the extent that one can extrapolate on the basis of the *musiqa al-ṭarab* singers now regarded to comprise the Golden Age pantheon, it appears that this distinction did not hold in earlier decades. If anything, one might expect this inverse relationship to have arisen during the period of the 1950s and 1960s, when low-modernist *musiqa al-ṭarab* began to proliferate alongside its high-modernist cousin, in concert with the slow shift toward direct emotional evocation in music and singing stars who offered a more overtly seductive style in compensation for their limited vocal technique. An examination of the public reception of one of the major culture industry stars from the low modernist period, Suʻad Ḥusni, however, disproves this suspicion.

Suʻad Ḥusni, the late actress and singer who was also a famous beauty, did not confront this inverse relationship between estimations of beauty and talent. Although no one would claim that she was the musical equal of Umm Kulthum, Ḥusni was respected for her singing voice on-camera as well as for her acting skills. No one to whom I have spoken has ever claimed that Suʻad Ḥusni could not sing well, and no one argued that her physical beauty necessarily precluded her from musical talent. This holds despite the fact that Ḥusni's reputation as a celebrity might easily have been based more on her personal behavior than on her professional achievements: much like Elizabeth Taylor, she was known partly for her long series of marriages and rumored affairs with other stars. Ḥusni was also a style-conscious woman who often dressed in chic designer clothes with plunging necklines, short hemlines, and form-fitting cuts, all of which were relatively unremarkable at the time but which would be scandalous on the streets of Cairo today. In this regard, she was of her artistic generation, entering the motion picture industry as a teenager in the late 1950s and working as a youngish contemporary of Shadiyya, Fatin

Ḥamama, and other such icons of the post-1952 Egyptian culture industry. Had she been born a generation earlier, she might have been publicly excoriated for her marital record and too-overt attention to her own beauty, as was the singer Asmahan (Zuhur 2000:78–89). Had she been born a generation later, she would have had to contend with a culture industry that was again growing more conservative, with celebrities accorded less leniency in how they dressed and comported themselves if they wanted to take major roles in serious films and television serials.

However, Su'ad Ḥusni's memory nowadays may have a different cast to it than the stardom she enjoyed during her lifetime. One of her more famous films, and the one for which she is perhaps best remembered now, is Ḥassan al-Imam's 1972 musical romantic comedy written by the great Nasserist poet Ṣalaḥ Jahin, *Khalli balak min Zuzu* (*Pay Attention to Zuzu*).[31] The film's protagonist, Zuzu (played by Ḥusni), is a charming and hard-working (and therefore, within the conceit of the film, rising in social class) student at Cairo University, apparently admired by all except some dour quasi-Islamist classmates. She takes up with her handsome, aristocratic young professor, who breaks his engagement to his shallow, spoiled cousin to be with her.

In the evenings, though, Zuzu also helps her family earn a living by moonlighting in the family's business of party entertainment: specifically, she and her mother are belly-dancers, and her father sings as musical accompaniment. Entertainers have traditionally occupied a position of very low prestige in Egypt, especially female dancers (see van Nieuwkerk 1995). To this day, many Cairenes consider the line between belly-dancing and prostitution fuzzy at best. 'Antar, the manager of a somewhat disreputable café at which lower-middle-class youth—*mutawasiṭin*, perhaps, but not *muthaqqafin*—belly-dance as amateurs to both live and recorded music (Gilman 2009), confidently informed me of this association: he claimed that all professional belly-dancers up to and including the major stars of the Cairene belly-dancing world, who generally perform only in their own nightclubs along Pyramid Road or within the floating restaurants moored along the banks of the Nile in Zamalik, are "professionals at sex." Within the conceit of *Zuzu* such a claim is clearly not true, but in the film the dancers themselves are clearly mindful of and anxious about the potential accusation.

What follows the budding relationship between Zuzu and her professor is a love triangle inflected by class snobbery. Bent on revenge, the jilted cousin spies on Zuzu and figures out her family's occupation, and arranges a party at which Zuzu's mother (portrayed by the famous belly-dancer and actress Taḥiyya Karyuka)[32] dances for the presumably upper-middle-class attendees, including her ex-fiancé and a horrified and humiliated Zuzu. When the youthful partygoers, at the ex-fiancée's instigation, proceed to mock Zuzu's parents as low-class and over the hill, Zuzu outs herself to her peers as the dancer's daughter, and out of a combination of proud defiance of her tormentor and loyalty to her mother, she performs the belly-dance in the older woman's stead.[33] Zuzu's university classmates publicly mock her for her scorned occupation and her supposed lack of morals, causing her to flee from campus and vow to become a full-time belly-dancer now that it seems impossible to continue her studies in peace. Her mother, however, has a nightmare in which she foresees her despairing daughter's impending descent into actual prostitution as a nightclub belly-dancer,[34] and when she wakes up in agitation, she orders Zuzu to dance no more, expelling her from the family business for her own welfare. Zuzu returns to campus chastened but dignified, and after delivering a speech shaming her accusers while also abjuring her earlier work, she is welcomed back as an honored classmate and love interest.

The film has retained its popularity over the years, and in particular Su'ad Ḥusni's role is well remembered. The melodramatic, almost tragic scene in which Zuzu defiantly dances in front of her peers in defense of her family's dignity is remembered with especial fondness: when a television serial, *al-Sindirila,* was produced of Ḥusni's life and work (Sayf 2006), this set piece was one of the classic cinematic scenes that actress Muna Zaki, portraying her illustrious senior colleague, had to re-create with great care. At the same time, it is hard to say with any certainty whether or not contemporary audiences, especially contemporary youth, take the same cinematic pleasure from Ḥusni's performance as did audiences in 1972. As Armbrust observes, the tendency for youthful viewers forty years later is to appreciate the film nowadays more for its sensual, eye-catching, well-choreographed dance scenes than for its plot (Armbrust 1996, 124). But in a sense, this shift in the focus of the viewership's interest underscores the point that audiences in the 1960s and 1970s considered Su'ad Ḥusni far more than just a pretty face. As Armbrust has analyzed it, the film's plot folds neatly into the vision of bourgeois nationalist modernity promulgated by the Egyptian state at the time of the film's production (Armbrust 1996, 117–25). Indeed, Ḥusni starred in serious artistic dramas as well as light musical comedies in the 1970s, including some hard-hitting films that dealt directly with the violence and corruption of the Nasserist state (Shafik 2007, 110–11)—hardly the venue for an actress valued solely as eye candy. And, in spite of the two-dimensional characters and the sometimes stilted dialogues, *Pay Attention to Zuzu* was written and produced as an honest social commentary, not (merely) as a vehicle for Su'ad Ḥusni. Had Ḥusni presented herself, or been presented by the culture industry, as a young beauty whose good looks superseded or overrode modest performing talents, she would not have had a career worthy of a biopic serial. The point here is that Su'ad Ḥusni was not unusual for her time; she only seems so if one assumes that Egyptian female performers were always valued primarily for their beauty *or* for their talent but never for both. Those paths to stardom have not always run in parallel but diverged at some point subsequent to Ḥusni's heyday.

Origins, Authenticity, and *Aṣl*

The desire to define oneself in opposition to musical tastes stands as a major subtext of a great many conversations that I had throughout my time in Cairo. I participated in these conversations with the same level of intensity as did my Cairene associates. The simple fact of my professional interest in *al-musiqa al-shababiyya* made my musical taste somewhat suspect to many Egyptians with whom I discussed such matters. While some people expressed affection for various singers and songs of the genre, others excoriated it wholesale, and one or two actually attempted to convince me to abandon my studies of *shababiyya* and reorient my scholarly interest toward *musiqa al-ṭarab*, a more worthy musical topic. None of this surprised me much, since I was already aware of *shababiyya*'s shaky stature in popular culture, and likewise aware of the high regard in which many hold *musiqa al-ṭarab* for reasons musical, cultural, and political.

I was, however, surprised to learn that a mirror-image situation often pertains between Egyptians and me when the music under discussion is American. In attempting to describe the beauty of *musiqa al-ṭarab,* a shocking number of Egyptians seized upon analogies to Michael Bolton, Whitney Houston, and Celine Dion. These singers, in my aesthetic judgment, represent many of the worst tendencies of American popular music, churning out emotive, histrionic performances of blandly formulaic and generic lyrical texts. American music snobs—a group in which I somewhat reluctantly situate myself—tend not to value such qualities in song, and accordingly place these singers in a sort of pop music rogues' gallery. Egyptians, though, and especially highly educated Egyptian intellectuals of my acquaintance, adore these same singers. The same scholar of Egyptian traditional music who finds most *shababiyya* exhausting to listen to claimed to me that he experienced a kind of *ṭarab* when listening to Whitney Houston and Celine Dion: "It is in the throat," he explained. Absorbing this attitude toward music gave me cultural vertigo almost as disorienting as when I first arrived in Egypt, unable to speak the local dialect and humbled by the difficulty of accomplishing simple tasks.

Aside from a love of emotiveness in itself, the tastes of most educated (and, no less important here, aesthetically discriminating) Egyptians whom I know differ sharply from that of their American counterparts, specifically regarding their relative lack of interest in irony in music—or, more precisely, ironic distance as a lyrical or narrative device. Michael Bolton's songs irritate me partly because there is never an indication that he himself is aware of the tremendously formulaic nature of everything he sings, the sense that all of his songs are variations on the same set of on-the-nose clichés and depend upon a level of emotionally direct language that has no place in the prose of everyday life.[35] To my friend Khulud, however, these qualities blend perfectly with Bolton's emotionally strained vocals to create great pop songs. It surprised her to hear that I am not a fan. At the same time, Khulud has little patience for the infamously "seductive"[36] Lebanese singer Hayfa Wahbi, whose songs and especially video clips evince—to my eyes, at least—a winking, ironic commentary on themselves. Where I see meta-commentary by a former fashion model who knows perfectly well that her talents are prodigious physical beauty, cultivated sexual allure, and a weak singing voice,[37] Khulud sees calculated whorishness and lack of musical talent. The most that Khulud will admit in favor of my argument is that, in comparison to other female singers whom she dislikes as sexually inappropriate, at least Hayfa possesses a modicum of charisma that makes her seem slightly more palatable.

Aḥmad 'Umran, one of the very few interlocutors whom I identify by their true names, is an established professional musician best known as the *'ud* player for the Cairo-based musical ensemble Wusṭ al-Balad (about whom much more in chapter 4). A *muthaqqaf* from a family of *muthaqqafin,* Aḥmad is the son of a professor of folklore who is himself known for his long study of Egyptian folk music traditions. Aḥmad studied *'ud* and flute at conservatory, and has lived abroad in Germany for periods of time. Like most trained musicians I have met in Cairo, Aḥmad is fluent in both Western and Arab musical idioms, and during the period of my doctoral research, he began experimenting publicly with a side project in electronica while continuing to play with Wusṭ al-Balad.

Aḥmad was far from the only serious student of music with whom I spoke, but he was the only working musician with whom I had significant contact young enough to qualify as a *shab* (youth). He kept an apartment downtown appropriately convenient to Makan, a performance venue closely associated with a variety of traditional music ensembles and performers, and he was often to be found in the various *ahawi* (traditional cafés) and upscale coffee shops in the downtown area favored by intellectuals. Aḥmad struggled personally as a musician with both the performing expectations for his ensemble, which he eventually found constricting, and the stuffy high-culture attitudes that surrounded the memory of the "Golden Age of *ṭarab*," which he considered injurious to a proper assessment of Egypt's musical patrimony.

In this iconoclastic vein, Aḥmad 'Umran dismisses the work of Umm Kulthum as inauthentic to Egypt's *turath* (cultural heritage). The corpus of *musiqa al-ṭarab,* which so many Egyptians told me was the only real music that Egypt had ever produced, strikes Aḥmad as adulterated by Turkish musical traditions and technical approaches, particularly in Umm Kulthum's choice of *maqamat.*[38] He declared to me once that his erstwhile classmate in conservatory, none other than Shirin 'Abd al-Wahhab, actually made use of far more "Egyptian" *maqamat* than her illustrious predecessor. In this regard, Aḥmad stands as a youthful analogue to the educated and formally trained music experts of the elder generations, whose erudite and, arguably, elitist understanding of what constitutes Egyptian music excludes cultural artifacts that most Egyptians would include without a second thought.[39]

In the discourses that young Cairenes experience and in which they participate as inescapable and essential parts of their lives in contemporary Cairo, there runs an underlying unifying discourse of authenticity of identity, which these young Cairenes are strongly inclined to understand and theorize in terms of Egyptianness *(maṣriyya)*. This phrase encompasses not only Egyptian nationality as political subjectivity but also Egyptian identity as cultural, ethnic, and even racial subjectivity. This overarching subjectivity depends upon a complexly structured and dynamic understanding of authenticity of the subject: one that cannot be taken for granted as a matter of birth, nor be mistaken for lifetime tenure. Rather, this subjectivity requires constant attention and performance, even though the kinds of performances demanded are not stable and the rules of action and reaction are sometimes unclear to participants.

Intersubjective practices of gendered comportment—that is, what a putative Egyptian subject can and cannot do with his or her body in various social contexts—comprise a major criterion by which Egyptians authenticate themselves or, to use John L. Jackson Jr.'s analytical term (2005), lay claim to the *sincerity* of their identity. Such gender relations are subtly linked nowadays to Arab political relations, since the erotically charged Lebanese singers (and, by association, Lebanese people in general) consumed as part of *al-musiqa al-shababiyya* figure into Cairenes' thinking as a sexual Other, a model of Arab subjectivity that is fundamentally incompatible with Egyptianness. While the West and especially the Western woman has long represented a kind of incompatible sexual Other for Egyptians, this fantasized Lebanese subjectivity represents a far more troubling and challenging problematic.

Another component in this subjectivity is the shift in preferred aesthetics of emotional evocation in popular music, and the consequent ways in which Cairene youth are capable of appreciating music and its potential to move the listener. Authenticity of musical performance has become a serious matter for Cairenes as an aspect of postcolonial modernity, and much of their judgment of this phenomenon rests upon their evaluation of a singer's success at communicating emotion and, thereby, evoking emotional response in the listener. As I shall discuss, Cairenes' aesthetic evaluations of *shababiyya* singers constitute a matter of both authenticity and sincerity, in that there exist overlapping subject-object and subject-subject relations in such evaluations, and both sets of relations contribute to Cairenes' understandings of their own subjectivity.

This evolving sense of national identity contributes to a kind of racialized fragmentation, most prominently, in the case of pop music, between Egyptians and Lebanese. This concept, which within scholarship is not yet commonly encountered outside particular social and historical discourses of interactions between people of very different phenotypes, requires some explanation here. I do not mean to suggest that Cairenes are moving toward a perception of themselves as, say, black in comparison to Lebanese people; to assume that this somatic and color-defined differentiation is the natural progression of such thinking is to view the phenomenon of racialization too narrowly. Rather, Cairenes, for reasons partly of phenotype but more fundamentally of imagined behavior and moral distinction, have begun an epistemological project of marking themselves as profoundly different from the inhabitants of Lebanon, in a way that can only be described as racial difference.

My thinking on this subject draws on the work of Bruce Baum (2006), who has described the prehistory of the category that Westerners and especially Americans now call "Caucasian." Baum observes that contemporary Western observers of racialization (or "race-making") scenarios in other historical periods and geographic locales may perceive these scenarios as fundamentally *ethnic* in nature, rather than *racial,* because they are unaccustomed to thinking about race in any terms other than the biological ones they have known. Nevertheless, since the end result in each case is a collection of phenotypic characteristics and cultural practices assigned some political and social value, racialization is the underlying phenomenon under discussion (Baum 2006, 10–11).

In these terms, then, Cairenes are engaged in a process of shaping their perception of Lebanese people into a perception of a new concept of race, within the Egyptian context—in short, race-making. I refer to the scenario under discussion as *incipient* racialization because, if we are to follow Baum's analysis, the fullness of the phenomenon requires an institutionalized system of privilege and discrimination of one group over another. At the very least, such a system does not yet obtain in Egypt, other than questions of citizenship and political subjectivity that pertain to any modern political state. In addition, the quasi-racial distinctions that Cairenes drew between themselves and Lebanese were never identified explicitly as racial; however, it is entirely possible that they have collectively begun to formulate such an idea before it can attach itself to an existing word in their lexicon (Baum 2006, 41).

I should also point out that the interplay of race and ethnicity in the Arabic language bears little resemblance to its counterpart in English and other European languages, as much for sociological reasons as for linguistic ones. In the United States, we tend to speak of race as a physiological, biological quality ultimately rooted in the color of one's skin and the features of the face, and of ethnicity as a cultural subset of race determined by the "original" language and geopolitical location of one's ancestors.[40] These criteria do not obtain for the same purposes in Arabic, at least not in Cairo. Cairenes tend to apply the word "race" (*gins* or *'unṣur*) to the various distinctions within the broader ethno-linguistic category of the entire worldwide population of native Arabic speakers, to which Cairenes refer as "the Arab nation" *(al-umma al-'arabi)* or more simply as "all the Arabs" *(kull al-'arab)*. More commonly, however, Cairenes break down the world according to "nationality" *(ginsiyya)*, a technical term of political citizenship that carries implications of both ethnic subset and racial category, depending on how it is deployed, or "origin" *(aṣl)*, which refers not only to the linguistic and placed implications of the English word *ethnicity* but also to the concept of *authenticity* (which I shall discuss in greater detail below). There is therefore an inescapable element of translation in my interpretation of my interlocutors' comments on the subject, which I have attempted to parse as precisely as possible.

The Lebanese are hardly the only Arabic-speaking people whose ethnic/racial identity Egyptians tend to perceive as fundamentally different from their own. Indeed, in an off-handed manner, most Cairenes of my acquaintance tend to speak of their identity in banally territorial-nationalist terms: that is, that they are first and foremost *Egyptians,* and Arab identity is something they feel only in comparison to Europeans, sub-Saharan Africans, et cetera. The word *Arab* itself has long been used in the spoken Arabic of Cairo with a pejorative cast: a hundred years ago in the time before the spread of Arab nationalism, the word referred to the nomadic Bedouin tribes who live in the Sinai Peninsula and the Western Desert, in contrast to both the sedentary villagers of the Nile Valley agricultural lands and the ostensibly more sophisticated inhabitants of the urban centers that punctuate the flow of the Nile and the Mediterranean coastline.[41] Nowadays, the word *Arab* in Cairene dialect often refers to citizens of the oil-rich countries of the Arabian Gulf, many of whom spend their summers in Cairo or Alexandria to escape the brutal heat of the Arabian Peninsula. Accordingly, the word now often implies not rusticity or lack of civilization but rather the crass *nouveaux riches* who, in the eyes of many Cairenes, come from the Gulf to lord their wealth and power over their relatively impoverished Egyptian neighbors. As one young woman helpfully explained the usage to me: "If you go to Arab League Street,[42] you might say, 'Ah, a lot of Arabs came this summer'."

Moreover, Cairo racial attitudes also encompass in some ways the negative valuations of dark skin that Western scholars of race tend to analyze. A conversation with Zaynab, one of my more style-conscious acquaintances in Cairo, illustrates this prejudice. Zaynab had the caramel *samra* complexion seen so often among Egyptians, and dark hair that she opted to dye jet-black for a more striking contrast with her skin. Like many young women in Cairo, Zaynab was fastidious in her personal grooming: her hair was always painstakingly coiffed, her eyebrows were always carefully plucked precisely into shape, and her make-up was always artfully applied to accentuate her eyes. A liberal Muslim who chose not to veil, she generally dressed on the flirtatious side of modesty, always properly covered but in very form-fitting clothing.[43]

Zaynab comes from what I understood to be, in the pre-independence era, a family in the lower ranks of the old Ottoman-Egyptian aristocracy. She had forebears who numbered among the titled effendis and beys who staffed the pre-independence government offices. This also meant that she could trace some of her lineage back to other Ottoman and Arab lands; she proudly informed me of her ancestry from Morocco and the Levant. Her family still travels to Lebanon from time to time to visit relatives, and Zaynab delighted in her acquired facility in the Lebanese dialect of Arabic. Since I was already beginning to mark the racial categories that Cairenes utilize, I asked her how she would put it across to me if her Egyptian background were mixed with Sudanese heritage, rather than Lebanese or Moroccan. "I would not mention it!" she promptly answered. "I'm Egyptian, period!"

Zaynab grinned self-deprecatingly as she said this, but she spoke candidly of the attitudes prevalent in Cairo on this subject. Cairenes do not treat all Arab ancestries equally, even when discussing admixtures of one's Egyptian bloodlines. The Sudan,[44] although it has often been part of the Egyptian political sphere, and although the northern portion has long been ruled by a Muslim majority with political and cultural ties downriver, is not a desirable family origin for Cairenes: the region of the Sudan has for many centuries[45] been associated with dark-skinned black Africans, and this fact holds racial implications for Cairenes. Despite being majority Muslim and Arabophone (at least in the north), the Sudan seems "other" to Cairenes, who view the region as a less prestigious origin than, say, Lebanon. It is a backwater to those who reside in Cairo and the Lower Nile Valley at large. More than simply the boondocks, though, the Sudan is essentially part of black Africa to Cairenes, where people's phenotypes, obviously enough, index blackness and Africanness, rather than Arabness or Egyptianness.

This indexicality of blackness is troubling to many Cairenes who prefer to perceive themselves as descending from a mixture of autochthonous Nile Valley populations—the pre-Islamic Coptic Christians, in essence—and the Muslim conquerors from the Arabian Peninsula. Egyptians, although they are quite literally African in terms of geography, almost never willingly apply such a label to themselves. They strongly prefer to characterize themselves in terms of geography as "Mediterranean," and even this identifier is not especially common. The word "African" is inflected with a host of negative valences, among them ignorance, stupidity, and ugliness. Indeed, the only time I ever heard a Cairene self-identify as African, it was sarcastic and pejorative: my friend Huda, berating herself for forgetting something that she was supposed to remember, mocked herself by saying to me, "Honestly, sometimes I really think I am African!" The western half of the Arab world, to which Egyptians are generally happy to ascribe themselves, sits loftily along the northern coast of the African continent, and all of its constituent lands south of the Lower Nile Valley—Sudan is one of several—can appear only partially or provisionally part of that world to the inhabitants of Cairo.

This anxiety about blackness articulates itself every day on the streets of Cairo, where many black people—Arab and non-Arab, Muslim and non-Muslim—have settled from other parts of Africa. Blackness, because of its traditional associations with evil and negativity, features in many idiomatic expressions in Arabic, and thus it is easily turned into a term of vituperation toward people perceived to be black. Partly for this reason, then, Cairenes commonly use the term *asmarani* (literally "brown") with a broad connotative meaning, as a way of describing the darker common complexions of Egyptians without seeming to insult them. *Asmarani* and its feminine-inflected form, *samra*, frequently refer to the breadth of shades of skin color seen throughout Egypt, among all social classes and geographic regions. By way of illustration, most Egyptians whom I mention by name in this book would likely classify themselves with this pair of words, and the few who might consider themselves too pale to be "brown" would likely opt for *qamaḥi* ("wheaten" or "wheatish").[46] Even when blackness is perceived to have some beauty or sexual desirability to it, this perception often comes through in a pejorative, racist way, as when dark-skinned girls are harassed on the streets by boys who jeeringly taunt after them, "*Ya shukulata* (Hey, chocolate)!"

These color terms occasionally make their way into popular music, where their meanings can be very much in the ears of the beholder. The "low modernist" *musiqa al-ṭarab* singer Shadiyya[47] recorded a song entitled *Ah ya asmarani* ("Ah, O brown one"), whose lyric text sensually describes the beauty of the title character. A plethora of *shababiyya* compositions also make use of the term, always with a positive connotation of beauty and desirability.[48] Most notably, perhaps, Muḥammad Munir recorded a new version of the old tune popularized by Shadiyya, with extensive electronic instrumentation and a driving, percussive rhythm. This recording, however, comes from a different cultural context than the original: whereas Shadiyya was a beautiful, light-complexioned woman, Munir is probably the most famous Egyptian man alive of Nubian background. Even though I find it hard to distinguish his coloring from that of many Egyptians of non-Nubian heritage, Cairenes—who, of course, are well aware of Munir's biography—perceive him as much darker than the average Egyptian, and certainly more so than the average Cairene. In Muḥammad Munir's hands, the song can take on resonances of Nubian ethnic pride and, in a larger sense, Egyptian national pride: Munir stands in contrast to the hundreds of almost interchangeable white-skinned singers from the Levantine countries whose songs, as well as their video clips, generally eroticize whiteness. Shadiyya, Egyptian nationalist though she may well have been, cannot imbue the song with the same resonances.

An astonishing number of my interlocutors unselfconsciously used the phrase "Egyptian voice" as a colloquial gloss for "good voice." Though this might seem to those with some familiarity with *shababiyya* to reflect the proper usage of Egyptian Colloquial Arabic (ECA) as a musical medium, it is not the case. In fact, until the 1990s, there were but a few notable Arabic-language singers—for instance, Fairouz in Lebanon, Cheb Khaled in Algeria—who ever sang in a dialect other than ECA and maintained a pan-Arab or at least Arab regional listenership. To this day, it remains common for ambitious *shababiyya* singers from Lebanon and Syria to record songs in ECA, although they may also choose to record some pieces in their native country's dominant dialect, or even in that of another country. Indeed, some of my interlocutors muttered glumly to me that nowadays, pop music stars are inclined to record at least a few tracks in *khaligi* (Arabian Gulf) dialect to court the favor of Prince al-Walid bin Ṭalal, the Saudi owner of the huge music label Rotana, as well as the wealthy listenership that his countrymen and those of neighboring Gulf countries constitute. When Cairenes speak of "Egyptian voices," they speak not of dialect (which anyone, theoretically, could learn to emulate), but of the essential quality of the voice itself (with which one must simply be born). While there certainly are non-Egyptian Arabs whose voices Cairenes openly admire,[49] listeners of my acquaintance take special pride in the skills of talented musicians from Egypt, and frequently identify Egyptian biographical roots as a determining factor in one's ability to perform vocal music well.

This typological maneuver applies to men just as much as to women, as I discovered. In particular, 'Amr Diyab and Tamir Ḥusni were often cited to me as male singers whose voices were markedly Egyptian. Upon close inspection, this notion has few if any concrete criteria; whenever I pressed interlocutors who made this claim to explain it in clear terms, they fell upon a variety of glosses and workarounds that often did not relate to either man's singing voice. Indeed, if one were to compare either of these men to their Golden Age predecessors, their voices would fall short of classical greatness. To put it another way, they are accounted good singers, but not according to the standards set forth in *musiqa al-ṭarab;* rather, they have good voices according to the looser and Western-influenced standards of *shababiyya.*

Much like their Western counterparts, 'Amr Diyab and Tamir Ḥusni are praised by fans for the sweetness of their tone, their ability to hit and hold notes, and the light melodic style of their recordings. The word "light" here is one that I have taken from my interlocutors; to the best of my understanding, young Cairenes use the term to refer to a pleasant, comforting tune and the sort of uncomplicated, undemanding melodic structure that requires little effort on the part of the listener. This compositional aesthetic differs sharply from *musiqa al-ṭarab,* which my informants frequently described as "heavy" and difficult to appreciate in its fullness. Vocal lightness and sweetness can also correlate with a gentleness of tone that very few singers can produce except at a volume just above a whisper, which means that this aesthetic expectation tends to demand the presence of electric amplification in order to hear the singer's notes at all—in other words, sweetness can favor a relatively weak singing voice. This contrasts sharply with the vocal aesthetics of *musiqa al-ṭarab,* in which the quality of the singer's voice is judged partly upon his or her reliable ability to produce notes at high volume, no matter what the emotional color of the passage.

In analogous fashion, the qualities of the two singers' voices differ from those of their predecessors. Speaking for myself as a Western-bred music listener, I found the voices of Farid al-Aṭrash and Muḥammad 'Abd al-Wahhab somewhat grating when I first heard them.[50] They do not correspond to the "sweet" tonal qualities that American music listeners tend to value; they can sound harsh, erratic, unconcerned with clear tonality or even consistent pitch. This is not to suggest that *musiqa al-ṭarab* possesses no useful aesthetic criteria; this is by no means the case. The aesthetics of *musiqa al-ṭarab* are, in their way, complex and demanding; but they simply do not map easily on to the suite of aesthetic criteria by which either Western pop music or *shababiyya* is judged. In spite of this disconnect—or perhaps, as I will discuss, because of it—my interlocutors had little trouble identifying "very Egyptian voices" among both modern and bygone music stars.

Among *musiqa al-ṭarab* artists, it is not surprising that Umm Kulthum received a great deal of praise from my interlocutors as "very Egyptian." If, however, we grant a fair degree of inclusivity to the category of *shababiyya*—which is essentially a catch-all category defined primarily by its listenership rather than its musicological qualities—then another artist generally associated with *musiqa al-ṭarab* actually was cited more frequently: 'Abd al-Ḥalim Ḥafiẓ. To clarify the matter somewhat, I only concerned myself with inquiring about the Egyptianness of *shababiyya* singers; some people would offer their thoughts on Umm Kulthum's Egyptianness without my prompting, but I did not interrogate this concept per se. In this sense, it is rather striking that so many of my youthful interlocutors would (still) think of a man thirty years in his grave[51] as one of the most Egyptian of *shababiyya* singers. In general, those interlocutors who dwelt on the specifics of his voice spoke more about its romantic, emotive qualities than about his technical virtuosity. My interlocutors spoke admiringly of current male stars like 'Amr Diyab, Tamir Ḥusni, and Hani Shakir in a very similar fashion. Their comments on such singers, including 'Abd al-Ḥalim, reveal a great deal about their thinking on the subject.

Alice, like many of her Cairene age-peers, mostly listens to *shababiyya,* and has little interest in *musiqa al-ṭarab,* except for 'Abd al-Ḥalim. Her first comment on him was, in fact, a foreshadowing of her later lengthy repudiation of Umm Kulthum: "His songs are very short; they are not seventeen minutes long, like Umm Kulthum!" When I asked her to explain what she found enjoyable in his songs, she thought for a bit, then responded, "I think he feels these words. I don't feel this with Umm Kulthum, for example, or [Muḥammad] 'Abd al-Wahhab. The old people [that is, Golden Age singers], of course, I don't know all of their names, but my favorite is 'Abd al-Ḥalim. He's the only one whose songs I listen to, from among the old people." Further probing uncovered another important aesthetic difference between the younger and the older subdivisions of *musiqa al-ṭarab:* pleasing lyrical compositions. "The poem[52] itself was written in a very good way . . . I hear some songs, for example, that—" Alice shrugged at this point to demonstrate her apathy, "—what then? Is that all there is?" Alice, in fact, privileges the composer of the lyric text above the vocal interpreter in her judgment of a song's worth, as suggested by her use of the word "poet" to describe the songwriter. "It all goes back to the poet. I don't despise the singer, but it all goes back to the poet."

Such comments as Alice's suggest the extent to which a "very Egyptian voice" depends not only upon sonic characteristics but upon the pleasurable reception of lyric texts and musical arrangements. While there are many fine distinctions between the common musical techniques of *musiqa al-ṭarab* and *shababiyya,* one stands as particularly salient in this context: *shababiyya* singers, unlike their *musiqa al-ṭarab* counterparts, shape the words they sing with far greater respect to a constant meter. That is, a great many songs in the corpus of *musiqa al-ṭarab* allow a high degree of interpretive license to the singer in deciding how long to hold a syllable on a sustained note, or to stretch the same syllable across several slowly produced notes, or across a rapid melisma. This has the effect in many cases—Umm Kulthum's renderings of the virtuosic passages in recordings of *Inta 'umri* or *Alf layla wa-layla* are but a few obvious examples—of making the featured singer actually sound slightly out of time or tune (in a Western, even-tempered sense) with the backing *takht*, or of interrupting the overarching time signature of the piece, with a resulting degree of disorientation for the inexperienced or inattentive listener. *Shababiyya* simply does not permit such individual variations or improvisations. The meter of practically any *shababiyya* song that one might encounter is far more dominant and dictatorial, and demands a higher degree of metric consistency than most of the Golden Age musical composers would ever have considered using.

Consequently, the ways by which *shababiyya* singers—and in this regard, 'Abd al-Ḥalim Ḥafiẓ may be numbered among such—must approach the endeavor of imbuing their singing with emotional resonance are quite different from the tactics that *musiqa al-ṭarab* singers could employ. The kinds of ornamentation available to them, while qualitatively similar to those that characterize *musiqa al-ṭarab,* are quantitatively constrained by the constant, consistent meters that characterize *shababiyya.* This fact has the practical effect of privileging the vocal qualities that 'Abd al-Ḥalim Ḥafiẓ, 'Amr Diyab, and Tamir Ḥusni often demonstrate in their recordings: their control of sustained single pitches, their precision in articulating lyrics to conform to a consistent meter, and their judicious use of *Sprechgesang* as a tool of emotional expression. The *Sprechgesang* used here does not correspond to, say, Hayfa Wahbi's usage of the technique, which serves primarily to intensify her seductive persona while compensating for her diaphragmatic weakness. Instead, in the hands of these popular male singers, it serves to emphasize what my interlocutors interpret as the emotional engagement of the singer with the text.

This discussion of aesthetic criteria is circumscribed by ethnicity, as my conversations with my interlocutors indicate. In particular, there are three highly regarded male *shababiyya* singers who utilize a good deal of the *musiqa al-ṭarab* toolkit in their *shababiyya*:Wa'il Kafuri, George Wasuf, and Kaẓim al-Sahir. Little was said about any of these singers in my interviews and conversations. There are two apparent reasons for their peripherality to my interlocutors' thinking. First, there are some received typological distinctions of a given musician's primary musical field that potentially exclude Wasuf and al-Sahir from a consideration of *shababiyya* artists: Wasuf and al-Sahir are generally considered by my interlocutors to be *musiqa al-ṭarab* artists who have crossed over to some degree into *shababiyya.* Second, and more important, none of them is Egyptian: Kafuri is Lebanese, Wasuf a Lebanese citizen of Syrian birth, and al-Sahir Iraqi.[53]

The discourse is also circumscribed by gender, although from a different perspective. Female *shababiyya* singers who earned the most praise for their vocal abilities are, in sharp distinction to their male colleagues, almost infallibly more skillful at the *musiqa al-ṭarab*-influenced techniques, as well as the *shababiyya* techniques that respond predictably to metric constraints. Shirin and Angham, the two female *shababiyya* performers whose voices my interlocutors consistently identified as "very Egyptian," gained this distinction in their admirers' eyes partly because they can (even if infrequently) demonstrate great skill in high-prestige musical techniques,[54] particularly sweetness of pitch throughout a tonally varied passage or melisma, sustained diaphragmatic breath control, and equal deftness in the use of head and chest resonances. Those women who could sing *shababiyya* only on par with 'Amr Diyab—that is, with significantly more skill in more recent technical standards than in older ones—did not qualify as "very Egyptian voices."

There are, in fact, just as few male Egyptian *shababiyya* artists who can demonstrate such talents. To my knowledge, there are only two who are both well known in the music industry and whom my interlocutors were likely to know: Hani Shakir and Ihab Tawfiq. While Hani Shakir came up once in a while among my interlocutors, he was not a frequent topic of conversation. This may be due to his advanced age (born in 1952), as well as to his professional association as a young man with some of the canonical singers of the Golden Age: Hani Shakir was one of the last protégés of Muḥammad 'Abd al-Wahhab. Neither reason, however, strikes me as especially compelling, given that many *shababiyya* performers have, if not a personal affiliation with musicians associated with the Golden Age, then at least some degree of culturally prestigious professional training in *musiqa al-ṭarab.* For that matter, Ihab Tawfiq himself has excellent professional credentials as a performer: he earned a doctorate in music from Helwan University in Cairo. In spite of the cultural capital this might win him, my interlocutors usually considered Ihab a disreputable clown, on account of his dull lyric texts and his video clips, which swarm with bikini-clad women and sexual innuendo. The former problem impugns his aesthetic taste, compared to colleagues who demonstrate superior judgment in the songs they choose to record; the latter problem impugns his moral sensibility among fans who consider sexual impropriety incompatible with Egyptianness in general and with a "real Egyptian voice" in specific.[55]

The way in which Cairenes young and old valorize skillful use of the vocal techniques of *musiqa al-ṭarab* reveals, by a negative comparison, how rare that skill truly is within the world of *al-musiqa al-shababiyya.* The techniques are seldom used, and then only by a small minority of singers. The musical aesthetics that appeal to listeners in *shababiyya* are, for the most part, totally different from those that apply in *musiqa al-ṭarab*—a fact that often leads aficionados of the older musical genre to conclude that *shababiyya* literally has no aesthetic standards other than visual luxury and seduction. Fans and even producers of *shababiyya* can appear to play into this understanding when, like the *muwazzi'* Murad, they take care to point out the vocal dexterity—and, thereby in some cases, the innate Egyptian musical skill—of particular singers tackling difficult *maqamat.* But when one examines the larger corpus of music that these youths prefer, another set of aesthetic preferences articulates itself. These preferences and their taxonomic implications constitute the next topic to which I turn.

3

"The Hardest Thing To Say"

Taxonomies of Aesthetics

Waḥid and Baligh, denizens of Café Horreya,[1] a well-known coffeehouse popular with expatriates and left-wing Egyptian intellectuals (Conant 2010), spent months trying vainly to convince me that I was wasting my time by focusing on *shababiyya,* finding it incomprehensible that I would pursue such a project when I came from the West (especially America), whose music they admired far more. Waḥid adored the British classic rock band Led Zeppelin, and often sat at Café Horreya attempting to perfect his Robert Plant impersonation. Baligh was a fan of the American heavy metal band Sabotage. Just as they shook their heads in confusion when I spoke at length about *shababiyya,* I felt hard-pressed to understand why Waḥid and Baligh disdained so much of the music in their daily ambience and valorized music that I find, at best, difficult to enjoy in any quantity.

Our arguments ran in parallel: we each found it hard to appreciate the other's musical tastes because each of us was too familiar with what we respectively considered "good music" in our home cultures. Waḥid swore to me that Led Zeppelin's lyrics were deeply complex and meaningful; I dismissed such claims by pointing to older blues songs that the band rearranged and, in my view, sang poorly in comparison to the originals. I would put forth the idea that a song by Shirin represented a contemporary example of the older standards of vocal talent; Baligh would smile patronizingly at me and say that I needed to listen to 'Abd al-Ḥalim Ḥafiẓ if I wanted to know what a really good contemporary Egyptian voice should sound like.

These youthful fixtures of the downtown coffeehouse scene became some of my more articulate as well as contrarian interlocutors during my doctoral research. Waḥid and Baligh were both twenty years old, and came from families that, as I gathered, lay somewhere in the middle of *ṭabaqa mutawasiṭa* socioeconomic status. The boys had received decent if non-elite primary and secondary educations, but their families could not afford to send them abroad for university, nor to the expensive private universities that cater to Cairo's elites. Both young men were students enrolled in the Faculty of Arts at Cairo University, one of Egypt's major public universities. They spent most of their waking hours, though, hanging out with friends at a rotation of coffeehouses in the Wusṭ al-Balad and 'Abdin neighborhoods; by their own account, they seldom attended classes, and often slept through the better part of the daylight hours. Their major was as much a social identity as a program of study: they reveled in dressing the part of a rebellious art student, with oddly styled goatees, shaggy, unkempt hairdos, and torn black T-shirts featuring ostentatious heavy-metal band logos. Waḥid and Baligh were themselves the singer and bass player, respectively, of a largely hypothetical metal band that, insofar as I could tell, had never actually met to practice. In support of his headbanger persona, Baligh liked to be called by an English translation of his name, the suitably metal analogue "Extreme." Indeed, Baligh was the more outgoing and confrontational of the two, and had been arrested several times on suspicion of being a Satanist—a charge commonly leveled against heavy-metal fans in Egypt that led to some sensational trials there as well as in several other countries in the Arab world, and which resulted in prison sentences that left a chilling effect on Egypt's nascent metal scene in the late 1990s (LeVine 2008, 29–31, 66–68).

Neither Waḥid nor Baligh seemed much concerned with acquiring money. In fact, Baligh seemed concerned with very little at all; by his own admission, he did not know his family's own street address,[2] and had always simply found his way around by landmarks. Their parents subsidized their rambles through the city, so that there was never an issue about paying for a snack here or a *nargila* (water pipe) there. For a short time, Baligh held a job as an assistant at a tiny garment store in one of the shopping malls downtown selling knock-off denim apparel, where he would fold and refold shirts and trousers to kill time in between customers, frequently shaking out the clothes and starting over as the ashes from his ever-present cigarette fell around the counter. Only a few months after taking the job, he quit, afterward explaining vaguely to me, "I could not bring myself to do it anymore." I had to agree that the workplace was physically stifling and depressing, but I watched with dismay as Baligh comfortably returned to idleness full-time, not seeking out another position.

As both young men expressed clearly to me, neither of them held much hope of obtaining a job in Egypt commensurate with their anticipated education level. Although both of them occasionally complained aloud that their postgraduate prospects for employment were dim, they expressed few ideas of just what they might do for a living once they earned their degrees. As they intimated, they would eventually need to prevail upon someone or other within their respective family networks to set them up in a position in some private company; they bitterly asserted that such personal *wasṭa* represented a far surer economic advantage than any professional credential. They rarely even spoke about their looming economic doldrums, except when I brought up the subject. They tended to discuss the future only in vague, fantastic terms, particularly the distant hope of going abroad for work in Eastern Europe. Baligh idly pondered the idea of migrating to Poland, where, as he had heard from someone, there was a welcoming scene for metalheads. Waḥid dreamed of emigrating to Lithuania, the home country of a former exchange student on whom he had nursed a crush. Whatever plans they seemed to be hatching at one time or another, they never failed to show up regularly at Café Horreya, leading me to doubt that they would ever end up anywhere else.

Aḥmad 'Umran, the *'ud* player in the Cairo-based ensemble Wusṭ al-Balad, had no patience for Egyptian music fans like Waḥid and Baligh. In his eyes, there was no aesthetic benefit in wholly imitating foreign musical styles, whether Western or Eastern, when Egypt offered its own rich musical heritage on which to draw. Moreover, he opined that Waḥid and Baligh could hope for nothing more than to be third-rate imitations of what he termed "real metal." "Why are they into this?" he asked me with genuine puzzlement. "Why would I want to hear them play that music if I can hear Metallica instead?" Egyptian metal, in Aḥmad's eyes, fails the test of cultural authenticity because it is not autochthonous to Egypt. The irony undergirding this conversation with Aḥmad is that the band for which he is known is a deeply eclectic and syncretic musical ensemble. I have seen and heard Aḥmad onstage playing compositions that draw freely from reggae, blues, klezmer, hip-hop, raga, and salsa, as well as a range of Egyptian and Arab musical styles. When it suits their creative purposes, Aḥmad and his bandmates are happy to combine numerous such styles into a fusion that both they and their fans consider "Egyptian music."

The King

Muḥammad Munir has been singing and recording professionally since the late 1970s.[3] Munir comes from a Nubian[4] family in Upper Egypt, near the city of Aswan, and established himself in Cairo when he moved to the capital to attend university. He has gained fame for his inventive arrangements, his selections of song texts that both celebrate and critique contemporary Egypt, and his perceived synthesis of folk melodies and motifs from both Upper and Lower Egypt—including, in the case of the former, Nubian elements that are otherwise rarely present in Egyptian pop music.

A number of interlocutors who freely disparaged contemporary pop music to me would change their tone entirely when Munir's name came up. Muḥammad Munir, as I learned, inspires a degree of respect that no other currently active Egyptian musician can equal. Students of music enjoy his arrangements and departures from the usual sound of *al-musiqa al-shababiyya;* nationalists appreciate his songs that sing of the goodness of ordinary Egyptian people; secular Egyptians admire his statements, musical and otherwise, in favor of secularity and non-sectarianism, and against the kind of Islamist political thought represented by the Muslim Brotherhood, the political party that calls for the institution of Islamic law as the basis for government. (The Muslim Brotherhood, while technically outlawed until the 2011 revolution, remained so popular and influential that the Mubarak regime found itself obliged to come to some *modus vivendi* with its enemy, including gestures toward Islamization of public and political space.) Even the Egyptian state under Mubarak, which was not well disposed toward social critics, treated him with some grudging respect: he recorded albums and video clips and performed freely throughout Mubarak's tenure, although Munir has made statements that could have landed a less exalted personality in jail, and has recorded a song and video clip, *Madad ya rasul allah* ("Help, O messenger of God"), which enraged the powerful Islamist political opposition led by the Muslim Brotherhood.[5]

Very few artists even attempt the sort of musical project that Munir espouses, although one would be hard-pressed to find an Egyptian musician who does not praise Munir's skill and creativity. The only artists I ever encountered who have expressed any interest in following in Munir's footsteps are the members of the band Wusṭ al-Balad, another Egypt-focused musical act who have concentrated on building a fan base in Cairo and

Alexandria, rather than in the larger Arab world. The apparent lack of interest of his colleagues in synthesizing traditional Egyptian music of all kinds with Western instrumentation and occasional stylistic influences throws Munir's music into higher relief, giving him the appearance of a visionary. While I cannot deny that he is such a figure in Egyptian music, I would also point out that, as the Arabic-language corporate music industry has developed, the kind of music that Muḥammad Munir performs has little commercial potential outside Egypt. By Munir's own admission, he has a large following only in Egypt and Germany, with relatively few fans in most of the Arab world. He styles himself as an Egyptian national artist, rather than an Arab artist from Egypt, and claims only the Egyptian people as his intended audience, and thus is not overly concerned with his reception in Lebanon or Saudi Arabia (Munir 2008). It is worth observing that this attitude requires both a relatively strong cultural politics and a firm position in the field, to say nothing of a blatant disregard for the ordinary mechanics of the contemporary pop music industry.[6] It would be exceedingly difficult for a musician starting out today to take Munir as both an artistic template and a business model, and still feed himself. Therefore, Egyptian musicians hoping to build careers for themselves in the sphere of *al-musiqa al-shababiyya* would naturally seek to perform music that would play well throughout a larger region—preferably the entire Arabic-speaking world. And thus, by contrast, Munir seems nobler than the average musician, and motivated by something other than profit.

Because of his unusual, eclectic musical aesthetics and his long-lived career, whose beginnings coincided with the time of 'Abd al-Ḥalim Ḥafiẓ's death, Muḥammad Munir represents a transitional figure in the world of Egyptian pop music. He studied music and began to perform publicly during the years that the stars of the Golden Age were either dying off or fading into the seclusion of retirement. When he began to release albums, they were published as both vinyl LPs and cassette tapes, during the time before piracy techniques allowed bootleg sales to destabilize the profit model of corporate cassette production. His albums have always featured arrangements that draw on numerous musical genres, among them the "late modernist" style identified with 'Abd al-Ḥalim Ḥafiẓ, *sha'bi* associated with urban working-class singers like Aḥmad 'Adawiyya, folk music styles from up and down the Nile Valley, and Western-influenced rock music production values, strongly associated in Egypt with the prolific Libyan-born producer Ḥamid al-Sha'iri. The resulting music is accordingly difficult to classify taxonomically; my inclination to classify Muḥammad Munir as a *shababiyya* artist derives much more from his widespread popularity among Cairene youth and my interlocutors' general insistence that he falls within the *shababiyya* purview than from any musicological trends inherent in his music.

Through some convoluted wheedling over the course of six months, I secured an interview with Muḥammad Munir, conducted at his home in Cairo. When I told my friend Ḥassan about the upcoming interview, he was visibly excited, even though he ordinarily denigrated *shababiyya* as worthless commercial pap. When I informed him that I was going to sit down for a formal interview with Muḥammad Munir, Ḥassan's eyes gleamed, and he told me, "For my generation, he is very important. He is the king!"[7] Ḥassan reminisced about when the singer released his album *Shababik* (*Windows*), and everyone in Ḥassan's class ran out to buy a copy of the cassette.[8] "There's none of this '*ḥabibi* I love you *ya ḥabibi*'," he noted of the lyrical content of Munir's recordings, "he sings about the people." To my surprise, the normally cool and artistically snobbish Ḥassan suggested to me, "When you go to his house, take a picture, because the house will be very beautiful!" I remembered this advice, and made good on it at the interview (Figure 13).

When I arrived at Muḥammad Munir's home, I was shown by the building's doorman to the formal salon, where I waited while my presence was announced. Munir soon appeared, greeted me, and invited me to follow him to the interior reaches of his flat: he himself, it was immediately evident to me, spent most of his leisure time in a much smaller room near the kitchen. Unlike the pristine and slightly sterile salon, this back room had a lived-in feel, with deep impressions on the couches and little scratches on the glass-topped coffee table from dishware, glassware, and ashtrays. In a corner of the room sat his computer and what I gathered was the server on which he maintained his official website. He was not alone in the room, but sat with one or two friends and assistants at all times. These were not so much hierarchical subordinates, such as a great many bureaucratic managers all over Egypt keep on hand, but friends and advisors to Munir who, as I learned, helped him especially to maintain his Internet presence and his public relations in general. They also spoke much more English than he, and occasionally played the role of interpreter. All in all, I felt pleased and flattered to be invited into relatively private space, where he would feel most comfortable talking with me.

FIGURE 13. The author interviewing Muḥammad Munir, March 31, 2008. Photograph from author's collection.

Munir had a great deal to say about good and bad music,[9] and how one could distinguish the two in the contemporary music industry. In fact, he and his two assistants all had a great deal to say on the subject, and took turns offering me their opinions while occasionally arguing with each other. Munir, as a secular nationalist who expresses himself musically, was reluctant to denigrate nationalist pop songs that others had mocked to me as shoddy work. He suggested that, despite the good intentions of the songwriter, some compositions were relatively "flat" *(musaṭṭaḥa)*—that is, they directly extolled the nation without framing the sentiment in the details of everyday life. "There is no such thing as bad art, even in terms of the nation," he told me. "Maybe it is nationalist art, but weak! But there is [also] powerful art! You as the listener and I as the artist are [both] responsible: you have to choose the powerful and not the weak."

Munir indirectly referenced the wealth of everyday detail in his song selections in his explanation of his reputation among my respondents. As I observed to him, his was the name most frequently cited by young people as "very Egyptian" among *shababiyya* singers. When I asked him why this should be, he answered, "[Because] I'm not a liar! I love them [the people] and I say so, that's all." Similarly, he spoke of his avowed aim in his art to speak to the whole of "the nation," explaining that he has no limited audience demographic for his music: as he sees it, his audience is "the father, the mother, the son, the daughter, and the grandchild. All the people."

Munir cited his personal sense of nationalism as an overt influence on his choice of songs to record. "In every song, there is this *taḥriḍ* . . .[10] You dream of a better life, of good people, of a good and strong society." This response allowed me to ask how love songs, the aforementioned bread and butter of the *shababiyya* industry, play into his thinking and his selections: was his song *Qalb faḍi* ("Free heart"; Munir 2005) somehow a political statement? Munir gently critiqued my received implication that love was somehow less important than politics: "Love is something big! Every song about love, yes! People love, people fight, people defend themselves, and their continent, and their nation, right? So all around us are people. Every instrument, you know." I took this somewhat cryptic answer to mean that it was foolish and shortsighted to expect even the most nationalist of pop singers to ignore love songs, on the aesthetic level no less than on the practical.

Munir's song "Free heart" is, in fact, an interesting example of a lyric text that, on the face of it, is simply about romantic feelings—albeit elegantly expressed—but refers obliquely to social issues beyond teenage romance. The narrator appears to resemble those of any number of other pop songs who long for an unknown and unnamed romantic partner, but he is unusually candid in his self-characterization, as well as in his characterization of his fantasized lover. The key verse is:

Qalbi shari, mish babi'uh
Qalbi ghali wa-mish ḥayirkhaṣ
Qalbi lissa fi 'izz rabi'uh
Bas nifsuh qalb mukhliṣ

(A loyal heart, I'm not selling it
A dear heart and won't come cheap
A heart still in the bloom of its youth
And yearns only for a faithful heart)

Upon close inspection, it appears that the narrator is not at all a teenager or adolescent youth whom one might expect to inhabit a *shababiyya* pop song. "A heart still in the bloom of its youth" does not, one would think, belong to an actual youth but to an older man; the narrator is not affirming his youth but denying that he is too old to be considered as a potential bridegroom. There is a sense that the narrator feels his opportunity for romance slipping away, especially in comparison to people around him. Such lyrics call to mind the economic constraints on marriage that many of my interlocutors detailed to me: it is now a common phenomenon to see Cairene men marry for the first time in their thirties or forties, because it has taken them that long to amass the capital necessary to put themselves forward as serious candidates for marriage. Such older men on the marriage market must know that the intensity of their predicament is a recent phenomenon; their fathers and grandfathers rarely would have encountered such obstacles to marriage, even if they too needed to work for a few years to accumulate marriage money. The reality that their prospects for marriage nowadays are much worse than their forebears', even with a much larger national population than in their parents' time, is a bitter pill to swallow.

In another change from the usual, the narrator does not long for the stereotypical girl of fantasy, who is surpassingly beautiful, graceful, innocent, and virginal. On the contrary, the narrator obliquely acknowledges in the chorus of the song that he would be ready to love a woman who has previously been involved romantically with another man: "It's even ready to love / A heart that wants to forget a past." At the very least, this would imply an unmarried girl who has previously been engaged; this situation is fairly common nowadays, and does not necessarily suggest any damage to the girl's reputation. However, since some Cairene men have explained to me that merely being acquainted with a boy outside her family makes a girl suspect, this status is also clearly not ideal. My language tutor Yaḥya informed me in a brotherly way that every woman necessarily remains in love with the first man with whom she had sex, as a way of explaining why he insisted on looking for a virgin for his bride.[11] 'Antar, the manager of a café I patronized for some time—himself the veteran of numerous premarital sexual affairs—swore to me that he would not have married his wife "if she had so much as kissed a boy" (Gilman 2009, 85). Moreover, the lyric encompasses more than this scenario; it could as easily be a divorced woman, or even—and this is the most emotionally resonant implication in the song—a woman who has previously fallen in love and had sexual relations with another man outside of any formal arrangement. Given the premium that most Cairene men place on the chastity of their intended brides, and their anxiety about the loyalty and trustworthiness of women with any degree of prior sexual knowledge, this is an extraordinary concession for the narrator to make.

In discussing the use of the word *taḥriḍ* to describe the sentiments in Munir's nationalist songs, his assistant Salma unexpectedly offered me some eyewitness evidence suggesting a link between Munir's music and *musiqa al-ṭarab.* As Salma described her associate's concerts to me, "he induces in [the concertgoers] a sense of positive passion, making them do things they wouldn't normally do because he sends powerful messages of inspiration . . . All the concerts, in the beginning, it's very slow, and very harmonic, and then all of a sudden, they start dancing and jumping and doing all kinds of stuff that they wouldn't normally do, that they would normally be ashamed to do. But in his concerts, people take off their shoes and start dancing, and hailing Egypt, or their loved ones, or whatever it is they want to hail!"

This reported behavior struck me as very similar to the physical expressions of aurally inspired *ṭarab* described by A. J. Racy (2003, 1–8), and I asked Salma if this behavior could be appropriately called an expression of *ṭarab.* This led to a four-way conversational interlude, with Salma being interrupted once or twice by her colleague, 'Ali. "*Ṭarab* is a very Arabic word," she began thoughtfully. "It moves the heart, because it's related to Arabic culture and it's related to"—'Ali interrupted to suggest "enjoyment" in English—"enjoyment, of course, it's all entertainment! But it's authentic entertainment! It's real entertainment!" In this sense, then, Salma used "authentic" to suggest "meaningful": that is, the pleasure glossed as *ṭarab* was not merely the empty or trivial pleasure of pleasant aural stimulation brought on by ordinary music listening but a richer experience of emotional movement grounded in Arabic cultural heritage. Due to the weight that she placed on this concept, Salma was somewhat hesitant to affirm that Munir's concerts constituted a venue for experiencing *ṭarab.*

At this point, Munir offered his own practical explanation of *ṭarab:* "*Ṭarab* is the moment in which the singer says to himself, '*Allah!*'[12] At the same time, the listener in front of him says to you, '*Allah!*' If the two of you at the same time say this, then you enchant me *(bitiṭribni)*—you as the singer enchant me, and you as the listener enchant me!" Munir's definition not only focused on the observable experiential results of *ṭarab* rather than its cultural origins but also slyly integrated his performances with the production of *ṭarab* in a way that Salma, focusing on the intellectual parsing of the concept, seemed unable to state confidently. Once again, there is an association of *ṭarab* with authenticity and ineffability, deployed here in a particularly sharp way meant to distinguish Muḥammad Munir's music and performance capabilities from those of his peers. Munir's explanation also reflects the traditional understanding, within the world of Arab music, of a great music performance necessarily being an intersubjective occurrence. Intersubjective pleasure, in fact, is one of the metrics by which aficionados and practitioners of *musiqa al-ṭarab* often judge the authenticity of a performance (see Shannon 2003, esp. 79–82).

A huge majority of song texts in the *shababiyya* genre focus exclusively on the subject of romantic longing and (ostensibly chaste) desire—what Cairenes refer to, approvingly and otherwise, as *rumansiyya* (romance). For that matter, the same can be said of *musiqa al-ṭarab;* as discussed above, the difference in lyrical texts is largely a matter of compositional style, rather than topic. Smitten people sing of their newfound love for someone whom they have not yet met formally, or of a brief social encounter that inspires romantic feelings, or of the confusion resulting from the mixed signals read into the love object's behavior. These topics are the bread and butter of *shababiyya* songwriters; very little other subject material ever finds its way into *shababiyya.* Muḥammad Munir represents an exception within the music industry, given the degree of fame he has achieved by singing about avowedly unromantic, unsexy topics such as bureaucracy (*Iqrar*), urban poverty (*Qalbi masakin sha'biyya*), and violence in the name of religious sectarianism (*Madad ya rasul allah*).[13]

Socially conscious singers such as Muḥammad Munir are exceptional not just for their acclaim and popular following but also for the fact that they perform such songs at all. Such compositions are favored in neither *musiqa al-ṭarab* nor *shababiyya,* as a rule. Too much lyrical specificity is itself out of favor, even in love songs. Arabic music's lyrical conventions allow (or force) composers to refer to heartaches both serious and trivial in highly abstract and allusive language. By comparison, Western pop songs that explicitly refer to—or even implicitly hint at—specific issues such as youthful sexual consummation, the more general possibility of sexual intercourse outside of marriage, or the pain of a marriage that ends in divorce can seem shockingly blatant, embarrassingly risqué, and even artless to those who have grown up listening to Arabic music. The Egyptian novelist Ahdaf Soueif uses this comparison as a plot device in her novel *In the Eye of the Sun* to underscore the awkward emotions that pass between an Egyptian married couple living in England and on the verge of divorce, after the wife's infidelity.

> Saif opens the car for Asya and lets her in. He closes it behind her. He walks round the car, gets in and starts the engine. The radio splutters to life.
>
> '—the future *is*
> About to unfold—
> Up*stairs* before the night's too old, *'cos—*'
>
> 'Crap!' says Saif.
> 'Switch it off?' says Asya.
> 'No,' Saif says, pulling out. 'We can't go round switching everything off.'
>
> '—To*night's* the *night*
> It's gonna be all right
> Ain't *no*-body gonna stop us now-ow—'
>
> Saif reaches out and switches off the radio. These days all the hits could have been designed with them in mind: *Torn Between Two Lovers, Lucille, Winner Takes It All, I Don't Wanna Talk About It*—not one that misses its mark. Songs here are so—so specific, she thinks; if they'd been in Cairo and switched the radio on they would never have got 'there's been another man—' and 'she'd made him look small'; they'd have got 'farewell, O world of happiness' or 'I shall not submit to what is written' (Soueif 1992, 664)

Still, the lyrical complexity and specificity of some songs by Muḥammad Munir drew positive comparisons to the most prestigious works of the Arabic musical canon by critically oriented fans. Firas, the cynical consumer of pop music, dismissed most of it as cheap commercial product but had totally different words for Muḥammad Munir. Using the research category terms that I had introduced into the conversation, Firas argued that Muḥammad Munir represents the "*musiqa al-ṭarab* of *shababiyya*," by virtue of the nuanced meanings of the texts he sings. "You need to listen to Muḥammad Munir's songs many times to understand what he's talking about." I wanted to ask what he meant, but I also wanted a practical example to work from, lest I lose the train of thought. The idea of nuanced textual meaning made me think of the recording *Qalbi masakin sha'biyya* ("My heart is popular neighborhoods"),[14] so I asked Firas if that was the sort of thing he had in mind. Firas took the example unhesitatingly to demonstrate his point. "Exactly, that's what I'm talking about! *Qalbi masakin sha'biyya:* what does it mean?" The ambiguity of the song's title and the subtle and complex potential meanings it implies is indicative to Firas of a higher standard of composition than most *shababiyya* can offer. Firas, as well as many others with whom I spoke, observed somewhat obliquely of the singer, "He has a message." Such a terse statement creates more ambiguity than clarity, so it is difficult to surmise exactly what my interlocutors meant when they made this pronouncement. Given Muḥammad Munir's association with critiques of Egyptian state and society that few Cairenes felt comfortable stating on the record before the 2011 revolution, this ambiguity may well have been intentional.

Muḥammad Munir himself does not accept any genre label for his music, much less shababiyya. When I asked him how he would classify his music, he deliberated for a moment, then intoned to me, "I am Muḥammad Munir." Despite his discomfort in being labeled as *shababiyya* (or anything else, for that matter), he is received by the vast majority of my interlocutors as part of the larger category of *shababiyya.* In terms of his music, his lyric text selections, and his mode of political engagement, however, he is a highly unusual performer within this genre, and hardly representative of the aesthetic norms that have developed in the commercial recording industry that produces and markets *shababiyya.* As many people informed me, "there is no one like Munir"; however, there are some musicians who take him as an influence on their musical aesthetics and their political engagements. Among the most important of these musicians are those who perform as the ensemble called Wusṭ al-Balad.

Wusṭ al-Balad

The idea of a musical ensemble is more commonly associated with *musiqa al-ṭarab,* or with the various kinds of folk music produced traditionally in different parts of the Nile Valley, than with contemporary popular music in Egypt. The *shababiyya* music industry is almost entirely populated by individual artists, rather than bands, so it came as a surprise to me that a number of my respondents enthused about the Egyptianness of a large band based in Cairo known as Wusṭ al-Balad (or Downtown). This group, formed in the late 1990s, relied exclusively on live performances for years—unlike the average *shababiyya* musician, who seeks label representation and its concomitant recording prospects as soon as possible, Wusṭ al-Balad studiously ignored the recording industry until 2007. Since they did not produce any recorded material during this period, their audience is naturally concentrated not only in Egypt but in Cairo and Alexandria.

The explanations offered by my respondents as to the Egyptianness of Wusṭ al-Balad differed significantly from those for most of the other artists whom I have mentioned, except for Muḥammad Munir. According to their fans, Wusṭ al-Balad's songs reflect the realities of life for young Cairenes, particularly in terms of romantic possibilities and oblique criticisms of the Egyptian government. The band also departs from ordinary *shababiyya* practice with some songs in its repertory that discuss, laud, or incorporate various aspects of Egyptian and Arab cultural history, including pre-Islamic poetry, rural folk songs, and Nubian instrumental techniques. That such statements and practices resemble those of Muḥammad Munir is no accident; several members of Wusṭ al-Balad told me themselves that they take Munir as a role model for their performing and songwriting careers.

Wusṭ al-Balad, in terms of aesthetics, bears little resemblance to most of the musical acts that populate satellite video channels. Many of their songs do not follow danceable rhythms, and their experimentations with an array of instruments and musical styles interfere with pop music's usual ability to let the listener drift off into a state of receptive inattention. What is more, their lyrics often describe situations of daily life—especially as Cairenes experience daily life—which hail listeners in a powerful fashion: when nearly all songs on the radio are generic love songs, listeners cannot help but prick up their ears when they hear a singer lamenting how expensive it is to acquire an appropriate wedding dowry. And, while the lead singer, Hani 'Adil, is a tall, good-looking man, the ensemble limits its use of sexuality to a joking reference on its website to Hani as "the cute one"; the lack of eroticism in their physical presentation limits their appeal to *shababiyya* video producers who regard eroticism as an indispensible tool of the trade.[15]

Adham Sa'id, one of the singers in the band,[16] explained to me once that politics, such as it might enter into the band's songs, is not a matter of parties and government factions but rather of social conditions on the level of daily life. If those conditions lead one to interpret the meaning as a critique of the government for causing or failing to fix them, then so be it. I asked him, as delicately as I could, about the presence of antigovernment protesters at a recently prior Wusṭ al-Balad gig, and he said they did not participate in that, but there are other people who, perhaps, enjoy their music, and who also see that "clearly, there are problems" *(waḍiḥ mashakil)* in Egyptian society and voice their opinions on the same.[17] No doubt I was not the first person to ask Adham about this matter; there was nothing off-the-cuff about his manner or his response.

Adham repeatedly used the expression "underground"—both the English term and its Arabic calque *taḥt al-arḍ*—to describe the band, which struck me as odd, given that they are one of the biggest local acts in Cairo. I understand this to be more a reference to their musical style and their grassroots fan base, rather than to a claim of outsider status. Then again, they certainly are outsiders in terms of their musical style and their relatively overt flirtations with political opposition. The fact that they pursue a career based not in the recording industry but by gigging in Egypt's major population centers does, in a sense, also qualify them as outsiders to the *shababiyya* music industry at large. At the same time, part of the band's outsider status has an elitist flavor, in that its eclectic musical aesthetics place it within the omnivorous taste culture that partly defines the *haute bourgeoisie* of Cairo. While Wusṭ al-Balad attempts to market its music to all Egyptians, the bulk of its fans come from the socioeconomic elite of urban Egypt.

When I sat backstage at a concert held at Culture Wheel, a popular Cairene venue for smaller musical acts that appeal to this elite taste culture, both the music and the audience drove home this class leaning. During the course of a single song, the band meandered through a klezmer-like melody, followed by Hani beatboxing, followed by a long blues guitar progression that gave Aḥmad, the *'ud* player, and As'ad, the classical guitarist, the chance to slip offstage to smoke a cigarette.[18] While this went on, I let my eye drift to the river only twenty feet from my perch in the corner of the backstage area, and saw a pair of fishermen in a rowboat with one's young son happily riding in the middle. They trawled by the theater and, dropping their net right next to the concrete embankment, began fishing by Culture Wheel. Well-to-do young fans of Wusṭ al-Balad, sneaking cigarettes themselves outside the stage area, took out their mobile phones and snapped photographs of the fishermen as Adham sang in Classical Arabic to a Gitano melody. The sight of people fishing for a living in Cairo was something remarkable and worthy of a photograph to these youth, particularly in juxtaposition to their high-culture hang-out where they could hear a variety of musical styles that most Cairenes have not been taught to appreciate.

Shababiyya and the Limitations of Taxonomy

The tripartite division of genres that I present here can be problematized in terms of terminology. Very few of my Egyptian acquaintances and colleagues ever disputed the substance of these categories—Muḥammad Munir being a prominent and self-interested exception—but a number of them took issue with my nomenclature. In particular, they argued with me about how to name the category of music to which I refer as *musiqa al-ṭarab;* they criticize my suggested usage as unforgivably foreign, although they themselves never came to an agreement on any other term. As I have mentioned, there are many terms that one might think to use but no term upon which everyone agrees even in a single conversation, much less across the field of scholarship. Given this situation, as well as Racy's observation (and my own) that the concept of *ṭarab* is closely linked with this genre of music, I am content to use *musiqa al-ṭarab* as a taxonomic term, with the recognition that Egyptians themselves rarely apply the term in quite the same fashion. I am likewise content to follow Middleton's advice (1990, 4–7) and accept a degree of contradiction in any possible system of classification applied to musical forms as the inevitable outgrowth of a classed society whose elites find ideological motivation to posit such distinctions among popular, common, folk, and so on.

I do not intend for the reader to understand these three musical taste cultures as rigid, mutually exclusive categories. Many Cairenes listen to all three on different occasions and for different reasons; performers can even slide between generic definitions. Early on in my research, I myself made the mistake of magnifying the degree to which such consumer practices exclude each other, and my friends patiently kept reminding me that even devotees of the latest *shababiyya* would occasionally listen to an Umm Kulthum record or a *sha'bi* song by Sa'd al-Ṣughayyar. They likewise pointed out that even microbus drivers, who are stereotyped as listening to *sha'bi* cassette tapes all day long, might like to relax at home by listening to *musiqa al-ṭarab* with their tea. Only the stuffiest and most isolated cultural mandarin could possibly listen to nothing but *musiqa al-ṭarab* all the time without hearing a well-known *sha'bi* song once in a while. Up to a point, people engage with these taste cultures in the same way that they engage with different registers of the Arabic language, grounding themselves in one register while dipping into another at need.

This intertwining of musical genres extends to performers as well. Ḥakim and several other *sha'bi* performers are attempting to forge careers that cross over into the higher-status musical genre of *shababiyya,* as indicated by their willingness to invest in the production of music video clips of some of their songs (Grippo 2010:155–56). These video clips, which air on various music channels through satellite television, stand out as oddities in a way, because the video clip as an aesthetic and commercial form is a hallmark not of *sha'bi* but of *shababiyya.* For possibly similar reasons of cultural prestige, several *shababiyya* performers working in Cairo who have studied Arabic classical music formally, Shirin 'Abd al-Wahhab and Kaẓim al-Sahir, have given well-received concerts entirely devoted to *musiqa al-ṭarab* compositions, although no one defines these artists as belonging primarily to the *musiqa al-ṭarab* fold.

The reception of both Muḥammad Munir and Wusṭ al-Balad among Cairene youth points to the limited utility of taxonomy itself, of identifying genres and attempting to make the names mean something. Infallibly, young people told me that both of these musical acts are part of *shababiyya,* albeit an unusually sophisticated and nuanced variety thereof. Both Muḥammad Munir and Wusṭ al-Balad told me, however, that they do not feel themselves at all part of the *shababiyya* world, with a noticeable measure of disdain in their voices. As discussed above, Munir is particularly resistant to participating in any discussion of genre identification. Insofar as he was even willing to entertain the idea that he comes out of a specific generic tradition, he attempted to trouble the categories by classifying a great many of his influences, up to and including 'Abd al-Ḥalim

Ḥafiẓ, as *sha'biyya* ("folk music" or "music of the people," in this sense). In a similar fashion, both Adham Sa'id and Aḥmad 'Umran of Wusṭ al-Balad preferred to complicate the question of their band's genre identification by distancing themselves from *shababiyya* on the one hand, and claiming a broad mantle of "Egyptian music" on the other—in essence, a closely related claim to Munir's affinity for *sha'biyya.*

In both cases, the artists made it clear to me that they disliked being identified as *shababiyya* acts partly because they associate this term with the domain of corporate capitalist music production that emphasizes what will sell over whatever might sound good, and its attendant implications of commercialized eroticism and superficial romanticism. Munir and his associates especially questioned my musical taxonomy on the grounds that the term *shababiyya* itself refers not to musical qualities but to a commercial audience. This compared poorly, they argued, with *musiqa al-ṭarab,* which refers literally to an evoked emotional state, and *sha'bi/sha'biyya,* both of which are taken by Cairenes to refer on some level to the people as the source of the music, rather than its audience. If a category were so broad as to encompass the work of both Muḥammad Munir and Nancy 'Ajram, then of what analytical use could it be?

They are not the first people to mount this critique of musical taxonomies. Richard Middleton, the scholar of popular music, has noted that every taxonomic system of musical genres is relatively easy to turn on its head, revealing its internal contradictions and absurdities. Touching on the exact problematic that a category like *shababiyya* presents, that of categorizing music by the social group that produces or consumes it, Middleton observes that musical arenas and social classifications can never be reduced to equivalents, since both production and reception have always sprawled across cultural venues and socioeconomic classes (1990, 4). It is dangerous, as Middleton suggests, to use a social group as the defining characteristic of a musical genre, because social groups are necessarily in conversation with each other, and such groups do not remain static for very long, if at all. In this regard, *shababiyya* is highly unstable, since it refers to those who are currently (or recently) in what Cairenes consider the period of youth or adolescence. What happens when they age? The phrase "rock and roll" in the late 1950s referred to an emphatically youth-oriented musical form in the United States, but now that same term, applied to the same music, has a distinctly nostalgic flavor to it. The youth of the 1950s have aged into senior citizens, while popular music in America has undergone numerous innovations and changes that have taken it far from the work of Buddy Holly or Chuck Berry. In this sense, I cannot defend my taxonomy from the criticism that it is not as unassailable or scientifically precise a system as one could apply to popular music in Egypt. But Middleton also raises the point that any taxonomic system of popular music is ultimately flawed and internally contradictory, because the music (and often the categorization as well) is created and deployed by the members of a complex society who have disparate and conflicting agendas that influence how they perceive the world (1990, 7).

It is worth examining the underlying assumption of Middleton's argument here, which is that socioeconomic class is the driving force behind any taxonomy of popular music. This idea follows from the fact that class, itself a powerful and often brutal distinction between human beings in a complex society, stimulates a wide array of other distinctions of human behavior in that society. As Middleton reads the practice of taxonomy, it is fundamentally tied to an attempt by the more powerful classes to further subjugate the less powerful, or to bolster a weakened or threatened upper class (1990, 248–49). This concept of distinction as a matter of class-inflected tastes, famously laid out by Bourdieu (1984), has become a central concept for analysts of popular music.

The class concept as an element of distinction holds true in the case of Egyptian popular music, but not to the degree that Bourdieu might have envisioned. While class certainly plays a role in who judges which music as good and the ways in which they do so, age groups are another important form of social category involved in this phenomenon. Witness the fact that young people from the elite families in Cairo and their middle-class, *mutawasiṭ* age-peers all tend to listen to *shababiyya,* and their parents all tend to listen to *musiqa al-ṭarab,* regardless of their socioeconomic circumstances. Where class distinction articulates itself most strongly is in the listening preferences of young Cairenes from the poorer segment of society. At least as a stereotype, poor youth in Cairo rarely listen to *shababiyya,* preferring *sha'bi* as their music of choice. Their parents and grandparents listen to *sha'bi* as well, but are also happy to relax by listening to *musiqa al-ṭarab,* which can be heard as often in *baladi* coffee shops as in concert halls.

A similar stereotype holds in terms of specific low-prestige occupations. Many Cairenes, who themselves rarely set foot in taxis[19] and likely never came near a microbus, stereotyped the drivers of those vehicles as listening to *sha'bi* endlessly; taxi drivers, in this classed view, would only vary their auditory diet by listening to cassettes of sermons by Islamic preachers.[20] Sometimes, as such thinking goes, cabbies will play something else, but only in an attempt to please a passenger; indeed, I have occasionally entered a taxi playing one thing or another, only to have the driver take stock of my foreign accent and my outlandish computer bag, and switch the radio to the Western pop music station. But taxi drivers, who are thought to be almost as addicted to *sha'bi* music as their microbus-driving brethren, can provide their passengers with a musical education, if one is paying attention. I have certainly ridden in taxicabs blasting *sha'bi* at the predictable ear-splitting volume, and have ridden in my share of taxis playing sermons on the cassette player. But, just as pious Muslim cab drivers will sometimes use cassette sermons to proselytize to their passengers, I have also encountered many taxi drivers who will gladly, even evangelistically play *musiqa al-ṭarab* while fighting their way through traffic. I have also spent plenty of time in taxis with youthful drivers who have no interest in the listening preferences of their passengers, but will contentedly navigate the roadways to the sounds of *shababiyya,* and can debate the merits of voices and songwriters with the full intensity and consideration of connoisseurs. And, just as some upper-class Cairenes make a virtue of disdaining all contemporary Egyptian music except for Muḥammad Munir, I have had taxi drivers who express similar attitudes. One memorable driver admitted that the 'Amr Diyab song on the radio was not very good, and asked me what I preferred. When I mentioned Muḥammad Munir, the driver was inspired to play on his mobile phone an old voice performing some music that I had never heard before. Growing a little excited, he informed me, "This is Aḥmad Munib: Muḥammad Munir's teacher!" (Aḥmad Munib was a professional mentor to Munir in the early days of the latter's career.)

Exceptionality and Marginality

Cairenes who speak contemptuously of *shababiyya* presume that it can only be frivolous, sex-saturated music. This way of thinking necessarily excludes "whatever I happen to like" from a person's categorization, since anything good and worthwhile is by definition outside the purview of *shababiyya.* This is a convenient rationalization of one's musical tastes, but it also points to the practical limits of taxonomy in popular music.

Since the entire set of musical aesthetics that Muḥammad Munir espouses exists only in his music and that of one or two groups influenced by him, it seems unreasonable to call those aesthetics a genre of their own. It is hard to imagine what term one would even select, given that Munir himself pointedly refuses to qualify his music by any market genre term. The members of Wusṭ al-Balad are similarly disinclined to define their music according to the current market terms and, much as Munir did, reacted with consternation when I suggested that the mass of my interlocutors consider them *shababiyya.*

This self-identification as different from the mainstream, and therefore somehow unclassifiable, cuts both ways in terms of its political import. On the one hand, the sense of esteemed distinction that both Muḥammad Munir and Wusṭ al-Balad enjoy allows them more space to make subtle political critiques and raise questions in their work, because that higher cultural prestige grants their music more credence among literati, and by association gives them the air of educated political sensibility—in other words, they are considered sufficiently cultured to make knowledgeable political critiques. (Compare this to the vitriol that intellectuals direct at Sha'ban 'Abd al-Raḥim for his supposed ignorance and the noncomprehension that characterizes his political songs.) On the other hand, the aura of prestigious difference—what Americans might call coolness—has the effect of marginalizing those same performers, due to the impression among many listeners that the political topics under discussion in the music constitute an intramural conversation between members of the cultural elite—people who may or may not belong to the effective political elite but have no ties to the large mass of political subalterns of which most Egyptians are part.

For both positive and negative reasons, then, Muḥammad Munir and Wusṭ al-Balad in the Mubarak era were at liberty to make veiled and subtle critiques of the state. The cultural intelligentsia appreciated them for this practice, and cited the high quality of their music as granting the musicians license to sermonize in oblique ways. Meanwhile, the Mubarak regime and its supporters looked at this opposition as mostly toothless and unworthy of serious concern. This is not to say that the state left the musicians entirely to their own devices: this became clear when revolutionary protesters stormed the State Security headquarters and confiscated its remaining documents. The state security apparatus kept tabs on *everyone,* as paranoid authoritarian regimes tend to do. It is only reasonable to assume that Muḥammad Munir and Wusṭ al-Balad were included.[21] If Muḥammad Munir were not considered a serious threat to the Mubarak regime, then that judgment could not have come about except through domestic espionage intended to gauge his potential to harm the state. If antigovernment protesters made a point of declaring their presence at Wusṭ al-Balad concerts, then it is certain that the state would have looked into that, too. The security state was so pervasive that it was not practically possible for a musical act to become an organizing locus for political dissent without the state examining the phenomenon at length.

We can see, then, that exceptionality and marginality are linked concepts. To be exceptional—for a musician to be so talented or insightful that he or she rises head and shoulders above all contemporaries—is also to be marginal, in the sense that the musician simply is not making the same kind of music as those contemporaries, and thus inhabits a sort of epistemological ghetto. Muḥammad Munir never found himself in jail because of his marginality to the larger political discourse, as well as his cachet among wealthy and privileged Egyptians. Wusṭ al-Balad was never blocked from performing because the state, even though it viewed the band with suspicion, may have judged the potential threat so minimal that it would not have been worth the effort to censor a musical group popular with the children of the elite.[22] Greatness can go hand in hand with obscurity or irrelevance, in popular music.

This marginality derives as much from the musicians' place in mass media and transnational broadcasting as it does from their musical aesthetics. As discussed above, both Muḥammad Munir and Wusṭ al-Balad have relatively narrow fandoms that are fundamentally tied to the territory of Egypt: they are nationally bounded in a way that most *shababiyya* acts would not wish themselves to be. Due to music executives' judgments of widespread appeal and economic viability, satellite music video channels are far more likely to air a video clip by one of the hundreds of generic and unremarkable singers who comprise the bulk of *shababiyya* label rosters than anything by a group with a following only in Egypt's urban population centers. The industry has evolved to focus on selling music to the wider Arab world, and this has meant, in practice, crafting music that is as broadly appealing as possible to the music-consuming youth.[23] Music that engages with the specifics of daily life in a particular locale, to say nothing of local political topics, does not qualify.

What is more, political songs that tackle issues of corruption, increasing poverty, and frustration or anger at the power-wielding elite can draw the ire of leaders of countries far from the songmakers' homes. A song written by an Egyptian about government corruption and authoritarianism may appeal on a visceral level to music consumers living in Morocco or Saudi Arabia or Palestine. In this scenario, the problem is not that the music holds no appeal but that it is all too engaging to other national publics. Such a song may irritate an authoritarian leader sufficiently that he will seek wider censorship than that already in force, possibly even a total ban on the singer in the country. While this would be phenomenal free publicity for a singer, and would very likely generate an enormous and sympathetic following among the citizens of that country, such an eventuality is anathema to music executives. The industry and its technocrats earn revenue not from repeated listening but from repeated exposure: mass-mediated exposure in the form of advertising-subsidized video clips, and direct exposure via expensive private concerts. An angry autocrat would likely find it difficult to ban a singer from the airwaves: with no brick-and-mortar building in his country to close and little effective means of blocking a satellite signal, the broadcasting ban would be largely symbolic. The ban on performing, though, would be easily enforced, and would greatly diminish potential returns on the music company's investment in the singer. Politics is bad for business, in the eyes of *shababiyya* industry executives.

Exceptional Aesthetics

As suggested by my discussion of the lyrics to *Qalb faḍi,* lyric texts form an important aesthetic component of emotional evocation in the outlying high-prestige variations of *shababiyya*—perhaps more so than in more mainstream *shababiyya.* In fact, a number of my interlocutors suggested that their appreciation for many songs in this exceptional category was predicated largely upon the value of the lyrics to them. Musical composition sometimes seemed a distinctly second-order criterion. This apparent prioritization of lyrics over music is less clear-cut than it seems, however, because youthful music fans are engaged in a subtextual discourse of nationalism, musical aesthetics, and identity. This discourse, which has by no means resolved at time of writing, gives music composition a more stressful and unstable position in their overarching aesthetic criteria, and therefore makes musical composition more difficult to analyze with confidence than lyrics. Such an anxious topic is, of course, necessary to analyze here.

One of the critiques, or at least observations, that fans of both *musiqa al-ṭarab* and *al-musiqa al-shababiyya* make is that relatively few *shababiyya* songs are composed in the traditional Arabic modes (*maqamat*), whereas such modes are essential for *musiqa al-ṭarab.* As discussed in chapter 1, this critique is not technically true for the most part, since a great many *shababiyya* songs are in fact composed precisely within one *maqam* or another, and acquire their patina of Western musical composition later in the recording process. But the larger point of the critique holds: *shababiyya* does not sound as indigenous to Egypt as does *musiqa al-ṭarab,* as a rule. At base, the critique implies that the more a given *maqam* can be arranged to harmonize with Western compositional style and instrumentation, the less Egyptian it will sound. The most Egyptian *maqamat,* then, would be the ones that most stubbornly resist Western harmonization, and—not by coincidence—are the ones that must be learned most thoroughly on their own terms, rather than taken as adjuncts to a larger body of easier musical theory. Murad, my *muwazzi'* friend, confidently identified these more difficult *maqamat* to me as *bayati* and *rast.* His explanation for the relative rarity of these modes in *shababiyya* turned upon an understanding of differences in how a prospective singer could acquire professional facility in singing techniques. Formal training was well and good, Murad explained to me, but it worked best with Western compositional theory and with the more common (and, following his line of thinking, easier) *maqamat* that accommodate polyphonic harmonies. The famously difficult *bayati* and *rast*, he said, could not be taught in a music school alone; rather, the singer needed to grow up immersed in such sounds from childhood. Once this was accomplished, formal pedagogy might add a bit of polish, but that was all. Long-term acclimation and attunement to the more difficult *maqamat* counted for much more, in Murad's view, than formal instruction.

Murad's understanding of skill acquisition in singing the difficult *maqamat* bears some obvious similarities to other explanations of musical skill and education in the Arab world. Notably, his suggestion of long-term immersion calls up a kind of embodied knowledge: that is, if you do not feel it from inside yourself, then you cannot learn it intellectually through pedagogy. Embodied knowledge or skill comes up with some regularity in discussions of the older corpus of Arabic popular music and its ability to evoke *ṭarab.* A. J. Racy quotes the Syrian writer Ḥanna Mina's memoirs, in which Mina recalls being told by a traditional music instructor in the 1940s that music—the kind to which I refer in this book as *musiqa al-ṭarab*—has some originary carnality to it, that it comes "from the belly" and requires various physical gestures to perform it properly, beyond those which are needed to play a given instrument (Racy 2003, 27). In a more playful tone, Jonathan Shannon was told by one of his elderly interlocutors in Aleppo that the increasing rarity of genuine *muṭribin* (those who inspire *ṭarab*) in Syria was due to the rising consumption of corn oil as a cooking fat, in place of the more traditional cooking fats, clarified butter and sheep fat (Shannon 2003, 73).[24] And, in a larger sense, this embodied understanding of musical skill reflects the common perception among my own interlocutors that there is some peculiarly indigenous musical genius that Egyptians possess, a natural inclination to be great *muṭribin* over and above the natural abilities of other Arabs.[25]

My youthful interlocutors indicated, by way of their general tastes in music, a preference for an artful blending of Arabic and Western musical styles, something that seemed neither excessively imitative of the West nor a slavish acquiescence to older indigenous tradition. Muḥammad Munir looms large here as an example of "good" aesthetics in *shababiyya,* not merely the exceptional, high-prestige fringe of the genre. The compositions he selects generally strike listeners as not merely artful but also innovative combinations of indigenous musical traditions and Western commercial music. After all, the huge mass of *shababiyya* contains some degree of an Arab-Western blending of musical compositional styles, but most of it is considered either marginally artistic or, at best, formulaic and genre-bound. Munir, on the hand, distinguishes himself by opting to record songs that draw upon a wide variety of musical traditions autochthonous to the Nile River Valley.

I say autochthonous because scholars of Egyptian musical traditions may not identify all of these styles as "originally" from Egypt. For example, Munir's song *Ṣayyad* ("Fisherman") makes use of a folk melody that I had heard elsewhere under the title *Ya banat iskandariyya* ("O girls of Alexandria"). When I played Munir's recording for Dr. 'Abd al-Laṭif, my instructor of Arabic music and an expert performer on the *'ud,* he waved his hand dismissively and said, "That's not an Egyptian folk tune, much less Alexandrian. That's a Turkish tune called *Iskudar.*" To 'Abd al-Laṭif, the melody's origin in what is now Turkey excludes it from a serious discussion of indigenous Egyptian musical traditions.

As an anthropologist, I feel obliged to disagree with the learned but aged 'Abd al-Laṭif and his colleagues, for several reasons. First, his objection appears to be based on the understanding that this cultural artifact arrived in Egypt only several hundred years ago: he regarded this tune as one of many such Turkish imports that entered Egypt with the large influx of Ottoman functionaries and technocrats invited by Muḥammad 'Ali Pasha in the early 1800s to leave Anatolia for Egypt. This assertion raises a question of historicity, since Turkey did not exist as a state until 1922, and Egypt was part of the Ottoman Empire along with Anatolia in the 1820s, when the pasha made his invitation. While this may seem recent history to a thinker attuned to the vast stretches of time that Egypt's written chronicles offer, it remains some generations removed from the present day—and it may as well be antiquity to my youthful interlocutors.[26]

Second, if one is to regard anything with identifiable origins outside Egypt as fundamentally un-Egyptian, then one could draw a deeply offensive and uncomfortable analogy with Islam, which, after all, was brought to Egypt from Arabia in the late seventh century CE. While I have occasionally heard Coptic Christians make the observation that Egyptians were originally Christian rather than Muslim, it was always within the context of speaking to me as someone understood to be non-Muslim to whom a disgruntled (and, often, anxious and frightened) Christian could vent about political maneuvering by Salafists, the hardcore political and religious fringe of Islamism in Egypt. Moreover, these same people were bemused—sometimes to the point of offense—when I responded that Egyptians were originally not Christian but pagan, a fact that everyone knows but that many people allow to slip conveniently from their polemics. I would no more agree that this folk tune is not now part of autochthonous Egyptian musical tradition than I would agree that Islam is not now part of autochthonous Egyptian religious tradition.

Third, the peregrinations of this particular folk tune tend to belie the perspective that it is "really" Turkish. The earliest version of what Dr. 'Abd al-Laṭif referred to as *Iskudar* indeed appears to come from Anatolia, and is known in Turkish as *Üsküdar'a gider iken* ("While going to Üsküdar"), after the first line of its lyric text. The melody, if not its text, has spread widely throughout the former Ottoman Empire, and has taken on a variety of names in different languages as it has reached populations increasingly distant from its original reference point. (Üsküdar is a city close to Istanbul.) The most distant such version that I have encountered personally is a klezmer recording by the clarinetist Naftule Brandwein, who recorded his arrangement in 1924 in New York City, under the Yiddish-language title *Der terk in amerike* ("The Turk in America").[27] However, it has traveled even further than that, both literally and figuratively: the scholarly record notes that the tune has been recorded multiple times in Indonesia, and in the Balkans it has acquired a multiplicity of competing and contradictory ethnonationalist, religious, and ecumenical resonances for listeners in different social contexts (see Buchanan 2007). If it began in Turkish-speaking lands, it certainly did not remain confined there, and in the Arabic-speaking lands to which it traveled, it has been folded into local musical traditions—frequently, as I had heard myself, under the title *Ya banat iskandariyya.* Classically trained musical experts such as Dr. 'Abd al-Laṭif are more likely to be aware of the tune's "Turkish" origins than the average Cairene. Musical experts of Dr. 'Abd al-Laṭif's generation are also oriented toward a vision of Egyptian nationalism focused upon the autochthonous and the indigenous, and are on some level suspicious of the syncretic. These experts' particular investment in indigenous practices leads them to exclude the tune from their taxonomy of Egyptian music, whereas most young people simply do not worry about such things.

Taxonomy, in fact, articulates itself again and again as a matter of scant interest for young Cairenes while simultaneously functioning as a stumbling block for their elders. The elders, who are generally the standard-bearers for the old-fashioned vision of Egyptian modernity tied to (among other things) the corpus of *musiqa al-ṭarab,* retain a distinctly modernist concern with proper taxonomy of popular culture. Taxonomy is never simply about distinguishing one thing from another; it is not, as can appear to be the case to outside observers, a matter of educated discrimination. Rather, taxonomy's larger purpose is in the control of knowledge, in seizing and maintaining authority of a process of knowledge production and dissemination.

In this regard, taxonomy bears some important similarities to the practice of collecting, a practice that itself is closely bound up in narratives of nationalism and projects of knowledge control. Speaking of collections, in the context of ethnographic museums, James Clifford writes, "Some sort of 'gathering' around the self and the group—the assemblage of a material 'world,' the marking-off of a subjective domain that is not 'other'—is probably universal. All such collections embody hierarchies of value, exclusions, rule-governed territories of the self" (Clifford 1988, 218). Also writing in terms of collections of material objects, Susan Stewart suggests a kind of epistemological and taxonomic project inherent in collecting. "The collection does not displace attention to the past; rather, the past is at the service of the collection, for whereas the souvenir lends authenticity to the past, the past lends authenticity to the collection. The collection seeks a form of self-enclosure which is possible because of its ahistoricism. The collection replaces history with *classification,* with order beyond the realm of temporality" (Stewart 1993, 151).

This epistemological project that Clifford describes can apply equally well, I would argue, to the establishment of taxonomies of popular expressive culture. Expressive cultural practices can assume powerful implications in narratives of self-identification, and for the kind of nationalist modernist project that took hold in mid-twentieth-century Egypt, the question "who am I?" is never far removed from "what do I do?" Although I do not wish to overstate the similarities between cultivating aesthetic judgments and amassing collections as a whole, I want to draw out the similarities in the two endeavors on the level of classification—which, as Stewart says, can substitute in some ways for a larger sense of history and temporality.

The seizure and maintenance of authority in knowledge production parallels the seizure and maintenance of authority in general in Egypt, dating back at least as far as the nationalist discourses of the 1920s and possibly further, but more closely associated with the regime that came to power in 1952. The self-appointed guardians of Egyptian and Arab culture who frequently produce hand-wringing essays on the impending degradation and self-destruction of the Arabo-Egyptian musical heritage are not randomly sprinkled throughout Egypt's socioeconomic classes. As is usually the case in such matters, such guardians come from the ruling class, and they disseminate their pronouncements through formal instruments of education, as with *musiqa al-ṭarab,* as well as informal cultural knowledge acquisition, which frequently comes in the form of having one's musical choices snubbed by someone else attempting to make a point. The constituents of the wider public that produces as well as consumes most music is almost never consulted about what taxonomy, if any, they might employ, and in any case their vote is never final. These taxonomic terms to which people tend to resort—*shababiyya, sha'bi, musiqa al-turath*—are of value primarily to those who wish to control the terms of debate over what Egyptian music can and should be. Musical taxonomy is of little interest to young Cairenes precisely because they exert very little control over the terms of this debate, and therefore to play this game wastes their time. So while the primary difference between popular music listeners in Cairo is generation, it should not be forgotten that the language that they can employ to make distinctions is more a product of class distinction than age distinction.

The Great Aesthetic Shift

Insofar as I am able to discern from my conversations with Cairenes of various ages, there has occurred within the past twenty to thirty years (and, therefore, during the span of Muḥammad Munir's career to date) a major shift in the desires and expectations of listeners of popular music, marked strongly by generation. Cairenes born or raised during this period of time generally employ a drastically different aesthetic for evaluating the worth of a pop song's lyric text than that employed by their parents and grandparents. Whereas the older generations look for poetic subtlety and metaphorical abstraction in lyric texts, and tend to disdain songs whose words are too "on the nose" in describing emotions, the contemporary youth generation holds no such disdain. Youthful listeners adhere to the opposite view of what constitutes a good lyric text: they love poetic directness in emotional description, and tend to display impatience or boredom with songs that delve too far into indirect, metaphorical depictions of people's emotional lives. What the fifty-year-old music aficionado hears as poetic beauty, his twenty-year-old daughter hears as overly mannered pretension. Subtlety and emotional indirection, in contemporary *shababiyya,* have been devalued from their former rank in the evaluation of Egyptian music; in their place, as it would appear, stands direct emotional appeal on both the textual and performative levels.[28]

This generational shift in compositional and performative emphasis dismays fans of *musiqa al-ṭarab,* who argue that such a change from more complex to less complex is a sign of degradation, apart from the similarity to erotic seduction that also strikes them as unacceptable in popular music. But many youthful fans of *shababiyya* who evince no lack of subtlety in their own thinking do not agree; rather, they tend to voice the sentiment that contemporary *shababiyya* expresses something true and resonant about their emotional lives. Likewise, such young people, whether highly educated or not, do not respond emotionally to high modernist music as do their elders: in other words, while they can identify and comprehend intellectually the subtlety of indirect emotional evocation in such music, it fails to work upon them. The aesthetic critiques of their elders thus rankle on a personal level: in the eyes of young Cairenes, to scorn the aesthetics of *shababiyya* is, by implication, to scorn their generation and its position in contemporary Egyptian society, and thereby diminish the authenticity of young Cairenes' Egyptianness.

This shift also explains the generational crossover appeal of the two transitional figures discussed in this book: 'Abd al-Ḥalim Ḥafiẓ and Muḥammad Munir. In a very real way, older people and younger people hear different qualities in each singer's output. The lyrical texts of both singers tend to impress older listeners with their variety of poetic metaphors and cleverly phrased sentiments, in combination with beautiful instrumental arrangements and, particularly in the case of 'Abd al-Ḥalim, the hypnotic beauty of the singer's voice. While a few youthful listeners expressed similar impressions, they also made clear that they valued the intensity of directly expressed emotion above the artfulness of the wording.

This preference extends even to Muḥammad Munir's nationalist songs that do not easily correlate with love songs: young people explained that you could hear in every word not just a good text, but Munir's real feeling in these national sentiments. A great many pop musicians in Egypt have recorded nationalist songs at one time or another, but usually consumers disregard these as cheap propaganda that either the government or, perhaps more likely, a particular satellite music channel has commissioned in order to curry favor with viewers. Even the few music fans who admitted to disliking Munir's music felt obligated to observe to me that they respected his personal commitment to the ideas about which he sings. Such critics referred not to overt political activism but to his talent for recording songs with relatively subtle secular-nationalist political implications and investing them with strongly received emotion—making them resonate in the same way that his predecessor 'Abd al-Ḥalim did with love songs.[29]

Likewise, this shift in evaluative aesthetics helps to explain why stars of *shababiyya* like 'Amr Diyab and Shirin 'Abd al-Wahhab are so often beloved by young people and so often scorned by the members of older generations. These singers perform texts whose emotional baldness drives older listeners to distraction; these older listeners perceive such texts—sometimes, perhaps, with some justification—as so similar from one composition to the next that they are essentially boilerplate, and thus not truly art at all. Youthful fans, though, do not necessarily seek unique poetic compositions in their music, least of all in love songs; since the language of direct emotional experience speaks to putatively universal human sensations (at least within a given cultural framework, such as Egypt or the Arabic-speaking world), uniqueness cannot be the whole point. Formulaic compositions actually offer a superior vehicle for much of *shababiyya* in this regard, because the lyrics need not distract consumers from the real focus of their attention: the singer's skill in direct emotional evocation, and ability to communicate to an audience that he or she truly "feels these words." This shift in aesthetics comprises perhaps the sharpest disjuncture between the visions of modern Egyptian subjectivity espoused by the older and younger generations. Not only do they disagree about the authenticity of various singers but they do not employ the same rubric of authenticity in the first place.

A particular discourse of authenticity emerges from this language of feeling and emotionality of music. Authenticity (in Arabic, *aṣala*) of music and musicians relates closely to notions of autochthonous forms of production—in both linguistics and in cultural practice, the concept of *aṣala* connotes origins in a particular place and milieu.[30] If the Egyptian youth whose words appear in my ethnography are to be believed, then authenticity of Egyptianness rests partially upon perceived indigeneity of musical style and content (as opposed to origin anywhere else in the world, whether in Arab lands or the West); partially upon the supposed innate musical talent that owes to Egyptian ethnic/racial affiliation; and partially upon the verisimilitude of the emotions expressed by the song and through the singer.

But this parsing presents us with an apparent paradox: how do Egyptian youth reconcile this understanding of musical authenticity with their own day-to-day listening habits? After all, Muḥammad Munir himself—the most authentically Egyptian pop singer alive, *per* my interlocutors—often delves into Western musical rhythms, melodic progressions, and stylistic touches; other singers in the *shababiyya* industry draw more heavily upon forms of musical production that owe nothing to the traditions of Arabic music in general, let alone indigenous Egyptian forms. Does not this heterogeneity or, more precisely, heterochthony impugn the authenticity of the listener as well as the producer?

The answer to this question is that Egyptian youth invest themselves in this discourse of authenticity as part of a much larger project of cultural and political subjectivity. This project has become something of an obsession for Egyptians of the current youth generation, fueled by the confluence of political, economic, and cultural forces that shape their lives at the everyday level. The kind of Arab nationalism that earlier generations espoused, and which is still taught to adolescents in high school, aligns poorly with the political realities discussed earlier in this chapter. Young people can see these political realities for themselves, essentially free of government censorship or even oversight, simply by logging on to the Internet (if they belong to the middle and upper classes who can access such technology) or by turning on the television and channel-surfing through the various satellite news channels (which are now available to nearly everyone in Egypt with access to electrical power, legally or otherwise) broadcasting in Arabic, English, and French.[31] They must grapple with the reality that their country's regime, both before and after Mubarak, is in some ways supported as well as dominated financially and politically by the United States—a very unpopular situation that nonetheless seems irremediable in light of the state's economic weakness, thinly stretched infrastructure, and enduring strategic value to the global power. In a way that their parents and grandparents did not, young Cairenes must now contend with an obvious and growing disjuncture between what the Egyptian state tells them Egyptian nationality and Arab supra-ethnic identity are, and what that nationality and ethnic identity in political practice appear to have become. This incipient project does not yet articulate itself as a coherent ideology, the way their parents and grandparents might claim a Nasserist or *infitaḥi* ideology from their own upbringings; rather, it is still at the nebulous stage of a "structure of feeling" (Williams 1977), a precursor of ideology that helps to give some sense of generational identity to these young people.[32]

This ontological project, although specific to the contemporary youth of Cairo, has some precedent within the Arab world, in terms of the linkage between musical consumption and authentic subjectivity.[33] As a prominent example of this, Shannon (2003) has described the distinctly anxious relationship that Syrian aficionados of *musiqa al-ṭarab* have to Syria's intensely pan-Arab nationalist discourse that dominates discussions of cultural authenticity. He writes that the emotional experience of *ṭarab* "rhetorically confirms individual claims to cultural authenticity and emotional transparency and operates as a frame for the enactment of conceptions of the self," and that this music serves "as an important and highly contested metaphor for what many Syrian artists, intellectuals, and patrons understand to be a realm of cultural difference from the West—one infused with what they call 'oriental spirit' *(rûh sharqiyya)*" (Shannon 2003, 74). Shannon observes as well that this concept of "oriental spirit" does not function as the last word on the subject but as a point of entry into a fundamentally dynamic debate on modernity and subjectivity in Syria. In similar fashion, Cairene youth do not foreclose further discussion of embodied and performed authentic subjectivity by invoking Egyptianness but rather invite such discussion.[34]

The same satellite dishes that offer young people nongovernmental news sources also offer them video clips, which present them with alluring and unsettling standards of Arab physical beauty and sexual comportment. Concurrent with the fragmentation of Arab nationalism, and even consumed through the same media forms, these new standards of looks and behavior contend with what many (if not most) of my youthful Cairene interlocutors consider their cultural patrimony. In a way that their parents and grandparents did not, young Cairenes must now confront questions of how their own sexuality and their own bodies' potential beauty reflect or conflict with their understanding of themselves as Egyptians.

Beyond visual imagery, young Cairenes constantly consume a huge amount of popular music, most of it *shababiyya.* This music, beloved though it may be of young people, also presents them with potential questions of autochthonous versus foreign influence. There is no precise formula to determine the indigenous authenticity of a given pop song—would 60 percent autochthony generate authenticity, or 85 percent?—but then there can be no precise formulae for any of these vexing questions of what counts as Egyptian and what does not. As with politics, economics, beauty, and sexuality, the realm of pop music production reflects an interconnected and interdependent world whose attributes do not easily reconcile to any kind of territorially bounded nationalism. Compounding the issue is the inescapable fact that the very qualities that young people often love most about their pop music are the same qualities that their own analysis devalues as superficially or inauthentically Egyptian. In a way that their parents and grandparents did not, young Cairenes must now decide for themselves how to enjoy the expressive culture that they love with a clear nationalist conscience, while adhering to some recognizable aesthetic standards of evaluation.

I emphasize the generational divide because, as much as young people question, critique, or reject their forebears' points of view and aesthetic standards, these older ways of thinking persist as larger societal standards. Young people themselves are born into and educated in these modes of thought, which is why they must labor to question and critique in the first place. This critique must occur, however, because young people are increasingly aware of the gap between Egypt as it was thirty years ago and as it is today. The standards of what (and how) to think, be, and do that sufficed for their parents and grandparents simply do not apply any longer. Contemporary youth must therefore suffer the judgment of their elders while maintaining sight of the fact that, nowhere so much as in the realm of popular culture, it is no longer feasible to practice authenticity of Egyptianness—or modernity itself—as the old folks would wish.[35]

Whether these young Cairene pop music consumers are fond of Lebanese pop singers or not (and most of them definitely are), they generally perceive the capacity for musical talent and emotional evocation as qualitatively Egyptian; they perceive Lebanese singers as, at best, glamorous-looking Western-style singers who must draw on a shallower pool of nationally derived talent to sing Arabic music. Those singers from other countries who have become famous working in the Cairo-based music industry, or even by singing in the Cairene dialect of Arabic, are not granted any particular imprimatur of ethnicity-bequeathed genius but are instead figured as tapping into Egyptian musical genius. This can be a positive thing, as with the Syrian-born Asmahan and Farid al-Aṭrash, whose professional lives were intimately connected to Cairo, or a negative, as with Nancy ʿAjram and Hayfa Wahbi, whom Cairenes often deride as seizing on the Cairene dialect as a linguistic vehicle by which to augment their nationally impoverished singing skills. Egyptians, Cairenes feel, possess an inherently valuable aura—which they often describe to me as "authenticity"—that distinguishes them from other Arabs, especially as other Arabs in the music industry often seem to mimic Egyptianness as a professional device.

This project of authentic subjectivity is not simply a reaction to recent historical events and economic forces in Egypt but part of the ongoing process of imagining and reimagining postcolonial modernity. The attempt to set forth a coherent set of touchstones by which an autochthonous Egyptian identity (and with it, a standard of authenticity) could be recognized goes back at least to the late 1870s, when a dissident political movement led by Egyptian army officer Aḥmad 'Urabi came to associate increased political participation by the nonaristocracy and anti-imperialist policy with nativist sentiment (Juan Cole 1999, 183–87). 'Urabi became a nationalist hero in the Nasser era, as a forerunner of both the twentieth-century anticolonial nationalist movement and the military-led political dissidence that led to Nasser and the Free Officers' seizure of power in 1952. From their perspective, a nativist emphasis on the autochthony of Egyptian identity was a self-evident political good that could and should be disseminated through cultural means, and both of Nasser's successors, Sadat and Mubarak, have continued this theme in history lessons even as they have pursued political and economic policies that conflict philosophically with such cultural nativism. As discussed in chapter 2, gender and sexuality have also played roles in authentic Egyptian subjectivity for decades, at the least.

It is, then, no simple matter to reconcile one's individual desires and convictions with one's claim to Egyptian authenticity. Claims to authenticity cannot necessarily be worn lightly; they must be practiced, acted out, *performed*—and performativity of any sort, no matter how naturalized or customary, is a variety of artifice. This point, while worth remembering, may be a relatively circular bit of philosophy, in light of the fact that there exists a degree of performativity in everything that people do for the benefit of other people's perception, and this is not about to stop just because one person or another suddenly becomes aware of his or her own naturalized performance. But it sheds interesting light on those qualities that my interlocutors value so highly in popular music.

As discussed in chapter 1, my interlocutors tend to dislike *musiqa al-ṭarab* partly because they regard it as fundamentally inauthentic: too posturing, too self-consciously poetic, too much about the music itself, rather than the emotional engagement between the singer and the audience. They understand that their elders do not have this problem with *musiqa al-ṭarab,* and they even acknowledge sometimes that they may someday metaphorically turn into their parents and suddenly appreciate the older music in a way that is currently inaccessible to them. But that day has not yet come for most of them, and they consider it a form of inauthenticity to themselves to pretend to share their parents' tastes.

It may testify to the deep naturalization of musical performance *qua* performance that no one ever suggested aloud to me that all of these singers, across every genre, are always performing roles of sorts, always constructing artifices intended to please the audience. Or perhaps more likely, youthful music fans in Egypt, like their counterparts in the United States, have naturalized a particular performative aesthetic that carries with it an assumption about a singer's authenticity, and thus they are more easily able to perceive the artifice of other aesthetics. Barker and Taylor (2007) have written on the development of a discourse of authenticity within rock and roll, paying close attention to the critical reception of Elvis Presley's music and persona through the decades. They observe that, since the 1970s, rock critics—that is, music critics who start from a position of treating rock 'n' roll as a serious subject of musical criticism—have frequently viewed Elvis's earliest rhythm and blues recordings at Sun Records as his most "authentic," revealing the historically naïve assumption that the singer was at base a passionate and uneducated rural whose true self expressed itself most honestly in music similarly presumed to be primitive or unsophisticated. "But if one listens closely, Elvis's voice just doesn't fit these descriptions. . . . He knew how to inject a snarl into his voice, just as he knew how to put a sneer into his smile. An arrogance came across in his singing, an arrogance that was—especially when compared to the obsequiousness he displayed in interviews—an act" (Barker and Taylor 2007:143).

With this observation in mind, we gain a new perspective on my interlocutors' near-universal appreciation for Elvis's Egyptian analogue, 'Abd al-Ḥalim Ḥafiẓ. 'Abd al-Ḥalim distinguished himself in performance from some of the aesthetic assumptions of high modernist music by his directness of audience address and unctuousness of seductive emotionality in his voice; critics who dismissed him in his early years as a "crooner" were in essence rejecting him as an inauthentic singer who tried to sell himself rather than the song. To such critics, 'Abd al-Ḥalim's vocal talent was undermined by his unavoidable emotional posturing, even though much of what they loved in high modernist music was a specific suite of vocal tics, mannerisms, and postures, deployed in aesthetically approved ways. Sixty years after the first of these critical dismissals was aired, my youthful interlocutors swoon in admiration of 'Abd al-Ḥalim's singing style, and dismiss his predecessors as overwhelmed by their high modernist tics and mannerisms.

Authenticity in *shababiyya,* in this perspective, is more properly seen as a suite of performative devices and artifices, ones that have come to represent an imagined ideal of authenticity and have displaced an earlier set. The most important of these criteria, which comes through in my conversations and interviews, is an assumed experiential knowledge of a song's lyrical content: the idea that the singer truly knows what heartache and romantic desire feel like, and that the (often generic) lyrics can and will become a vehicle for the specific feelings the singer has experienced. After that comes the much-remarked-upon authenticity of Egyptian identity: the impression that the singer is an Egyptian born and bred who may partake of the imagined national birthright of prodigious musical talent, and who (as my interlocutors hope) will behave modestly and unpretentiously, without the dual airs of cosmopolitan sophistication and louche snobbery that my interlocutors associate with the Lebanese singers.

Observe, then, that 'Abd al-Ḥalim has found a completely different reception of his emotional sincerity among contemporary youth than he found (or finds) among devotees of the old high modernist aesthetic. In a sense, the intensity of his seductive emotional appeal sets up the high modernist aficionado's objection: 'Abd al-Ḥalim is too effective in his emotional appeal through words, and as with all smooth talkers, "the power to use words is a power to deceive and manipulate" (Frith 1996, 168). But, to the younger generation that reveres 'Abd al-Ḥalim, the sense that he directly addresses their emotions—that he, as it were, plainly attempts to seduce them—is a cornerstone of his appeal. Remember that contemporary music listeners tend to associate 'Abd al-Ḥalim with experiential authenticity in sharp distinction to his *musiqa al-ṭarab* predecessors; the younger singer's reception is partially dependent upon the melding of his personal biography with his performances. In Western pop music, it has long been the pattern that music listeners perceive a singer's biography and vocal performance as mutually constitutive and mutually expressive (Frith 1996, 185–86); this phenomenon simply did not occur in Egyptian popular music, prior to 'Abd al-Ḥalim's rise.

I wish to make clear that under discussion are two different interrogations of authenticity that, in the context of contemporary Egypt, relate to each other strongly. Within the broad discourse of cultural modernity, there is the aesthetic matter of authenticity of musical performance, and then there is the cultural and political matter of authenticity of subjectivity. Within this latter heading, there are two closely related branches:

authenticity of the postcolonial subject, and intersubjective authenticity, which Jackson (2005) distinguishes as sincerity. Among my Cairene interlocutors, all these forms of authenticity not only relate to each other historically but are, in fact, constantly in dialogue with each other.

Since at least the time of Umm Kulthum, Cairenes have spoken of musical performances, especially vocal performances, as authentic or inauthentic in accordance with a perceived ideal of cultural modernity. As I have discussed, the criteria for these judgments have changed a great deal over time, but the idea that such an ideal could be identified has held steady through the years. Moreover, this concept has long stood in fundamental opposition to a sense of excessive heterochthony, a critique that carried as much political charge in 1940 as it does today (Danielson 1997, 172). This concept was closely juxtaposed to the corresponding concept of authenticity of the postcolonial subject, which in many ways was judged against the same scale of autochthony versus heterochthony. Furthermore, these authenticities were meant to interrelate: after all, who else would make the ideal consumer of an authentically modern(ist) musical performance but an authentically modern(ist) Egyptian?

As Cairene ideas of desirable postcolonial modernity have changed over time along with aesthetic ideals, and as the putative ideal of autochthony has receded in confrontation with Egypt's multifarious engagements with the West, especially the United States, it has become easier to question a person's Egyptianness. It is more difficult than formerly to convince a skeptical questioner—the doorman who notes when you come home alone late at night, the union boss uncertain that you deserve to have your petition heard, the prospective father-in-law sizing you up—of one's cultural authenticity as an Egyptian, with whatever degree of respect or access such status might grant in a given scenario. But, perhaps more to the point, the most serious interrogations of authentic subjectivity come from the subjects themselves. Modernity and authenticity in Egypt are closely bound up with national identification, and being Egyptian, as the interlocutors who appear in this book make clear, is inextricably connected to being a moral and aesthetically discriminating person, as much as any legal qualification. My interlocutors therefore invest considerable energy in distinguishing good music from bad, just as they distinguish moral behavior from immoral. And, since aesthetic distinction goes for naught if others do not know about it, my interlocutors are similarly invested in a continuing discourse and embodiment of intersubjective authenticity: communicating the sincerity of their Egyptianness to others by means of the singers they listen to under various circumstances, and how they claim to receive performances as indicative or not of Egyptian subjectivity—subjectivity of the singer *and* subjectivity of the listener.

The intersubjective nature of this authentication process distinguishes it from the subject-object authentication of a piece of visual art. As a rule, my interlocutors felt no compunction about saying unprompted that a particular singer was authentic or inauthentic, even though they formulated this judgment on the basis of the singer's artistic output. Such a discourse does not seem as commonplace among Egyptian visual artists and art collectors, for example, who pass judgment on the authenticity of a given painting or sculpture, but do not (usually) extend that judgment to the fundamental character of the artist who produced it (see Winegar 2006).

All of this makes sense as long as the discussion is confined to Egyptian singers, but of course my interlocutors do not at all confine themselves to listening to their compatriots. Lebanese singers are very popular among young Cairenes, even if they do not rate as highly by certain metrics, and, as I have noted above, to consume that popular culture that is excluded from aesthetic authenticity is to invite a critique of one's own authenticity. I have written elsewhere (Gilman 2009, 91) that middle-class Cairene youth in particular seem to be actively rewriting the rules of respectable gendered comportment in a spirit of pragmatism, in response to social and economic circumstances beyond their control that make older standards of behavior quaintly impractical. I suggest that, in similar fashion, young Cairenes make room for Lebanese singers in their aesthetic tastes not by suppressing their desire for an aesthetic of experiential authenticity but by expanding it. Even the music fans most harshly critical of the Lebanese arm of the *shababiyya* industry acknowledge that young Cairenes evince an insatiable appetite for the kind of sexuality expressed therein, and that this appetite suggests that young people may have more trouble conforming to the nationalism-inflected standards of gendered comportment than they may wish to admit.

Of course, one might argue that such contradictory desires that seem to bubble up despite overt claims to the contrary constitute plain hypocrisy. While I cannot vouch for the intellectual integrity of every person with whom I spoke, neither can I dismiss these feelings and wishes as hypocritical. I am more persuaded by Samuli Schielke's assertion that morality, and especially sexual morality, is "an incoherent and unsystematic conglomerate of different moral registers" for young Egyptians, a complex and internally contradictory terrain in which everything that people say and do simply will not add up in orderly fashion (Schielke 2009, S30). Cairenes may deride the Lebanese *shababiyya* singers as artificial and inauthentic (and worse) for their studio-engineered voices and their surgeon-engineered faces, but they also yearn—albeit guiltily—for what they perceive as the lack of sexual inhibition in Beirut in general and among singers in specific. That perceived lack of inhibition itself represents an alternative kind of authenticity that, although it seems counterintuitive, resonates with young Cairenes; behind the comments of "But we are not like that" and "this is not our culture" lurks a powerful wish that things *could* be like that, that it *could* be their culture, and that they could incorporate such pleasurable, self-indulgent behavior into their behavioral options without any corresponding loss of authentic Egyptian identity.

The self-interrogation in which my interlocutors engage as part of their engagement with their state and society in many ways mirrors this aesthetic engagement that I have described. The desire for authenticity of subjectivity is hardly confined to musical matters, as the political and social parallels I have drawn illustrate. I cannot say precisely how close an analogy one might draw between Cairenes' political engagements and their consumption of pop music, and I am well aware that such posited allegories often stretch the bounds of credibility. I consider the parallel stronger between pop music consumption and the engagement with postcolonial modernity at large: in both arenas, the rules of evaluation periodically shift, forcing people to question whether or not the old ways really worked that well, encouraging the young to move away from or against the worldviews of their parents, and requiring that youth find a way of being in the world that allows them to feel true to themselves, without ever feeling truly as confident as their forebears felt toward that world. That confidence, however, is a feature of an outmoded vision of Egyptian postcolonial modernity, and young Cairenes are, in my experience, too pragmatic to follow an outmoded trend. The youth generation's way of being in the world is their own retuned vision of modernity—and thus, as it must come to pass, Egypt's emergent iteration of modernity.

When I began to conceive the analysis that I have presented in this chapter, the political consequences of the ideas that I theorized were considerably more difficult to envision than since the January 25 uprising. When I flew home to Texas from my doctoral field research, Hosni

Mubarak was firmly in power, showing no sign of departing for any other place in this world or the next. The state's neoliberal economic program—which seemed all too facilely to shade into kleptocracy—continued unabated. Despite what history and common sense suggested, it was shamefully easy to imagine on some days that Egypt would never change, that nothing better would ever happen for its increasingly burdened inhabitants, except for the powerful few who reaped the financial rewards of the system. Even the long-circulating jokes about Mubarak's resistance to change and refusal to submit to death itself began to mock the joke-tellers, as the system and its leader endured beyond the apparent limits of nature (El Amrani 2011).

This situation persisted when I returned to Cairo for my postdoctoral fellowship at the American Research Center in Egypt. Three months into my stay, however, the parameters of the possible began to stretch in ways that I would like to claim that I anticipated years before—but I would be lying. I turn now to the 2011 Egyptian revolution and the ways in which the pop music industry and its consumers' constant attention to authenticity and sincerity engaged with the changes on the ground.

4

"A Poem Befitting of Her"

Ambiguity and Sincerity in Revolutionary Pop Culture

Artifice

My friend Alice, whom I had met through her Evangelical church youth group in 2008, hoped and expected to gain employment after graduation by virtue of her skills and, as I suspect, with the additional asset of her family's *wasṭa,* especially within the somewhat rarefied Evangelical community that, by her family's own claim to me, maintained close cultural and economic ties with their co-religionists in Great Britain and the United States. Sure enough, when I met up with Alice several years later during my postdoctoral research, she was working in an entry-level administrative position for an American company that maintained a branch in Cairo. By that time, though, whatever anxieties she may once have had about acquiring a good job had been supplanted by her family's general anxiety about their status as Christians in Egypt: as luck would have it, I caught up with them on January 7, 2011, only a week after a car bombing had slaughtered twenty-three Coptic Orthodox worshippers and injured a hundred more in Alexandria at the Church of the Two Saints.[1]

Alice's grand-aunt Bushra had given me a lift to her aunt's home in Rehab City, her family's usual gathering place, from the Kubri al-Qubba metro station, along with a first-year college student from the Upper Egyptian city of Minya, Elaine. Bushra and I arrived at the station long before Elaine did, so we had ample time to chat before picking up the student. As Bushra, a dean at Helwan University, had explained to me, Elaine was studying at her faculty, and the older woman knew that Elaine had virtually no social circle in the city, except for a very few of her fellow Evangelical Christians.[2] With emotions in Egypt's Christian community running high in the aftermath of the bombing, Bushra had already found herself, to her dismayed surprise, doing damage control at work.

A Christian student under her charge had posted some angry invective on her Facebook page accusing Egypt's Muslim majority of stoking anti-Christian violence, offending both her Muslim classmates and much of the university staff who learned of it. Bushra had had to give the student a serious talking-to that, in my understanding, was less of an institutional reprimand than a familial scolding from an elder Christian to a younger one. Bushra had invited Elaine because she was attending Helwan University in Cairo and could not afford to travel back to Minya to celebrate the holiday with her family. (I had been invited simply because I had not seen the family in several years and it was a convenient occasion to catch up with everyone.) Given the volatile tensions she had to mediate between rash young people, to say nothing of whatever malevolent forces beyond the university might have been brewing, Bushra thought it both a kindness and a safety measure to offer Elaine the company of coreligionists.

The past week's events strongly colored the atmosphere at the gathering. One could hardly have called it a party, considering the pall of mourning cast on Coptic Christmas that year. Despite mundane topics such as how relatives were performing at school and the cost of this and that, the conversations were all dominated by the bombing and what it might portend for them as Christians. One person said that he was upset, but that he could not even imagine how the Christians of Alexandria felt. His cousin disagreed, venturing that he felt under direct threat himself as a Christian and that he feared this was the first skirmish of what could grow into a civil war. They agreed, however, that at least the bombing had made Egyptians acknowledge aloud what both men perceived as the rising sectarian tensions in the country.

The subject continued even after we took our leave and Bushra drove us to the metro station. Bushra, a secularist as well as a firm supporter of the Mubarak regime, observed optimistically that she had seen on television that Muslims had formed chains of human shields to protect other churches from similar attacks on Christmas Eve, and that a large number of Muslim guests and dignitaries, including the actor 'Adil Imam and President Mubarak's sons 'Ala' and Gamal, had personally attended Pope Shenouda III's own mass at Saint Mark's Cathedral in Cairo in a show of solidarity. Elaine was thoroughly unswayed by such public gestures, however, and sourly responded to Bushra that she considered the displays of national fraternity artificial (*mufta'ala*),[3] and that all of it was mere public relations. Although Bushra tried her best to persuade Elaine that her Muslim countrymen and political leadership meant what they said—perhaps thinking of her own students and staff simmering at the outburst on Facebook—the young woman would not be convinced. Sensing that she could only go so far in arguing with her own host and dean to boot,[4] Elaine allowed the matter to drop, guardedly saying that she was not as optimistic as Bushra, then sighing "*bas rabbina mawgud* (but our Lord is present)."[5]

The key point here is Elaine's assertion of artifice in the public discourse, the notion that public figures' sentiments of solidarity and religious respect were not genuinely felt. Her accusation was certainly not new, and likely not entirely in error, either, at the very least with regard to some of the politicians who were present at the mass. But the more important concept at play here is not hidden malice, but artifice of emotion in public discourse deployed in the effort to say what the speaker believes people want to hear. As I shall discuss in this chapter, such an idea featured in some of the first artifacts of popular culture to appear following Mubarak's ouster, as well as in the political rhetoric that appeared concurrently. Elaine's critique of the public gestures of solidarity was based on the understandings of sincerity and authenticity that I have discussed in the previous chapter; it was a political statement couched as an aesthetic critique.

Egypt Next

The first sign I saw that something large was brewing in Egypt was the newspapers on the metro. Due to the relatively low levels of literacy in Egypt, printed materials have never acquired the same degree of mass circulation as radio or television. Newspapers, in my experience, are a more widespread form of print media than books in Cairo. Newspaper articles are, increasingly, written in a simpler prose register of Modern Standard Arabic than are novels—language scholars often refer to this register as "media Arabic"—and people of modest education can master this style with relatively little trouble.[6] Traditionally, literate people would read the newspaper aloud to their illiterate companions, giving the press far greater exposure than literacy rates or business figures might indicate (Juan Cole 1999, 124–25).[7] In recent decades, however, newspapers have declined, partly due to the proliferation of satellite television news channels, which can provide essentially the same service to viewers as the village *shaykh* reading aloud in his local coffeehouse. In my observation, people would often pick up a newspaper or two, but it generally took them only ten minutes or less to skim through a paper, determine that nothing substantive had changed from yesterday, and abandon the paper on a bus seat or restaurant table.

January 15, 2011, was not like this at all. The day before, Zayn al-'Abidin bin 'Ali, the dictator of Tunisia since 1987, had resigned as president in the face of intense mass protests and fled his country, ignominiously flying around the Mediterranean looking for sanctuary in one country after another before being granted safe harbor in Saudi Arabia. It was lost upon no one in Egypt that bin 'Ali, a secular nationalist authoritarian leader from the military establishment, in power for decades and steeped in corruption, bore a close resemblance to Hosni Mubarak's professional profile. One Egyptian friend of mine commented on Facebook that she thought she must have been dreaming to see an Arab dictator forced from power by an ecumenical popular uprising. The same day that bin 'Ali fled, a crowd gathered at the Tunisian embassy in Cairo to chant, "Egypt next, Egypt next!" The next morning, the newspapers being read by passengers on the Cairo metro became an indelible image in my mind: I have never, before or since, seen so many people anywhere reading so many newspapers so intently. I counted at least ten different daily newspapers in people's hands, all of them declaring the news in massive bold type: THE FLIGHT OF BIN 'ALI. The papers were lit up with garish color photographs of the fires of the riots in Tunisia, and—depending on the political orientation of the publication—either anxious or gleeful descriptions of the collapse of the dictator's rule.

The Tunisian revolution inspired innumerable conversations across Egypt, including some that I never thought I would have. The night before Egypt's own revolutionary uprising began, I spent the evening with my friend Huda and her parents, discussing current events. Huda's father Gawhar, the retired army colonel who tended to view the military through rose-colored glasses, had insisted to me for years that, whatever mistakes the cabinet officials had made over the years, Mubarak himself was an honest and decent man. It was only a few months before, in November 2010, when the regime perpetrated election fraud of such crass obviousness that even some die-hard regime supporters complained aloud of corruption, that Gawhar hesitantly allowed himself to admit to me his fears that his government (and the military that supported it) was not only incompetent and corrupt but also possibly inimical to the state itself. But on the evening of January 24, 2011, Gawhar's entire demeanor was crestfallen. The former colonel looked and sounded strikingly like a child who has just learned that Santa Claus does not exist as he mused to me, hardly above a whisper, "The people are very angry, as in Tunisia, about all the money that the government has stolen from the public: sixty billion dollars, they say, Mubarak has stolen and hidden in Switzerland."[8] I found myself oddly moved to comprehend how deeply this idea wounded Gawhar, a career military man who fought in the 1967 and 1973 wars, and who had struggled for years to reconcile his love of the armed forces with his rising suspicions of the harm that the military-industrial complex had done to his country.

The Revolution?

During my doctoral research, I lived a few steps from Tahrir Square. When massive protests broke out in other parts of Egypt on April 6, 2008, I witnessed the square become a sea of security forces in which a dismally small group of protestors was quickly and efficiently arrested and carted away. My politically active Egyptian friends had long ago explained to me that this procedure was so common as to seem scripted: a small hard core of activists would be arrested the moment they showed themselves, and any number of their compatriots would flee to (or would already be seated at) Café Bursa, a large open-air coffeehouse near the old stock exchange in downtown Cairo favored by young secular leftists. The police would eventually drop by Bursa to question and harass any known activists they found there, possibly arresting them but more likely leaving them alone after making the point that the security forces remained in control, and knew where to get their would-be opposition, if they so chose. By the time I left my flat and started walking around Tahrir, about two hours after the scheduled start to the protest, no protestors were left in the square. There were, however, hundreds of security personnel: traffic cops, local police, Cairo Security, Central Security, and, perhaps most threatening of all, the plainclothes officers—unidentifiable agents of the Ministry of the Interior—dressed in civilian clothes, but lined up in telltale neat rows at street corners and by metro entrances, wearing hard expressions on their faces and looming grimly over everyone moving through the square.[9]

I carried this understanding of the cat-and-mouse game of public protesting with me when I returned to Cairo for my postdoctoral research in 2010. Through the usual channels of security information—the U.S. State

Department email listserve for expatriates and word-of-mouth rumors—I knew that there would be a demonstration in Tahrir Square on January 25, 2011. People claimed it would be big, but I was skeptical: I had seen how the planned massive protests of April 6 had dissipated, after state security had infiltrated the protestors' information networks. I expected more of what I knew: a few activists arrested, many more harassed while sipping tea at Bursa, an extra show of state power in Tahrir Square, and then business as usual in the city. There seemed little reason to travel uptown to see the sideshow myself; and, in any case, I had plenty of work to do at home. I spent the day inside my apartment. I was blindsided when I learned that evening that 15,000 protestors turned out on the square, refusing to cede the field to the police, and chanting (among other slogans), "Tunis is the solution."[10] My field notes for that day began with the heading: *Revolution?*

The week that followed was a bizarre amalgam of meals with friends, grocery shopping in siegelike conditions, avoidance of tear gas and machine-gun fire, and obsessive viewing of satellite television news channels. Only the first of these had played any role in my previous experience in Egypt. The rest were direct responses to new circumstances: military checkpoints that discouraged merchants from trying to haul any products by land or air into Cairo; sporadic battles between security forces, military forces, and a variety of civilian groups; and a new compulsion to follow current events on television, a device that had played hardly any role in my life in Cairo until that time, except as a medium for music video clips.

Television news, in fact, became bracingly interesting to watch as much for the reporting personnel as for the news itself—if one could even distinguish between the two. American news followers may recall that U.S. reporters sometimes became stories in and of themselves: the CNN reporter Anderson Cooper was beaten by pro-regime thugs as he covered events in Tahrir Square (Goodman 2011), and in a notorious incident, the CBS reporter Lara Logan was sexually assaulted in Tahrir Square by an entire mob of men on the evening of Mubarak's ouster (CBS News 2011). The phenomenon extended to television news reporters and anchors from the Arab world, some of whom spoke on-camera of their political concerns and their personal encounters with government repression even as the Egyptian Ministry of the Interior tried to silence them. On January 28, some friends and I were watching a report on Aljazeera International by the reporter Ayman Mohyeldin when some branch of the security forces attempted to gain entry to the studio to stop the broadcast—we could hear someone pounding on the door as Mohyeldin spoke. As we watched, Mohyeldin, who had been speaking in English to his anchor at Aljazeera's headquarters in Qatar, broke off to address the situation, and quickly shouted in Egyptian Colloquial Arabic to an off-camera colleague, "*Ma taftiḥish al-bab, ma taftiḥish al-bab! Khallih!* (Don't open the door, don't open the door! Leave it be!)"[11]

A reporter for the Al Arabiya[12] news channel also caught my attention, less for urgent drama than for her embodiment of the loss of on-air composure that the emergency situation forced upon news personnel. News anchors on Arab satellite channels tend to be as carefully made-up and blow-dried as pop stars, much like their American counterparts, and one such female anchor, Al Arabiya's Cairo bureau chief Randa Abu al-'Azm, was on duty on January 28, the day that security forces began to unleash large-scale violence against protestors to drive them from demonstration locales, most famously Tahrir Square. Abu al-'Azm, encased in foundation make-up and hair spray, spoke in pristine media Arabic, maintaining a calm demeanor until late in the evening, when protestors attempted to storm the building housing Al Arabiya's studio as well as the Cairo branches of numerous other satellite news organizations. The heavily deployed police forces defending the television building opened fire, killing a number of protestors, while Abu al-'Azm sat at her anchor desk many floors above, within at least partial eyesight and earshot of the massacre. When a news commentator in Dubai suggested to her that the claims of regime violence were overstated, Abu al-'Azm agitatedly demanded, "Do you know what I can hear from this seat? Do you know that there are people being shot right below me?" Several days later, as Abu al-'Azm continued to report for long hours each day, the mannequin-like perfection of her toilette faded, and a (presumably native) Egyptian accent in her Arabic began to assert itself. By February 1, Abu al-'Azm appeared to have aged ten years, and, in the middle of an interview with Essam el-Erian, a high-ranking spokesman for the Muslim Brotherhood, her media Arabic vanished entirely: she began to speak in pure Cairene Arabic, a dialect I had never heard before out of the mouth of a television news reporter. Both of these phenomena went against professional norms in Arab television news, and both of them underscored the anxiety and strain under which the journalists inside the television building had to work.[13]

It should not come as a shock that the popular music industry, unlike the news media, gave no indication whatever that something large-scale was about to happen. *Al-musiqa al-shababiyya* is not a proactive media form, and political commentary has never been its strong suit. I noted nothing unusual in the pop music world right up to the day that the revolution began—after that, I was unable to pull my mass-media attention away from the satellite news channels. By the time I became aware of political *shababiyya* engaging in any way with the revolution, I was living in temporary evacuation in Cyprus, keeping track of events through the Internet.

Post-Ouster Cairo

Once Hosni Mubarak was forced from power in February 2011, Cairo was suddenly filled with prorevolutionary citizens. This seemed to include not only those who had come out to protest and those who had more quietly voiced their opposition to the regime, but also a large number of people who had previously practiced quietism,[14] as well as some people who simply seemed desirous to associate themselves with the majority opinion. (As I shall discuss, public personalities, especially actors and musicians, were especially associated with this last maneuver.) Some of my friends who had participated actively in the initial uprising grumbled to me that too many people in the early months of 2011 acted as though the revolution were the latest fashion trend, and had neither a clear idea of its purpose nor any firm commitment to its cause. Others of my acquaintance complained that many of their newly revolutionary compatriots were hypocrites who profited from the Mubarak regime's pervasive corruption until the day of Mubarak's ouster, and then immediately declared themselves revolutionaries who had always despised Mubarak.

A conversation I had in May 2011 about pop music singers illustrated this latter point. Giselle, an employee at the American University in Cairo, expressed her contempt of singers who had supported the regime one week and turned on a dime to support the revolution after Mubarak fell from power. She cited the much-discussed singer Tamir Ḥusni, who drew widespread opprobrium after he was chased from Tahrir Square, the epicenter of Cairo's protests, by protestors who judged him a shill for the regime. "It would have been better if he at least kept his [original] opinion [after the revolution], but the way he ran around singing about the revolution after Mubarak fell!" Giselle was referring to Tamir's heavy schedule of prorevolution publicity events and music production, mere weeks after he had sung panegyrically of Mubarak as the nation's father; his abrupt about-face struck her as hypocritical (see Gilman 2011).

Giselle also observed that the singer Muḥammad Fu'ad, who had recently released a song and music video clip in tribute to the martyrs of the revolution, had his own close relationship to power. Leaning forward in her chair to emphasize her righteous indignation so that the large Coptic cross around her neck swung like a censer, Giselle told me, "I'll tell you something else as well, Muḥammad Fu'ad is a close personal friend of 'Ala' Mubarak!"[15] Giselle considered the recent musical efforts by Tamir Ḥusni and Muḥammad Fu'ad sheer pandering to popular sentiment, and an attempt to deflect attention from their own links to the disgraced regime.

The irony of this conversation is that Giselle was employed in the Office of Alumni Affairs, the arm of university governance that, until the Mubarak family fell from power, aggressively courted them for philanthropic contributions. Beyond financing, the university generally boasted of its close associations with the ruling elite of Egypt, including its alumni Suzanne and Gamal Mubarak—the wife and heir apparent of Hosni Mubarak, respectively. In fact, the conversation took place a short walk away from a lecture hall that had only recently been stripped of its original name, the Her Excellency Suzanne Mubarak Conference Hall. If Giselle was aware of this irony, she never once hinted at it during our time together.

This is not to suggest that the American University is the sole hypocritical party in post-Mubarak Egypt. Indeed, as an anti-Mubarak activist observed to me, toadying to the regime despite one's personal distaste for it seemed a prudent and pragmatic thing to do. Sirag al-Din, the son of an elite *muthaqqafin* family in Cairo, mostly held his tongue about his political views until the January 25 uprising began, at which time he and his friends began to participate in the daily protests in Tahrir Square. I spent several hours chatting with him in a café, not long after my conversation with Giselle. Curious about other opinions on the matter, I mentioned to him her claim that Muḥammad Fu'ad had been a fair-weather friend of 'Ala' Mubarak.

Somewhat to my surprise, Sirag al-Din responded not by excoriating the singer, but by indicting himself and his entire socioeconomic class. "You know what? Before the revolution, every one of us would have done anything to get the business card of someone inside the palace. We were *all* corrupt, and we all worked with corruption to get things done: me,

Muḥammad Fu'ad, Wa'il Ghunaym,[16] all of us! If I got stopped by a policeman for driving while talking on my cell phone, would I accept the ticket and pay the fine? Or would I just give fifty pounds—the same cost as the fine—directly to him and get my license back? He is happy, I am happy. I felt good doing that: I felt smart, like I was doing something smarter than just going through the legal process. When I had to take care of my military papers, I either had to wait in line for hours at a police station and then wait for months while they processed the papers, or call up a friend of mine who works in the Ma'adi[17] police station and have him take care of it in ten minutes. Of course I called him, why wouldn't I? Of course Muḥammad Fu'ad was friends with 'Ala'; it made sense." In other words, the upper-middle socioeconomic classes of Cairo had made their peace with the Mubarak regime's rampant corruption, and all of them were complicit—even those who, like Sirag al-Din, later went down to Tahrir Square and braved gunfire and mounted assaults to demonstrate their opposition to Mubarak.

From this pragmatic point of view, it seems only reasonable that Muḥammad Fu'ad, a professional singer whose livelihood derives primarily from concert fees, would seek to curry favor with the ruling elite, no matter what his personal feelings might be. It also explains why so many *shababiyya* singers who had recorded nationalist songs that toed the party line in years past were suddenly eager to eulogize the revolution and its martyrs. Such a change of tone probably did not represent a change of political convictions so much as a recognition that the political landscape had altered, and working singers who hoped to remain popular with their fans needed to acknowledge this fact somehow.

The only professional in the *shababiyya* industry with whom I managed to speak after Mubarak's ouster was Murad, the studio producer whose recording session I attended just before the revolution broke out (see chapter 1). I met with Murad at his home since, as he explained to me after I arrived, there was essentially no work for him at the time. The *shababiyya* industry had ground to a halt at that point, he told me, because the financial backers of nearly all pop culture ventures had become skittish about investing in Egypt's culture industry.[18] The revolution, in the context of the expanding Arab Spring political turmoil across the region, was playing havoc with the culture industry. Investors suddenly had a variety of frightening scenarios to consider: chiefly, that serious political violence could prevent stars from traveling, or prevent engineers from meeting to craft a finished product from the artists' raw material, or more generally keep things from moving through the production process to the market. It also seemed possible, in a way that it had not mere months earlier, that an album or a film might be made at the investors' expense, only to find that the public was uninterested in consuming the sort of disposable, "fast food" music and cinema that usually earned an acceptable profit in the market. A film or an album can fail at any given time, of course, but such a failure is ordinarily attributable to the vagaries of public tastes and the particulars of the product under discussion. The idea of a categorical lack of interest in cheap pop culture was entirely new to the people who earned their livings from the culture industry.

Even worse, the deeply interconnected world of Egyptian pop culture—music, films, and television—was also tied to various elements of the state, and the nature of the state itself was now under open discussion. The Egyptian state has overseen and invested in the television and cinema industries since the early days of Nasser's regime, for propaganda as much as profit. Investors generally assumed that the Egyptian state would purchase high-prestige projects, especially the Ramadan television serials that not only represent the best of Egypt's acting, directing, and writing talent but also frequently serve as showcases for specially commissioned songs by famous singers. Now that the entire concept of the Egyptian state was no longer a stable if stagnant entity but a fluid and dynamic set of assumptions being reconsidered at all levels of public and private discourse, no one knew what the effects would be on the culture industry that had grown fat and complacent under the regime. And, of course, there was also the matter of a potential sweeping regime change that could bring with it, among other things, a new and unknown set of censors whose preferences, sensitivities, and "red lines"[19] could only be determined by an expensive and perhaps even injurious process of trial and error.

Beyond the national borders, the larger universe of Arabic-language mass media also suffered a slump, even where it interacted only indirectly with the Egyptian production apparatus, as Murad sighed to me. Notably, Bahrain and Qatar had both cancelled big music festivals they had planned, thereby eliminating work for many musicians and engineers, including Murad. In this case, it was less that these countries relied on Cairo's music industry or Egypt's consumer market for their respective culture industries, but that their own involvement with various aspects of the Arab Spring—sometimes in deeply unflattering ways—made it seem diplomatically inadvisable to play host to large public parties. At the time, Bahrain had been suppressing its own national protests in brutal fashion, and Qatar had been negotiating the politically delicate matter of contributing formally to the NATO campaign of bombardment of Muammar al-Gaddafi's forces in Libya.[20] Given the negative publicity that both states were attempting to fend off, they each decided that the prudent public relations move would be to cancel their music festivals. Dubai had also cancelled a large concert that had been planned, although Murad was less certain about the reason for this. He suggested that perhaps, like a great many singers in the *shababiyya* industry whom he knew personally, Dubai simply found it potentially dangerous to appear luxurious and celebratory amid the upheaval of the Arab Spring. Whereas Dubai may have dealt with this concern by cancelling a music festival, Murad's professional acquaintances dealt with it by choosing not to perform on their usual circuit of weddings, engagements, and other such ostentatiously joyous occasions.

Revolutionary *Shababiyya*

As many scholars have observed, authenticity is a particularly stressful problematic of modernity, no less so in Egypt than in other places. Authenticity (in Arabic, *aṣala)* of music and musicians relates closely to notions of autochthonous forms of production—in both linguistics and cultural practice, the concept of *aṣala* connotes origins in a particular place and milieu.[21] Among habitual listeners of *shababiyya,* the authenticity of pop music and pop musicians as Egyptian rests upon a variety of musical and aesthetic criteria. The factor of interest to this discussion is the verisimilitude of the emotions expressed by the song and through the singer. This aesthetic criterion throws into relief the difficulty in which Egyptian pop singers found themselves in 2011: it is highly likely that many of them literally did not know *what* they thought about the revolution from day to day,[22] in the same way that every Egyptian I know has a range of intellectual and emotional responses to the period of revolutionary transition that Egypt is currently undergoing. One cannot sound convincing if one does not even know how one feels about a topic. And again, this is only natural: I do not know anyone who is happy about every aspect of revolutionary transition—not when they are experiencing it. The sense of instability and insecurity, the fear that one's political enemies will seize or consolidate power, the concern about the economy and one's livelihood within it: these are not trivial matters.

Taking this anxiety into account, perhaps it makes sense that most of the popular music that was recorded and released since the January 25 uprising until the end of 2011, and which explicitly tackled political topics, came from musical acts that, like Muḥammad Munir and Wusṭ al-Balad, seemed somehow outside of genre even as they engaged with particular aesthetic aspects of *shababiyya.* Munir himself released a song in the fall of 2011 entitled *'Ala min* ("Who are you kidding?"), which commented upon the apparent continuation of Mubarak-era repression and authoritarianism under the Supreme Council of the Armed Forces (SCAF). The lyrics, while as accusatory and transparently metaphorical as those of his earlier hit *Izzay,* remained slightly oblique in style—it was metaphorical, not direct in its composition.

Wusṭ al-Balad, while not at the forefront of revolutionary music production, grew in reputation after its lead singer, Hani 'Adil, collaborated with members of another popular underground Cairo ensemble on what became an anthem of the revolution. Amir 'Id,[23] the lead singer of Cairokee, wrote a song during the January uprising entitled *Ṣawt al-ḥurriyya* ("The voice of freedom"), which he recorded with members of his band and with Hani 'Adil. With the ordinary channels of recording and distribution frozen during the uprising, they chose to create a video clip for the song themselves, using a handheld video camera and smartphones to record footage. Amir 'Id uploaded the resulting video clip (Fahmi, Khalifa, and Shakir 2011), which shows the members of the group walking through the crowds of protestors in Tahrir Square and getting many of them to sing the song, to YouTube on February 10, 2011, whereupon it became a viral hit. Hani 'Adil also contacted several satellite television channels and offered them the use of the video clip, free of charge—it received particularly heavy airplay on the channel OnTV, which is owned by the Egyptian billionaire Nagib Sawiris, a telecommunications magnate who flirted with opposition politics in the pre-Mubarak era (al-Faramawi 2011). Months after Mubarak's ouster, I still frequently heard both *Izzay* and *Ṣawt al-ḥurriyya* blasting from car stereos; both songs struck a powerful chord in listeners.

Cairokee has grown in stature as it has become identified with prorevolutionary anthems, for which Amir 'Id generally writes the lyrics, around which the band collectively composes the melody. In late 2011, the group recorded a video clip for their new song *Ya al-midan* ("O Square"), a proud but somber meditation on the newfound sense of Egyptian political activism and potential for change. The song was both intended and received as a commentary on the growing repression of the SCAF, and the resulting popular backlash that stimulated large numbers of Egyptians to return to public protests of the regime, after some months of relative lack of mass protest. The band recorded both song and video clip with the highly regarded Egyptian singer and *'ud* player 'Ayda al-Ayubi, who had been semiretired for years. The visual contents of the video clip are so striking and emotionally resonant for supporters of the revolution that it is worth looking at them in detail.

The video clip (Shakir 2011) presents the song as an anxious sequel to the unabashedly optimistic and cheerful "The voice of freedom": the video clip of "O Square" begins with a close-up shot of the handwritten lyric text of the earlier song. The camera cuts to shots of a variety of visual reminders of both the initial uprising and the subsequent incidents of violent state repression that became almost commonplace in the latter half of 2011: a used tear gas canister, apparently kept as a souvenir; a jacket pierced by shotgun pellets at the shoulder; a homemade armband identifying its wearer as "Square Security," the protestors' form of internal law and order during the periods of time that they held Tahrir Square; an onion and a spray bottle of liquefied baking soda, both used to ameliorate the effects of tear gas; a megaphone; a smartphone accessing Facebook; broken eyeglasses, famously associated with the protestor Aḥmad Ḥarara, whose right eye was blinded by a shotgun attack by security forces during the January uprising, and whose left eye was blinded in similar fashion months later (Mourad 2011); homemade flyers encouraging Egyptians to vote "no" on the referendum amending the constitution in March 2011; a poster reading "the people are peaceful"; the simple food that protestors ate in the encampments; a shirt with the words "my brother" written on the back, followed by a mobile phone number;[24] a blood-stained physician's white coat, with the breast pocket identifying the wearer as a doctor in the "Square Hospital"; a spent shell casing refashioned into a key ring; a framed newspaper headline declaring "The people brought down the regime"; a riot shield confiscated from Central Security forces. The chorus of the song constantly reminds the listener/viewer of the intended meaning of these images: "*Ya al-midan, kunt fayn min zaman?* (O Square, where have you been for so long?)"

The melodic progression largely resembles a Western rock song built around a tempered scale, although, as discussed in chapter 1, there remains a hint of an underlying *maqam* in the compositional architecture. This compositional aesthetic is common in Cairokee's songs, as the band is somewhat more rock-oriented than most other formerly "underground" acts in the Cairo music scene. 'Ayda al-Ayubi's instrumental performance indicates the even-tempered inclination of the song: her *'ud* playing is limited to hitting relatively precise notes in the Western harmonic scale, rather than the quarter-tones and micro-tones that characterize *musiqa al-ṭarab*—the traditional home genre of the *'ud.* Al-Ayubi's singing has historically inclined toward the intersection of "low modernist" *musiqa al-ṭarab* and high-prestige *al-musiqa al-shababiyya,* and so her singing techniques in "O Square" fit her professional profile: a mixture of clearly sustained notes and melismatic variation, both of which are stretched across a constant meter with essentially no variation in tempo.

This compositional aesthetic, which is largely shared by Cairokee and Wusṭ al-Balad, drew some criticism from some elite commentators, even those who generally appreciated the songs' meanings. Amira el-Noshokaty, a music critic writing for the weekly English-language supplement of the daily newspaper *al-Ahram,* gave a year-end overview of music of the revolution, and cited both "O Square" and "The voice of freedom" as "inspirational." In particular, el-Noshokaty praised the lyric texts and the video clips of both songs, saying of "O Square," "this tribute to the square brought out the best in all of us," and of "The voice of freedom" that it "captured the spirit of the revolution." Simultaneously, however, el-Noshokaty criticized the compositional and performing aesthetics of both ensembles. "However, the pronunciation and vocals of Cairokee and Wust al-Balad lean very much towards the Western style, which detracts somewhat from the spirit of such patriotic songs" (el-Noshokaty 2011). In other words, she suggested that the musical architecture on which both groups habitually depend can impugn the authenticity of their message—despite the fact that, throughout the issue of *al-Ahram Weekly* in which her article appeared, and which devoted significant space to interviewing revolutionary protestors and discussing matters with them, the only person who voiced such complaints was the writer herself.

Beyond the compositional style, there is another aesthetic question that arises from these prorevolutionary songs. With the exception of the visual reminder in "O Square" to vote against the constitutional referendum, there are few indicators of the artists' political inclinations beyond a general opposition to Mubarak and a populist joy in seeing the masses congregate for large-scale protests. In each case, this lack of a more specific political program is understandable: after all, they are not standing for election, but announcing their support for a mass movement. Nevertheless, the listener even more than the viewer is left with little clear idea of what the musicians would like to see result from such mass actions. In terms of this possibly unintentional and perhaps even unavoidable obfuscation, even the prorevolutionary songs and video clips bear some likeness to the decidedly more ambiguous output of the major recording stars of the *shababiyya* industry: the martyr pop video clips.

Martyr Pop and Public Image

A curious phenomenon coming out of the 2011 Egyptian revolution is the emergence of a subgenre of popular music videos dedicated to the memory of the people killed during the eighteen days of protests that brought down Hosni Mubarak's government. This short-lived phenomenon was a notable change of pace from the mass-media Arabic-language music industry's usual stock in trade—schmaltzy songs of chaste romance—for several reasons. First, songs that aired as music video clips via satellite channels in Egypt during the Mubarak era were generally devoid of domestic politics, except for nationalist pablum that either avoided politics entirely or portrayed Mubarak as the legitimate leader of his people. Second, the visual imagery was usually carefully storyboarded and filmed: pretty people in pretty places is the norm in the world of Arabic video clips.

The video clips that memorialize the martyrs differ on both counts, in that simply referring to the revolution in mass media is itself a political act, albeit not necessarily a very clear one. And, in sharp contrast to the elaborate, soap opera–like mise-en-scène that predominates on the satellite music channels beamed across the Arabic-speaking world,[25] the new genre of video clips—to which I refer as "martyr pop"[26]—tended to eschew studio visuals in favor of news footage. Above all, there is a powerful emphasis on photographs of the martyrs. Despite the inherently political nature of singing about the revolution, however, most of the singers actually appear to seek a middle path in which their political sympathies are not truly disclosed.

The reason for this middle path is more economic than political: the Egyptian pop music industry is highly risk-averse, and both singers and executives fear alienating a significant segment of their potential markets (Frishkopf 2010, 17–18). The revolutionary desire to oust Mubarak from power was by no means universal among Egyptians, and there remain many who, out of personal interest or political conviction, believe that he should have remained in office. Since a large portion of Mubarak's supporters belong to the wealthier segment of society, upon which professional musicians depend for their livelihoods, those singers who have produced videos about the revolution apparently feel an obligation to steer clear of broadside partisan statements—even if, as may have been the case, such politics were genuinely important to them.

These video clips bear some close study, in terms of their musical as well as their visual aesthetics. Although I have generally tried throughout this book to focus more on musical aesthetics than visual imagery, I would be remiss if I ignored the salient visual tropes that emerge in these videos. This imagery, in fact, is not confined to music videos, in the way that the usual stock in trade of *shababiyya* videos appears nowhere else. These video clips are drawing on many of the same arresting images that lend weight to media coverage and political appeals in revolutionary Egypt, and therefore speak to something larger than commercial pop culture.

The earliest martyr pop video clip that I know of is a duet between the singers Rami Gamal and ʻAziz al-Shafʻi, "I love you, my country" (Muḥy al-Din 2011): the first upload of the clip to YouTube seems to have occurred on February 9, 2011, two days before Mubarak's ouster (BlancoTV CH 2011). Al-Shafʻi elaborated the words and melody from a song by the old composer Baligh Ḥamdi that memorialized people killed during the 1967 War. The tune accordingly echoes an old-fashioned style of nationalist song whose musical aesthetics more readily evoke a song of unrequited love than a patriotic anthem. The first verse of the sentimental text is:

Qulu li-ummi ma tizʻalish wa-ḥayati ʻandik ma tiʻayyiṭish
Qulu liha maʻlish ya ummi, amut amut wa-baladna taʻish
Amana tibusuli idiha wa-itslamuli ʻala biladi

(Say to my mother "do not be sad, my dearest, do not weep for me"
Say to her, "it's okay, Mother, I die, I die but our country lives"
I beg you, kiss her hand for me, and give my regards to my country)

There are occasional insertions of news footage, particularly those showing people being shot down in the streets, but the bulk of the visual imagery is photographs of the young protestors who were killed. Most of the photographs bear no indication of mourning, such as a black stripe near the left-hand corner, but a number of the faces of the dead have become well known, thanks to wide dissemination of the photos in Egyptian national media—for example, Aḥmad Bassyuni, the curly-haired gentleman in glasses, and Sally Zahran, the only female martyr depicted in this video. On a more subtly political level, the first martyr's photograph shown is not, technically speaking, from the uprising at all, but the famous photograph of Khalid Sa'id, a young man beaten to death by police in broad daylight in the Sidi Gabir district of Alexandria, six months before the uprising began. Khalid Sa'id's brutal murder aroused a great deal of popular anger, which was compounded by the police force's half-hearted and contemptuous excuse that Sa'id was a petty drug dealer who attacked his arresting officers.[27] The popular outrage over the murder of an innocent person by some apparently corrupt and brutal police officers was a contributing factor to the sense of injustice that motivated people to attend the first protests of the revolution, on January 25—a national holiday known as Police Day in Egypt. Due to the understanding many Egyptians have of Khalid Sa'id's death as an inciting incident of the revolution, he is commonly considered to be an early martyr for the cause.

Another early martyr pop video clip is "The martyrs of January 25," by the singer Ḥamada Hilal (Ḥarbi 2011). Released within a day or two of Mubarak's ouster,[28] this song is by far the clearest of the bunch in its singer's politics. A great deal of the news footage that made its way into this video clip plainly includes photos and videos of (often very angry) protestors calling for Mubarak and his government to leave power. The news footage is intercut with footage of Hilal himself walking around the environs of Tahrir Square and participating in various ways with the protests: posing with other protestors for photographs, praying with them, and generally interacting with the scene. It is difficult to guess exactly when the footage was shot, but since the video clip appeared so quickly after Mubarak left power, it is reasonable to estimate that the footage of Hilal was shot over the course of several days in between the time when the numbers of the dead and their photographs were released, and February 11, the day Mubarak stepped down. Much of the video is also dedicated to showcasing a lachrymose Hilal literally weeping about the martyrs, which is more in keeping with scripted studio-produced visuals than with the aesthetic that other martyr pop videos seem to pursue. The song begins:

Shuhada' khamsa wa-'ishrin yanayir matu fi aḥdas yanayir raḥu farqu al-ḥaya
Shuhada' lazim nitbaha bihum wa-kaman mabruk 'alayhum, al-ganna wa-l-sama'

(The martyrs of January 25 who died in the events of January went and parted from life
The martyrs, we must be proud of them and congratulate them, [they have] paradise and heaven)

Hani Shakir's song, "The voice of the martyr," has some of the most referential lyrics of any of the songs in this group, specifically discussing the fact that people protested for freedom and against corruption by demonstrating in Tahrir Square. Interestingly, the production credits take care to identify "the Palestinian poet" Rami Yusuf as the author of the lyrics.[29] Like Ḥamada Hilal's video, and unlike "I love you, my country," this video clip (al-'Aṣi 2011) includes unambiguous footage of people calling for Mubarak to step down, as well as a considerable amount of the violence perpetrated by the security forces. Hani Shakir, who composed the melody himself, is one of the oldest singers still popular with young people—he is about sixty years old now—and is known partly for being one of the last musicians trained by the old masters of the previous generation. Unsurprisingly, then, he chose to write a relatively old-fashioned nationalist melody, which would sound more recognizably like a military march or dirge without the electronica in the arrangement.

'Amr Diyab, perhaps the biggest star in the Egyptian musical universe, incurred some bad press during the early days of the revolution: not only did he make no comment at all about his political views, but he gathered his family on his private jet and flew them to London to wait out the uprising and see how things developed. Egyptians were especially irked that the wealth that they have given him over the years was spent on the means to escape Egypt altogether, with no apparent loyalty or sense of obligation to stay and, if not participate, at least lend his voice to whatever he believed in. It is probably not a coincidence, then, that 'Amr Diyab later released an extraordinarily somber martyr pop video clip (Ra'fat 2011)—indeed, it is hardly recognizable as a video clip in the usual sense, in that there is no living being shown at all. The whole of the video, entitled "Egypt said," is a series of photographs of some of the martyrs, edited together with a heavy, dolorous melody that would sound pretty depressing, if not for Diyab's beautiful voice.

Of special note are two editing choices regarding the photographs. First, the only female martyr included is the now-famous Sally Zahran, who died on January 28, 2011, known as the "Friday of Rage," and she is depicted wearing *ḥigab* (a veil covering her hair). As Walter Armbrust has elucidated, Zahran chose to veil herself for a relatively short period of her life, and at the time of her death, she was no longer a *muḥaggaba.* Zahran's unveiled face became famous as part of a feature story on martyrs of the revolution printed in the newspaper *al-Maṣry al-Youm* on February 6, whose photographic insert of eleven portraits of young martyrs (Figure 14) now seems an "*Ur*-text of January 25th martyrology" (Armbrust 2012). A number of pious Muslims, in the belief that Zahran was in fact a *muḥaggaba* until the day she died, began to object to her unveiled portrait, insisting that it should be replaced with other photographs showing her wearing the *ḥigab,* and in some cases covering the original photograph with a veiled photograph by means both physical and digital. The editing choice to include a veiled portrait of Zahran in this video clip, which was released even before some of the confusing claims about Zahran's religious practice were aired, suggests that the editor felt the more apparently religious visage conformed better to this somber exercise in national martyrology.

Second, the mourning photographs include several uniformed police officers, who were killed in such a way during the January uprising that they were regarded as martyrs. Given the rage directed toward the Egyptian police and security forces—notoriously corrupt at every level—as a root-and-branch element of Mubarak's dictatorship, and which still simmered for months after the uprising, this was a surprising choice.[30] These police officers, however, were distinguished from their colleagues by refusing in various ways to participate in suppressing the revolution: one in particular, Muḥammad al-Balṭran, was a police commander in charge of a prison in the city of al-Fayum who was shot, apparently by security forces, when he refused to open the cells and release prisoners into the streets as part of the regime's attempt to frighten the protesting public into going home.

Muḥammad Fu'ad was one of a number of popular musicians who issued a public statement praising Mubarak and hoping that he would continue to

شهداء ثورة ٢٥ يناير

الورد اللى فتّح فى جناين مصر

الشهيد مصطفى الصاوى

الشهيد كريم بنونة

الشهيد سيف الله مصطفى

الشهيد أحمد بسيونى

الشهيد محمد محروس

الشهيدة سالى زهران

الشهيد إسلام محمد عبد القادر بكر

الشهيد أحمد إيهاب

الشهيد محمد عماد حسين

الشهيد حسين طه

صيادلة يحذرون من وفاة آلاف المرضى بسبب نقص الأدوية

مؤتمر فى نقابة الصحفيين غداً لكشف ملابسات مقتل صحفى من «التعاون»

FIGURE 14. "The martyrs of the January 25 revolution" from *al-Maṣry al-Youm*, February 6, 2011. The red text beneath the title reads "Roses that bloomed in the gardens of Egypt." Captured online in the *Egypt Independent*.

be the president, during the early days of the revolution. While Fu'ad was not as harsh in his comments as other artists, some of whom hyperbolically insulted the humanity of the protestors, in hindsight his comments now appear a public relations gaffe. As with 'Amr Diyab, then, there is a sense of penance in Fu'ad's video clip (Nashat 2011)—and it is this video clip upon which Giselle commented when she voiced her suspicions to me about Fu'ad's political sincerity.

Fu'ad's martyr pop song, "I resemble you," is addressed directly to one of the martyrs, remarking at length on how much they looked like any ordinary Egyptian that one could have bumped into in a variety of everyday settings. (The martyrs' published photographs enhance this impression: they are mostly not formal portraits, but informal shots of them playing on the beach, grinning at friends at a café, and so on.) This ordinariness contrasts with the greatness of what the protests accomplished, which the lyrics note at the end in a deliberately vague way:

Kan nifsi bas aqulak inta ma ruḥtish hadar
Dilwaqti ṣawtna 'ali wa-khalaṣ khawfna inkasar
Baqa fi qulubna raḥma wa-laylna fi qamar

(I just had to tell you that you did not shed your blood in vain
Now our voice is loud, and gone and broken is our fear
There remains in our hearts compassion and in our nights there is a moon)[31]

These lyrics clash somewhat with the editing choices in the video, which mingles photographs of the recently killed protestors with stock footage shots of Egyptian soldiers in long-ago wars, and exemplary, stock-footage ordinary Egyptians who had nothing to do with the protests. In a strange intermingling, Khalid Sa'id appears here, as well as several police officers. Possibly in an appeal to more conservative sensibilities about visual depiction of females, none of the female martyrs is shown. While a few photographs are shown of events at the protests, they flash by quickly and somewhat out of focus, and none of them has any legible protest signs that might indicate what the protests were about.

Tamir Ḥusni, a very popular and ambitious young singer, committed a huge public relations misstep during the protests by going to Tahrir

Square and, under government pressure, trying to convince the protestors to disperse and go home. Amid a sea of protestors recording the incident on their mobile phones, which they later uploaded to YouTube, Tamir was chased from the square to a safe spot in which he sat and wept, apparently in self-pity that no one appreciated his good intentions. The video uploads of the failed political appeal and its aftermath led to widespread and widely discussed public contempt of Tamir, unlike the relatively low-level grumblings about 'Amr Diyab and Muḥammad Fu'ad. Once it became clear to Tamir how badly he had injured his public image, he threw himself into a number of prorevolutionary endeavors as public relations opportunities, in an effort to salvage his reputation (Gilman 2011).

His video, "The martyrs of 25" (Ḥusni 2011), is one such endeavor. Tamir, who wrote and composed the song himself, opted for a contemporary sound that would not be out of place in a standard-issue love song. The lyrics are quite vague about who or what the titular martyrs might be, leaving it to cultural context for the listener to understand why such martyrs are being honored. The visuals are likewise referential and vague, carefully avoiding anything that spells out the protestors' opposition to the continuation of the Mubarak regime, much less why they had come to such opposition. The martyrs themselves, though, are clearly designated, and are depicted with their names beneath their photographs. There is also some footage of people either being shot down or their corpses being buried as national martyrs, with the Egyptian flag draped around the coffins or the bodies on stretchers.

Political Rhetoric and Strategic Ambiguity

Egyptian mass-mediated popular culture has long engaged with national and nationalist politics, often in such a way as to accord with the state's official ideological position while simultaneously leaving open the possibility of a critical, oppositional interpretation.[32] The more satirical forms of opposition that directly challenge or demean official state dogma, especially those classified by Armbrust as "antimodern," tend to appear in less centralized and thus less easily controlled media forms and genres (Armbrust 1996, 231n32). In this line of thinking, music video clips represent a middle-of-the-road category: as Armbrust reads them, popular music genres that are easily and cheaply distributed lean toward the less official, "vulgar" end of the spectrum, and thus have the ability to mount more strident critiques at the cost of being dismissed as culturally irrelevant by the intellectual elite. On the other hand, since the artists and technical producers associated with martyr pop engage directly with the medium of satellite television channels—a business model run on the corporate model and subject to at least some degree of state oversight—martyr pop is far more beholden to corporate norms of conduct than the music genres that circulate almost entirely outside of television.

Television, in fact, has historically been a closely controlled media form in Egypt, as a powerful tool to educate the masses[33] as well as an absorbing medium of spectacle (Abu-Lughod 2005, 10). As Abu-Lughod has shown at length, television (in the presatellite era) was perhaps the single most powerful mass-media form in Egypt in terms of politics and state control not only for its broadcasting capabilities but also for the way in which social and political discourses have often been larded into the Ramaḍan *tamsiliyyat*, the much-anticipated yearly serials aired in installments throughout the Islamic holy month, during which people frequently gather in the evenings for meals, constituting what television producers recognize as prime audiences. Even now, as the proliferation of satellite channels has circumvented some of the Egyptian state's censorship, television has retained its educational role, enabling the intelligentsia to lecture the subaltern masses in proper nation-building behavior. Although *tamsiliyyat* play a far larger role in the nation-building project than do video clips, the latter form can also draw the participation of urban technocrats interested in pursuing this Gramscian project of supporting state hegemony.

As I have argued in this book, young Cairenes have cultivated an aesthetic preference for direct emotional evocation in popular song lyrics, in contrast to the preferences of their elders for more metaphorical and indirect emotional evocation. This aesthetic preference, however, is complicated when the form under discussion is a music video clip about the 2011 revolution—or, indeed, virtually any Egyptian nationalist song. The more explicit nationalist lyrics are about their subject, the greater their power, at least in the short term. At the same time, the nationalist songs that appear to hold the greatest staying power are indeed more allusive and less historically fixed. Umm Kulthum's recording *al-Aṭlal* ("The ruins") is a prime example: the text, while technically apolitical, has been invested and reinvested with political resonance—often nationalist—depending on time and place (Danielson 1997, 199).

Directness of lyrical content creates a particular anxiety for producers of Egypt's pop music industry when political songs enter the discussion: about what events can one sing directly? About what emotions? The January 25 uprising was not the nationalization of the Suez Canal: the national unity that people now recall for nationalization was not there for the revolution. And even among passionate supporters of the uprising, there existed a diversity of opinions about what the revolution ought to achieve, how people should go about it, and, not least, who ought to be in power when the transitional period ended. Being too direct in a pop song could make a person a lot of enemies and, potentially, scuttle a singing career.

In fact, frankness concerning political sympathies quickly landed a number of artists in the doghouse with the public: the actors ʻAdil Imam[34] and Samaḥ Anwar infamously went to great lengths to align themselves publicly with Mubarak, and denigrated the protestors as worthy of suppression and even mass murder. There simply is no equivalent among popular musicians. An arguable exception to this statement is the composer and would-be singer ʻAmr Muṣṭafa, who repeatedly gave television interviews in which he made risibly wild accusations of foreign conspiracies and illicit drugs fueling the revolution. He made his strongest statements weeks after Mubarak's ouster, however, and by all appearances he seemed genuinely to believe what he was saying. His statements were apparently not merely misgauged pandering to his public. Prorevolutionary Egyptians responded by uploading satirical videos to YouTube mocking ʻAmr Muṣṭafa not as corrupt—as they tended to do with other pro-Mubarak figures—but as clinically insane.

While no musician made quite as extreme a miscalculation of public sentiment as Imam or Anwar, a great many of them either issued pro-Mubarak statements or remained conspicuously silent throughout the uprising. Correspondingly, very few corporate-industry musicians[35] dared to say anything in favor of the protests (or the protestors) before Mubarak fell from power. Revolutionaries tended to take the proregime statements by pop culture celebrities very much amiss, and a "blacklist" poster indicting such celebrities circulated informally, both through the Internet and as one of the countless items of revolution-themed merchandise for sale in Tahrir Square in the early months of 2011. Perhaps in recognition of the large number of actors who embarrassed themselves by supporting Mubarak's regime in the last few weeks of his rule, the poster was designed to resemble a cinematic advertisement, with head shots of the actors, singers, and athletes lined up in a satirical mockery of an "all-star cast" (Figure 15).

Instead, the majority of singers who opted to create songs and video clips referencing the revolution have chosen to sidestep questions of their personal politics by singing about the martyrs. This was relatively safe territory: it is easy to feel sorry for people who died untimely deaths, and one need not have been prorevolution in order to mourn the loss of life incurred. Such a serious and weighty topic has rarely been broached in *al-musiqa al-shababiyya,* the musical genre in which all of these singers are figured by their listening public. The only time, to my knowledge, that it has done so before this year was during the second Intifada, when Egyptian pop singers, with the encouragement of the state, recorded a number of songs and video clips in support of the uprising. Such productions draw a sharp contrast to these video clips under discussion, largely because, as Elliott Colla (2005) reads them, the pro-Intifada video clips often suffered from semiotic incoherence stemming from the attempt to cram too many images signifying too many concepts into a single video. In extreme cases of this, Colla applies the term *preposterous,* in its original Latin sense of "topsy-turvy, disordered"; or, to be more precise, Colla uses the term *preposterous* with a broader meaning not of nonsense or absurdity, but an incompetently structured rhetoric (Colla 2005, 348–49).

The rhetoric of the 2011 martyr pop video clips was usually not so incompetent as to qualify as preposterous; rather, the rhetoric relied, with varying degrees of success, on a strategic ambiguity of meaning intended to please supporters of the revolution without (excessively) alienating its opponents. This ambiguity rested not only on the noticeable lack of a clear political position, but also on the human emphasis of the songs. As mentioned above, it is easy to evoke pity for young people who died sudden, violent deaths. These martyr pop songs and videos focus on pity for the dead, rather than sympathy for their cause. Pleading for sympathy for the martyrs' political purpose would inevitably evoke as well sympathy for their common cause with the millions of still-living protestors and revolutionaries: not pitiable corpses, but fellow subjects of the state still noisily agitating for their political aims and attempting to persuade others of the justice of their demands. Since the Egyptian body politic has articulated clear and mutually opposed factions, it would be exceedingly difficult to create a song or video clip glorifying any one position without alienating a large segment of another; it is precisely this potentially bitter alienation

FIGURE 15. The "Al'ar" (Shame) poster, displayed for sale on the ground in Tahrir Square, May 27, 2011. The red text near the top reads "Against the revolution." The "leading man" at the top center is 'Adil Imam. To the right of him is Muḥammad Fu'ad, and to the right of Fu'ad is Tamir Ḥusni. Photograph by the author.

that the producers of the corporate music industry seek to avoid at all costs. We therefore see that, at least in this case, to glorify the martyrs of a revolution can deracinate and in fact *depoliticize* their martyrdom.

Subjectivity and the Mediation of Sound

Lori Allen describes the visual presentation of Palestinian martyrs' corpses and the raw grief of their surviving relatives and friends as a project of immediation that its practitioners intend to circumvent political narratives in favor of a vivid, visceral experience that will impress upon viewers the unjust nature of Palestinian suffering (2009, 171). In Allen's analysis, the people engaged in this political project grant the sense of vision not only privileged access to material truth, but also superior capability of inspiring affective intensity. From this perspective, the feelings inspired by visual imagery are "somehow presubjective" and linked to an "unmediated, direct connection" with the truth (172). It seems reasonable to guess that the Egyptian martyr pop video producers were aiming for the same effect, since they utilized many of the same kinds of images—very likely influenced by Palestinian television coverage as well as by an earlier generation of music video clips celebrating Palestinian martyrs.

But look, then, at how far from immediacy the martyr pop video clips must fall. Very much unlike the scenes that Allen describes, a martyr pop video cannot in good faith attempt to present an immediate, unmediated image of martyrdom, since the whole purpose of the visual imagery is to accompany the song. Martyr pop videos, like most other televisual forms, are intensely mediated productions that bootlessly try to claim some immediacy. In all of the martyr pop videos, images are ultimately subjugated to a carefully mediated auditory experience. Assuming for the moment that the producers have the same understanding of vision as having "special access to truth," then it follows that perhaps they are unsettled or frightened by the implications of that reality demonstrated by footage of martyred protestors.

Naturally, one could hardly expect a music video clip to omit sound in favor of purely visual imagery, or to omit music in favor of the uncontrolled ambient sound that originally accompanied the visuals. But one can imagine a form of musical or sonic mediation that does not so obtrusively tell the listener what to think about those images. For instance, rather than composing songs in a contemporary form of Arabic, the producers could have opted to recite suras from the Qur'an, mirroring common Muslim funerary practice. Such a decision would have foregrounded the martyrdom of the dead without making any political comment, although of course that choice might have propagated a sectarian understanding of the martyrs in a way that most of the producers seemed anxious to avoid.

Sound and song differ in their relative implications of fact and veracity: songcraft is fundamentally different from the ambient or incidental sonic components of an event occurring within mundane (or tragic) daily life. If sound contains the potential to move a listener emotionally, then song contains not only that possibility but the potential to seduce, as well. The Islamic understanding of the ecstasy inspired by hearing the Qur'an recited is not about hearing material fact that could be encountered anywhere in any state of mind, but about hearing a unique emotional truth that should convince the listener, but can only do so if the listener's heart is open to that truth (Hirschkind 2004, 134). This in turn implies that, although most martyr pop video clip producers would likely be scandalized to hear the idea phrased this way, they do not want to let the facts speak for themselves, and feel obliged to push the consumer's emotional understanding of the images in a particular direction. In Hirschkind's terms, the immediate experience of viewing and hearing scenes of martyred protestors presumes a particularly *active* viewer and listener, whereas video clip producers seek to take the agentive role in comprehension out of the hands of the listener and to place it in the hands of the rhetor (2004, 138).

Within the epistemology that Allen and others describe, the sense of vision is taken to represent access to a presubjective, unmediated, and therefore immediate truth. In this epistemology, the sense of hearing is ultimately associated with subjective claims and rhetorical appeals, if not actually with falsehood, duplicity, and sophistry. To follow Allen's thinking, the preference for immediacy suggests an awareness that anything spoken in narrative voiceover or broadcasting context has a way of being coopted by the larger political narratives in the global media—even well-intentioned, sympathetic speech. The entire point of the politics of immediacy is to circumvent that which is *told* in favor of that which is purely *seen*. From this perspective, it simply is not possible to structure a sonic accompaniment to the visual images of martyrs that does not potentially undermine their affective power.

Moreover, such analysis assumes the sympathetic intentions of the mediating entity, which neither Palestinian activists nor Egyptian revolutionaries can take for granted. It is not a coincidence that Allen, in the same article, observes that the Palestinian activists' affinity for a politics of immediation is to some degree born out of disappointment with the work of international human rights NGOs. In her telling, these NGOs sometimes balk at engaging with Palestinian organizations to address human rights issues whose direct implications or accusations of Israeli state violence are seen as too partisan and therefore likely to draw criticism from Israel, if not from their own donors (Allen 2009, 166–67). This reticence leaves the international NGOs with little to say except anodyne wishes that both sides could talk out their disputes peacefully, with relatively little acknowledgment of the somatic consequences of those disputes. In essence, their desire to remain "nonpolitical" (read: nonpartisan) bollixes any attempt to make a coherent political statement.[36] Such thinking suffuses the martyr pop video clips as well.

The epistemological distinction between sound and vision has wide-ranging ramifications for the analysis of political rhetoric in popular culture, which is, of course, heavily dependent on sonic communication. Popular media in Egypt, in the sense of media readily accessible to the populace at large, is fundamentally tied to sound as well as image, since full literacy in the written word remains unavailable to much of the population, if not the majority (Haeri 2003, 117); that which is truly popular in this classical sense must also perforce be nonliterate. Television viewing (and listening) has long been associated with passivity, but the swift demise of the martyr pop video clip genre suggests that Egyptian television viewers exercised an actively engaged form of listening alongside their literal viewing, and judged the rhetoric of the video clips wanting.

But wanting what? To judge by the evaluations that many acquaintances in Cairo offered me, martyr pop videos lack a sense of sincerity—that is, authenticity of intersubjective emotion. Or, to put in the terms that Elaine used on Coptic Christmas, the sentiments of these videos are fundamentally artificial. The obvious commercial and public relations motives of the singers only serve as a partial explanation of this artifice, this failure of sincerity. The video clip itself as an object may be inauthentic, but it makes no sense to describe that object in terms of sincerity. Rather, it is the video clip's singer—and by extension, the other principal characters who participated in the video's production—whom consumers evaluate for sincerity, since sincerity is always an intersubjective rather than a one-sided subject-object relationship (Jackson 2005, 14–15). Cairenes tended to suggest to me not that the video clips were fake, but that the singers were fakes in terms of their political commitments. Those powerful visual images may speak for themselves to viewers, but there is displeasure in receiving such images with the overlay of blandly nonpartisan eulogy. While my acquaintances all seemed to receive the images in accordance with their personal political views, no one could detect a satisfactory message in the sound that had been interwoven with the images in martyr pop videos.

This judgment comes through in discussion of any martyr pop video clip, although I was struck most by its application to Ḥamada Hilal. Hilal, who practically reinvented himself[37] by releasing "The martyrs of January 25" immediately after Mubarak's ouster, soon thereafter found himself combatting public criticism couched in the form of satirical mockery. Only several months after Hilal's video clip debuted, Sirag al-Din, the young revolutionary who acknowledged to me his own complicity in the prerevolutionary status quo, snickered at the mention of Hilal's name. "We laugh at that song, you know," he told me, speaking of himself and his friends who shared his political views. "It doesn't *say* anything! 'The martyrs of January 25 who died in the events of January.'[38] What events? Why doesn't he tell us?" The tautological, circuitous phrasing irritated these critically minded listeners, who judged the lyrics as an attempt to avoid taking a firm political stance by naming the uprising a revolution or even by explaining why the dead qualify as martyrs—and this despite the seemingly self-evident visual imagery included in the video clip. Sirag al-Din then referred to the recent storming of the State Security headquarters by revolutionaries, who recovered a number of sensitive documents detailing the extent of domestic espionage and intimidation of the regime's political enemies, and jeered that Hilal should write a song about "the Amn al-Dawla documents which were found in the Amn al-Dawla building." After having gone to some lengths to style himself as a semi-official singer of the revolution, Hilal was increasingly sniffed at by the wider body of pop music consumers, who tended to consider him a cynical self-promoter (Ḥamdi 2012).

The martyr pop videos enjoyed a very brief vogue: their production ceased by the latter half of 2011, and all such songs and video clips seemed relegated to archival obscurity a few months later. It was during this time that a variety of political fissures began to reappear in the Egyptian polity. Political factionalism had always existed, of course, but with Mubarak deposed and the government undergoing reorganization—ostensibly to accommodate free and fair elections that genuinely mattered to a government accountable to its citizenry—these disagreements quickly became more vehement and indicative of the irreconcilability of competing political philosophies in Egypt's public discourse. If not truly irreconcilable, then at least these philosophies were intractable, and required painful compromise between parties to allow for effective governance.

The increasingly factionalized political landscape and its attendant bellicose rhetoric, in tandem with consumers' disinterest, scuttled the possibility of further martyr pop video clips produced by the corporate music industry and its associated artists,[39] even though there was no shortage of martyrs to commemorate. Those video clips had always evinced an anxiety about forthright political statements or affiliations, as discussed above, but by the close of 2011 it was distressingly clear to video producers, as it was to Cairenes in general, that even this anodyne political commentary no longer had any receptive audience, and could no longer hope to achieve any level of mass cathexis.

The rhetoric of martyr pop videos was never exactly preposterous in the way that Colla attributes to Egyptian pro-Intifada video clips, but it depended on a broad, shallow level of connection among the listenership and viewership, and on an awkward dance around the major political grievances that underlay the uprising. Such a political connection is inherently unstable within domestic politics, and even at its most opportune moment, martyr pop tended to rely on weak, insincere rhetoric that treated the immediate imagery of the martyrs as an adjunct to the lyrical message, rather than the other way around. Cairenes, at least, seemed more inclined to demand clear, even factional political stances as a requirement of rhetorical sincerity, and this was a demand that the corporate music industry and its associated artists simply could not satisfy without sacrificing their own careers. And, since Cairene audiences were more attuned to the meaningfulness of the literal sacrifice of the martyrs in the streets than to the metaphorical sacrifice of an inconvenienced singer, they responded by changing the channel and tuning out the ambiguous and ultimately unsatisfying rhetoric of martyr pop.

Whither the Pop Culture of the Revolution?

Even during the relatively short span of time during which I lived in Cairo after the fall of Hosni Mubarak, it was easy to mark the commodification of the revolution. The first time I went to Tahrir Square after returning to Cairo, on March 6, 2011, there were already dozens of vendors positioned around the square, hawking revolutionary paraphernalia of all sorts, ranging from the simple and obvious, such as Egyptian flags, to the kitschy and absurd, such as keychains and cigarette lighters emblazoned with photographs of martyrs or patriotic icons like Gamal Abdel Nasser. A few months later, during what seemed to be the doldrums of the revolution, I was again walking through Tahrir Square when I heard the purest commodification of those seismic political events that I ever encountered. A street vendor, his kitsch and tat spread out on a blanket on the ground by the corner of Tahrir Street, nasally voiced a well-rehearsed refrain, "*'Andina al-sawra bi-ginay, bi-ginay* (We have the revolution for one pound, for one pound)!"

This commodification extended far beyond the low end of the commercial spectrum to include popular music. Of course, one may well charge that all of the martyr pop music video clips that I have described in this book are themselves inherently a commodification of the revolution, even though they likely operated as a source of revenue for their creators only at a secondary remove. Certainly, some of my friends and acquaintances in Cairo considered the entire phenomenon of the martyr pop videos this way, viewing the creation of such videos as a crass and cynical attempt by mercenary singers to portray themselves as retroactively prorevolutionary. But even those songs and video clips released during the height of the January 25 uprising, when they could only be disseminated online as nonprofit artistic propaganda, were quickly assimilated to the existing capitalist structure of Cairo's pop culture industry. *Izzay* and "The voice of freedom," which had originally spread in *samizdat*-like fashion, became programming staples of Mazzika and Mazzika Zoom, the two Egypt-based satellite channels specializing in music video clips—complete with ads for snack foods popping up over the videos, and with the channels exhorting its viewers to purchase patriotic songs such as those two as downloadable ring tones for their mobile phones.

For *shababiyya* singers who came late to revolutionary sentiment, especially those who released martyr pop video clips, business does not appear to have picked up much. As Murad suggested to me, the apparatus of the transnational Arabic-language culture industry has largely stalled out. With opportunities to perform limited by finances or by concern for public image, singers and other pop cultural artists find themselves sitting at home more often than not, and a martyr pop song on one's résumé does not appear to ameliorate the situation much at all. As a case in point, Muḥammad Fu'ad admitted to a reporter, nearly a year after the start of the revolution, that he no longer understood his audience and feared exacerbating the public opprobrium he suffered after initially supporting Mubarak against the revolution. Even Muḥammad Munir, with his decades-long track record of social commentary and thoughtfully nationalist recordings, acknowledged some uncertainty about how to proceed with his career (Giglio 2012). Ḥamada Hilal, who practically reinvented himself by releasing "The martyrs of January 25" immediately after Mubarak's ouster, had to combat public criticism less than a year later couched in the form of satire: Hilal, who went to some lengths to style himself as a semi-official singer of the revolution, was increasingly sniffed at by consumers who considered him a cynical self-promoter (Ḥamdi 2012). Tamir Ḥusni, once one of the most popular singers in Egypt, seemed in 2011 hellbent on chipping away at his fan base by making one politically maladroit piece of pop culture after another. Following an entire album of songs about the revolution (including "The martyrs of 25"), which was generally received poorly, Tamir starred in a Ramadan serial about the revolution that, as far as I could determine from all of my friends in Cairo, earned tepid admiration at best. Cairenes generally seemed to agree with Giselle, the AUC employee critical of Muḥammad Fu'ad, that the more one sings for profit about the revolution, the less sincere one appears.

One of the boldest statements on the break with historical precedent represented by the 2011 revolution came not in the form of a song at all, but poetry. A pan-Arab television show called *Amir al-Shu'ara'* (Prince of Poets) has, since 2007, featured talent competitions between poets from across the Arab world—the elimination format, in which audiences watching at home vote for contestants via text message, is typical of numerous reality television and contest shows in the Arab world (Kraidy 2010, 8–12). In the fourth (2010–2011) season, the Egyptian finalist was Hisham al-Jakh, a well-known colloquial poet in his native country. Among other public venues, al-Jakh had previously appeared on Muna al-Shadhli's program *10:00 PM,* during which he recited one of his more famous compositions: a cynical and mordantly satirical poem entitled "Juḥa," named after the everyman character of Egyptian folklore. Both the recitation itself and its broadcasting venue—the same television program that would later popularize Muḥammad Munir's song *Izzay* (see the introduction to this book)—index al-Jakh's public association with relatively sharp critique of Egyptian society and, as far as was safe, critique of the Mubarak regime.

On February 9, 2011, Hisham al-Jakh returned to compete on the show after missing the previous week's round: he had chosen to participate in the protests in Cairo against the Mubarak regime. On his return to *Prince of Poets*, al-Jakh presented a poem describing his emotional experiences as a protestor, entitled *Mashhad ra'si min midan al-taḥrir* ("Main perspective from Tahrir Square"), composed in a poetic register of Modern Standard Arabic and recited in al-Jakh's characteristic Upper Egyptian accent. The poem not only impressed the panel of judges, but nearly every line also brought thunderous waves of applause from the audience in the studio, many of whom had come prepared with Egyptian flags to cheer on al-Jakh as a representative of the revolution. Al-Jakh recited the first lines as follows:

Khabbi' qaṣa'idak al-qadimata kullaha
Mazziq dafatirak al-qadimata kullaha
Wa-aktub li-miṣr il-yawma sha'ran mislaha

(Hide away your old poems, all of them
Tear up your old notebooks, all of them
And I [shall] write for Egypt today a poem befitting of her)

Hisham al-Jakh's poetic word choices in some ways mirror the aesthetic choices of *shababiyya* singers who have recorded martyr pop songs. The first two lines of his poem, the most powerful in the whole recitation, boldly suggest that everything that has come before is so out of touch as to be irrelevant. Given the recitative context—a poet addressing a panel of poetry experts, on a show devoted to Arab poetry—the initial demand resonated deeply with the audience. Poetry is a highly respected and widely admired art form in the Arab world, and often carries associations of Arab heritage (*turath*) and authenticity (*aṣala*)—far more so than does *musiqa al-ṭarab,* which, as even its most ardent fans will usually admit, is the younger and less pedigreed artistic endeavor.[40] Al-Jakh was in some sense suggesting that perhaps the entire history and heritage of the Arab world, and certainly the entire history and heritage of Egypt, had passed a point of disjuncture after which nothing would be the same, and after which historians and poets alike would need to consider everything afresh.

At the same time, the skeptical reader (or listener, in the case of the original recitation) cannot help but notice that al-Jakh, throughout the remainder of his reading, never actually specifies what he means by "a poem befitting of" Egypt. His poem runs for another ten lines, in none of which does he express a clear vision of what he believes to be the character of Egypt in any way that would lend itself to literary paean. That unanswered question hangs in the air, as it does in the carefully and unavoidably vague pop songs memorializing the martyrs; as it does in the earnest and yet lyrically oblique revolutionary music created by once-obscure artists of the great Egyptian population centers; and as it does as well in the utterances formal and informal of Egyptians who continue to struggle through a period of intense revolutionary and counter-revolutionary change.

Epilogue

On the Counterrevolution

The public euphoria over Hosni Mubarak's forced departure from office proved shortlived. The Supreme Council of the Armed Forces (SCAF), the transitional government comprised of senior military officers that succeeded Mubarak's administration after the governmental shake-up precipitated by the January 25 uprising, soon began to reconsolidate power in the hands of the old guard. The military in Egypt has not always represented a clear ideological perspective, but by 2011, the upper echelons were strongly identified with the secular neoliberal political stance of the ousted regime, known after Mubarak's ouster as *al-fulul* (the remnants). Since 1991, the Egyptian Armed Forces has increasingly limited the disbursement of well-paid post-retirement civilian positions to generals, all of whom have risen to that rank only after being vetted carefully for political loyalty (Sayigh 2012, 5–8). This arrangement has led to some long-simmering discontent among the junior officer corps, as SCAF and its membership appear just as bent on reserving their class and political privileges to themselves as Mubarak and his cronies did in the civilian arena; even within the military, then, there could appear a distinction between ordinary membership and *fulul* elements.[1] Concurrently, the Muslim Brotherhood, Egypt's long-standing and powerful Islamist political and social movement, provided the likely front-runner for a parliamentary majority or plurality, in the form of a newly established political party that the group hastily registered, the Freedom and Justice Party (FJP).

Cairenes who had once cheered the military as a stabilizing force that supported the people began to reevaluate this notion as it became clear that SCAF hoped to retain power until it could arrange for an elected civilian government to its liking, one that could check the political ambitions of the Muslim Brotherhood, if not actually reinstate the *fulul* as the governing elite. Election dates were set, postponed, canceled, and set again as SCAF and the FJP began to play a hard-to-predict *pas de deux* with each other. Many Cairenes had formerly held entirely sympathetic views of the military as Egypt's sole national institution above politics, and began to express dismay tinged with a loss of innocence to behold SCAF engaging in naked partisanship. The eventual run-off election for president pitted FJP candidate Muḥammad Mursi against the *fulul* candidate Aḥmad Shafiq, with Mursi emerging as the winner. However, even as the *fulul* interests symbolized by the military leadership continued to dominate Egypt's economy, the FJP-led government carried on the neoliberal economic and governmental policies of its predecessor (see Armbrust 2011; Rizk 2013).

During this same period, partisan discourse emerged between participants and supporters of the revolution, as old political factions began to reassert themselves and new factions began to form. The body politic seemed to fragment further every month as hard-headed political calculations between revolutionaries and counterrevolutionaries, Islamists and secularists, the moderate left and the hard left, and moderate Islamists and radical Islamists displaced the utopic (and perhaps partly fantasized) unity of "the square," much less of the Egyptian people. Even some revolutionaries inclined to distrust the military were stunned to see their former comrades turn upon each other: many idealistic young revolutionaries had convinced themselves that all traditional political factions in Egypt had been rendered obsolete by the need for unity in the face of Mubarak's intransigence. The experience of seeing liberals, leftists, and Muslim Brothers who had once supported each other in the square come into direct political conflict—and sometimes outright physical violence—registered with such idealists as a painful (and personal) moral defeat.

By the end of 2011, the hopes of a great many Egyptians for a smooth transition from a temporary military junta to a freely elected civilian government answerable to the people had faded. Protests in October and November of that year had been violently suppressed by security forces, with alarming numbers of new martyrs among the protestors, and some Egyptians held SCAF responsible as the ruling entity. Others blamed the violence primarily upon the protestors themselves, sometimes claiming that the focused political goals of the January 25 uprising had been forgotten by fickle youth, and sometimes that the continued political wrangling was beginning to constitute not legitimate civil discourse but *fitna* (strife). My friend Marwa (among others) voiced this latter critique to me, admitting that it felt strange to echo one of the accusations that Mubarak's regime had leveled at the protestors, but she was convinced that she was right in this instance whereas Mubarak had merely been attempting to delegitimize his critics.

Mursi and his FJP colleagues quickly alienated and sidelined their secular political opposition, and maintained only uneasy relations with the more hardline Islamist parties, such as the Salafi party Nur. Within a few months of taking office, Mursi granted himself wide-ranging powers in order to, as he claimed, root out the *fulul* elements that sought to undermine the rewriting of the constitution and the prosecution of those responsible for the murder of protestors during the uprising. He then presided over a rump parliament composed almost entirely of FJP and Nur representatives, who railroaded through a constitution that my friends argued was at best a poor first draft, and at worst categorically invalid.

Throughout Mursi's year in office, every one of my friends in Cairo, no matter the precise shade of politics they espoused, increasingly complained aloud of diminishing political freedom in general and of the government's slide toward authoritarian Islamist government. Among my friends' greater anxieties was that the Muslim Brotherhood—the "Freedom and Justice Party" was rarely mentioned in these contexts—would engineer a transition to an absolutist Islamist state on the model of Iran, with neither dissent nor religious practices other than the MB's interpretation of Sunni Islam permitted. As the national economy went from bad to worse, Mursi and his allies seemed more occupied with prosecuting people for alleged insults to Islam or to the president himself (Hellyer 2013). In an absurdist comedy of an incident, one such litigant called for the arrest of the television satirist Bassem Youssef for insulting both President Mursi and Islam itself. Youssef responded by arriving in public for his questioning wearing the oversized hat he had used to mock Mursi in one of his sketches several months prior to his arrest (Young 2013).

The humor of the situation was only small comfort to my friends who distrusted the Muslim Brotherhood and felt that the revolution had been betrayed by the Islamist organization, which had resisted joining it until public opinion demanded it. The leadership of the Muslim Brotherhood had initially forbidden its members from participating in the January 25 protests. Many young followers of the organization were incensed at their leaders' disregard for a popular uprising against the regime, and disobeyed the orders. In a famous instance of this, many youthful Muslim Brothers went to Tahrir Square and held it through the night of February 2, 2011, against the assaults of the security forces. The few people of my acquaintance who belonged to the Muslim Brotherhood formally broke with the group shortly thereafter, convinced that the Brotherhood was more interested in power than in liberation. By the middle of 2013, the Brotherhood had lost a good deal of support among middle-of-the-road Egyptians who were not necessarily strong supporters of the FJP's vision of Islamic governance, but who had given the party a chance as the lesser of two evils compared to the *fulul* candidates and the smaller, less efficiently organized parties.

On June 30, 2013, over 17 million Egyptians took to the streets to demand that Mursi resign the office of the presidency and trigger new elections, under the banner of a popular protest movement known as Tamarod (Rebel).[2] The massive protests, the largest that anyone in Egypt could remember, were treated with scorn by Mursi and his allies, in keeping with the unilateral majoritarianism that the Muslim Brotherhood argued was the nature of an elected democracy. Pro-Mursi and anti-Mursi demonstrators began to clash violently. With the country increasingly ungovernable due to mass protests, and with the president unwilling even to speak with his opposition, much less alter his stance, the military, led by Mursi's minister of defense General 'Abd al-Fattaḥ al-Sisi, seized the opportunity on July 3 to execute a coup d'état, forcibly removing Mursi from office, dissolving the parliament, and scrapping the Islamist-crafted constitution. Rather than appoint a new iteration of SCAF, which had ended its rule in 2012 amid much public acrimony, the military appointed an interim executive branch in consultation—as it seemed in public, at least—with the major opposition political groups and both Aḥmad al-Ṭayyib, the Grand Imam of al-Azhar, and Pope Tawaḍrus II, the head of the Coptic Orthodox Church.[3]

SCAF commissioned a small number of video clips during its transitional administration in 2011, often built around the theme of the army as the viewer's friend; the few mentions of these that I heard from friends and acquaintances were infallibly derisive and contemptuous. In the same way as the martyr pop videos—or perhaps even more so—the pro-military video clips lacked any convincing sincerity of purpose, and consequently failed to win over "fans." In 2013, the military tried this tactic anew, with a song and video clip entitled *Tislam al-ayadi* ("Kiss the hands") featuring more high-profile singers—among them the *sha'bi* virtuoso Ḥakim and the *shababiyya* artists Hisham 'Abbas and Ihab Tawfiq—if not better production values, and nearly seven minutes' worth of footage of military maneuvers, parades, and training exercises (Kamil 2013). The video clip seems to have garnered more positive and more numerous views on YouTube than had its (even more) mediocre predecessors, although it is quite nakedly another piece of military (and soon thereafter government) propaganda. The video clip appeared very shortly before the coup in July 2013, and commentators quickly identified it as yet another media tool to win the support of the masses for the military, and away from Mursi and the Muslim Brotherhood (Andeel 2013, el-Nabawi 2013).

To bolster support for the coup that drove Mursi from power, General al-Sisi called upon the country and especially upon the membership of Tamarod to demonstrate in favor of the military and its actions on Friday, July 26, 2013—in addition to Friday being the by-now habitual protest day of the week, the date was the sixty-first anniversary of the 1952 revolution that brought Gamal Abdel Nasser to power. Much as Nasser and the Free Officers had done, al-Sisi and his allies had perpetrated a military coup d'état against an unpopular leader who nonetheless had his passionate supporters. No doubt al-Sisi was keen to emulate Nasser as well by garnering popular approval for such an act, and thus the military emphasized the anniversary in its celebrations, even though it was a gamble to portray themselves as participants in a coup against an elected leader when the Free Officers had overthrown a monarch with no such claim to democratic legitimacy.[4]

The leadership of Tamarod responded effusively in favor of the military in general and al-Sisi in particular, and indeed millions attended pro-military rallies that served the dual purpose of rebuking the Muslim Brotherhood and giving a popular air of legitimacy to the interim government and especially the military brass who evidently steered the ship of state. In a tragic irony that the historian Khaled Fahmy presciently compared to Marx's "Eighteenth Brumaire of Louis Bonaparte" (Fahmy 2013a, 2013b), the military immediately embarked on a campaign of brutal suppression of the Muslim Brotherhood and its Islamist allies, committing many of the same crimes as its predecessor regime in the name of defending the security and freedom of Egypt. Now, once again, it was a *fulul*-aligned military-oriented regime—the interim government being overseen nominally by President ʻAdli Manṣur and *de facto* by General al-Sisi—which spoke of its political opponents as "terrorists," rather than an Islamist regime that fulminated against the "infidels." Horrific violence occurred as the military government increasingly followed a scorched-earth policy of removing the Muslim Brotherhood from the political scene (Fadel 2013), and the majority of anti-Mursi activists who had made their public voices heard quickly gave their support to such violence, often derogating their opposition in precisely the same derogatory language as Mubarak and his cronies directed at those activists in 2011. It was, to say the least, a depressing state of affairs for those who hoped to see political discourse take a more honest and critical turn in post-Mubarak Egypt.

Along with the hardening of partisan lines came a new surge of conspiracy theories and accusations. Within Egypt, the supporters of the military accused the Muslim Brotherhood of stockpiling weapons at its main protest site of the Rabi'a al-'Adawiyya Mosque, and augmenting their numbers by buying mass political support with the sexual favors of zealous Islamist prostitutes working within the protest camps. For their part, Mursi supporters charged that Coptic Christians who opposed any sort of Islamist political project had actually orchestrated the coup.[5] Both sides proffered byzantine conspiracy theories of Israeli or American skullduggery designed to destabilize and conquer Egypt, each claiming that the other was the ally or pawn of foreign forces that wished to gain control over the country.

These warped perspectives led to concurrent tragedies of equally cruel irony. As the military cleared the pro-Mursi protest camps by enormous brute force, military supporters made heartlessly far-fetched claims that the pro-Mursi demonstrators killed by security forces were morally culpable for their own violent deaths by continuing to protest the coup, whether or not any of their number had taken up arms against the state.[6] At the same time, Mursi supporters throughout the country acted on their suspicions of their Christian compatriots by attacking Christian-owned homes, businesses, and dozens of churches, many of which were burnt to the ground in the absence of even token security measures by the state (al-Tawy 2013).

These manifold tragedies piled on top of each other remain difficult to process at the time of this writing; grief and anxiety do not aid analytical faculties. I would observe, however, that the trend that I have discussed in the latter chapters of this book has continued unabated: one can already see a continuation of the trend that I have explicated in this book toward direct emotional evocation in political rhetoric. Indeed, this trend has taken a powerful turn in the post-Mubarak era, as Egyptian political partisans have learned that they must exhort the body politic not merely to mobilize on election day, but also—and more important, as events appear to dictate—to mobilize on the streets at moments of crisis in support of one political wing or another.[7] Political rhetoric in Egypt increasingly tends to focus on calling masses of people—many millions, to take the recent example of the June 30 revolution—out into the streets to protest a government in which they have no confidence, but also to perform similar feats of public gathering in support of their elite power of choice.

This style of public declaration of allegiance is less striking in and of itself than for the political forces that can call for and be championed by such demonstrations. Now both the leader of an embattled political machine with a diminishing base of support and the chief of the Egyptian Armed Forces can beseech the masses to demonstrate their love for one oligarchic power or another. The sense of duty to nation or people—historically a winning rhetorical device for Egyptian political leaders—is thus gently subjugated to a sense of love for, rather than responsibility to, a powerful and politically uncompromising force. Stranger still, al-Sisi persisted in this rhetoric after he was functionally in control of the government: he explicitly sought the affirmation of the public to attack the protest camps when he was already free to do so without serious repercussion. Whether or not the coup d'état was morally defensible, and whether or not al-Sisi was legally empowered to conduct such an operation, are trivial questions in the moment when the leader under discussion has the rank-and-file support of the country's military, has already dismissed and displaced the prior governmental cabinet, and can bring the military's might to bear on anyone who opposes him.

Yet al-Sisi seemed to think it necessary to ask Egyptians to demonstrate their love. What is more, masses of Egyptians responded positively to the exhortation to display their love for the military and its leader, suggesting that they too considered such a request necessary. Even as governance of Egypt turns toward the overt deployment of the state's capacity for mass violence—as opposed to the semi-covert deployment of Central Security to commit violence upon its citizens on an individual basis—Egyptians responded positively to al-Sisi's demand. Perhaps such demonstrators also thought it not only prudent but obligatory for a political leader to implore them in direct emotional terms to articulate an emotional response. Perhaps they, against the expectations of those who did not hear or appreciate the tune, admired the sincerity of the singer's voice. It remains to be seen for how long a critical mass of Egyptians continue to appreciate the song, how far they are willing to be convinced by its emotional appeal, and when they may lose that ephemeral connection and change the station.

Notes

Introduction

1. Zayn was making an ethno-national distinction between Arabs who originated in the Arabian Peninsula, and Egyptians who originated in the Nile Valley from the time before Arabic was spoken there.

2. "Video clip" is the common term in Egyptian Arabic for a music video, and does not imply any sense of excerption.

3. The Internet, which had been shut down completely throughout Egypt for nearly a week, had been restored on February 2.

4. Due to the many "informal" neighborhoods of the city that have been built by their residents without official permission and consequently are not counted in the census or other government considerations, Cairo's actual population remains a matter of guesswork to demographers.

5. I do not, however, suggest that this diminishes the cultural value or political meaning of such music to its listeners, as some critics of Arab nationalism have tended to do in scholarly analysis (see Khalidi 1991).

6. See chapter 1 for an explanation of the aesthetics of production and consumption of *musiqa al-ṭarab.*

7. Nor, for that matter, to a particular musical genre.

8. Although I should note that this includes many people who are not fond of *musiqa al-ṭarab,* and thus have little investment in such specifics.

9. Muḥammad ʻAbd al-Wahhab was most prominent among these.

10. That is, transposable scales structured with the same number of half-steps and whole steps.

11. Muḥammad ʻAbd al-Wahhab was especially known for his experimentation with Western instrumentation and theory as elements to combine with Arabic musical compositional theory.

12. Readers should not take this to mean that there is no optimism for Egypt's political and social future, especially since the 2011 revolution began. However, the nature of the changes under discussion in the present day is quite different and, in some ways, smaller in scale than the nature of those discussed in Nasser's day.

13. While there is some apparent influence from oral tradition in commercial, urban *sha'bi,* musical purists draw a sharp distinction between *sha'bi* and the rural folk traditions termed *sha'biyya*—the correct gender-inflected adjective for

music in Arabic. Professional folk musicians in particular tend to bristle at researchers' usage of the word *sha'bi* to describe the low-prestige urban genre as a smear on their own specialization (Grippo 2010, 145).

14. The class-inflected disapproval of *sha'bi* has even extended to outright governmental censorship (Grippo 2010, 154–55).

15. Ḥakim, as I was told by some of my interlocutors, was selected to perform at the 2006 Nobel Prize ceremony as a representative of Egyptian culture, although I was unable to confirm the exact nature of the engagement.

16. Oddly, Sha'ban has been cast in several television serials that have aired during the Ramadan high season; these Ramadan serials are, in the hierarchy of Egyptian popular culture, leagues above the kind of music he performs.

17. As in much Egyptian traditional music, the double-reeded flute known as the *mizmar* is particularly noticeable.

18. See, *inter alia,* Swedenburg 2012 and Burkhalter 2013.

19. Such an attitude is not limited to music, for the cultural elites of Cairo: Jessica Winegar describes an encounter with a Cairene art collector who spent a huge sum of money on a painting that, while created by an Egyptian, telegraphs a thoroughly Orientalist nostalgic memory of colonial Egypt (Winegar 2006, 244–45).

20. While I am not fond of this reductive media term, especially with its resonances of doomed Soviet liberalization, I recognize that this is how many readers will think of the collection of political and social revolutions launched in parts of the Arab world in 2011. It is also quicker to write.

21. It is worth noting here for readers attuned to sectarian matters that Muslims and Christians who participated in my research did not differ in any way in their discourses, other than in referencing Allah or Jesus as their spiritual lord, respectively.

22. The idea of a fourteen-year-old marrying is not at all popular in Cairo, and the more anyone thought aloud about what qualified a person as "youth," the more likely they were to set the low number at sixteen or seventeen. Since the starting point of youthfulness is essentially the indistinct moment at which one begins to look more like an adult than like a child, there is a healthy dose of "more or less" in this categorization.

23. Although the newlyweds increasingly expect to live by themselves, there is a corollary expectation that, insofar as possible, they will both live relatively close to their respective parents. Anecdotally, I have been told the priority is to live close to the groom's parents, with the bride's natal household a secondary concern.

24. Very roughly analogous to what Americans might call working-class neighborhoods.

25. For an in-depth treatment of the genesis and valences of this term in Egyptian society, see el-Messiri 1978.

26. In this sense, the term is comparable with Americans' use of the terms "trash" or "white trash" (see Hartigan 1997).

27. It is possible as well that some Cairenes, like their American counterparts, might use it to refer to themselves or others who belong to the wealthy, although I have never personally heard this usage.

28. Such behavior is often censured even among the socioeconomic elite whose livelihoods are frequently predicated on being polyglot and fluent in cosmopolitan knowledge and practice (Peterson 2011, 104–5, 188).

29. This is supposition on my part, since I did not question them about their family backgrounds in detail. Helwan University is free for Egyptian nationals, although majoring in any instrument other than voice usually requires at least a moderate outlay for the instrument itself.

30. The Mubarak regime was deeply paranoiac about ethnographic researchers, as authoritarian regimes tend to be, and imposed such restrictions as it was able. The Fulbright-Hays Doctoral Dissertation Research Award, which funded my doctoral research, was a notable exception to this tendency.

31. This process included not merely posing questions to myself but also consulting senior colleagues considering similar issues of their own.

1. "My Patience Is Short"

1. More commonly known in English as the Six-Day War.

2. As Khaled Fahmy has demonstrated at length, Muḥammad 'Ali's intentions for his army had little to do with emancipating the Egyptian nation, but everything to with seizing a kingdom for himself and his descendants (see K. Fahmy 1997).

3. Mubarak came up through the officer ranks of the air force, and became part of the inner circle of governmental advisors of his predecessor in office, Anwar Sadat, during the 1970s.

4. Nearly always, this critique was actually directed at the head of SCAF, Field Marshal Muḥammad Ḥusayn Ṭanṭawi, rather than at the council in general.

5. It is also worth noting that both men are Muslims, and thus have no sectarian reason to mourn the monarchy's passing. A number of Christian Egyptians, in comparison, have declared to me that they hate Nasser for what they perceive as his Islamic chauvinism in both his rhetoric and in his nationalization of various Egyptian business concerns, which affected Christians and Jews in disproportionate numbers. At the same time, some other Christians have remarked that Nasser, as the implacable enemy of the Muslim Brotherhood, seemed more secular and salutary toward religious minorities in his outlook, in comparison to Sadat, who made overtures to the Muslim Brotherhood as a counterweight to the political left.

6. Mahmoud Salem, a Cairo-based blogger and political activist, has noted sardonically that the only thing upon which the entire Arab League membership

seems to agree is the censoring of free information access under the guise of vice prevention (Salem 2008; see BBC News 2008).

7. Notably, Egypt and Saudi Arabia were vehemently opposed to Syria's aims at the 2008 Arab League Summit, held in Damascus, whose stated goal was a resolution of the political future of Lebanon. To communicate their displeasure, each country's head of state stayed home, and sent low-ranking diplomats instead (Worth 2008).

8. Approximately US$37 at the time.

9. In fact, the concept of a prestigious occupation may itself be a shaky construct in Cairo nowadays, as prestige seems to be linked more and more closely with the direct exercise of political authority, rather than the indirect deployment of elite cultural authority.

10. That said, we should not ignore the fact that the revolution succeeded in pushing for Mubarak's ouster partly because the youth were soon joined by large numbers of their elders, many of the latter themselves veterans of an earlier generation of youthful political activism (Winegar 2011).

11. Especially those songs composed in Egyptian Colloquial Arabic, and which refer explicitly to Egyptian nationalism rather than Arab nationalism.

12. This situation may well have changed since the 2011 revolution began: in the wake of the January uprising, a wide variety of formerly obscure nationalist songs experienced a resurgence amid the wave of revolutionary patriotism. See chapter 4 for a longer discussion of pop music released after the fall of Hosni Mubarak.

13. They did, however, keep an eye on the musical theater, in case a playwright or composer should craft a scene or song too much like a revolutionary exhortation.

14. ʻAbd al-Ḥalim had in fact trained as an oboe player before concentrating on his singing.

15. The song's structure allots more time and emphasis to the bridge than the English word might imply to readers. Musically, the melody of the second part forms the bridge of the song, although, unlike what most Western music listeners might anticipate, the verses of the second part are repeated almost as many times as those of the first.

16. And, for that matter, Nasser cultivated a similar image, as the son of a mailman from the provinces who rose to command Egypt through the opportunities afforded him by the military.

17. Technically, Cairo's twin city of Giza, on the west side of the Nile.

18. It is possible that he had yet other forms of recording media stashed away somewhere out of sight, but these are all that I saw.

19. In fact, much of the material and presentation of Umm Kulthum's concerts

abroad from Egypt referenced or bolstered Egyptian cultural hegemony throughout the Arab world (Lohman 2009, 45–46), in support of the Egyptian state's political agenda. There is some evidence that Umm Kulthum devoted more effort and attention to the cause of Palestinian national liberation than the Egyptian government would have preferred (Lohman 2010, 86–87), but Manṣur never raised this specific point.

20. Then again, this is hardly certain. 'Abd al-Ḥalim Ḥafiẓ, the still-idolized music and film star of the same era, sang almost exclusively in ECA, and, as Shannon has noted (2006, 49–50), he retains a great deal of popularity in Syria as well as Egypt.

21. This phenomenon stands in sharp contrast to contemporary Cairene youths' understanding of vocal talent in *shababiyya,* which seems almost diametrically opposed to physical beauty.

22. The Arabic term for the *oeuvre* of Umm Kulthum, as well as concerts dedicated to such material.

23. Although I did not inquire closely about these naming conventions, I gathered that there is some dispute among adherents whether the word "Copt" properly should refer to any member of the indigenous Christian community of Egypt—a choice that implies a degree of ethnic differentiation from Muslims—or only to a member of the Coptic Orthodox Church. In any case, however, I should note that I only heard the phrases "Coptic Evangelical" and "Coptic Protestant" from members of the Coptic Orthodox Church.

24. The peculiar-looking name is due to the common English form of the name in Arabic, *Riḥab.*

25. For a rich analysis of such eateries, see Peterson 2011, especially chapter 6.

26. See Shannon 2006, for example, which I have quoted in the introduction.

27. One must also note that Said was a famous aficionado of European classical music, another high-prestige cultural form whose aesthetics of composition, performance, and listening, in many ways, contrast sharply with those of *musiqa al-ṭarab.*

28. As I described in the introduction, Murad used this phrase to denote what I term *musiqa al-ṭarab.*

29. A percussive technique of playing a stringed instrument, very difficult to imitate even with advanced software.

30. In his native Moroccan dialect of Arabic, his name would be pronounced as *jarini.* The fact that culture industry professionals across nearly all of the Arab world refer to him and even address him directly by the Cairene pronunciation *garini* is yet another subtle indication of how much influence Cairo continues to exert in Arabic-language mass-mediated culture.

31. A Syrian musician in Aleppo's *musiqa al-ṭarab* scene commented to

Jonathan Shannon that this technological mediation is exactly what the Egyptian *shababiyya* singer 'Amr Diyab required in order to have a musical career, due to his "*nashaz*" voice (Shannon 2006, 154).

32. In fact, it is even possible to achieve this effect in live concerts, by plugging the singer's microphone cable into a computerized amplification system running Autotune, which can be programmed to anticipate and fix certain errors as they occur.

33. In addition to fixing wrong notes, Autotune is also sometimes used to distort notes as a stylistic production flourish. This technique was first used, famously, in Cher's 1999 song "Believe" (Sillitoe and Bell 1999), and has since become commonplace in the commercial genre of R&B and, to a lesser extent, *shababiyya.* In America, this technique has also been put to use by parodists, notably the comedic musical group the Gregory Brothers, to "remix" spoken statements into dance music.

34. McCormick appears to have been unaware that Autotune, even as he was writing this article, was already capable of aiding a singer in live concert performance.

35. Indeed, Jonathan Shannon describes one of the more unsettling ethnographic encounters I have read, in which a *musiqa al-ṭarab* aficionado in Syria challenged him explicitly to reflect on Adorno's writings while pursuing his ethnography (2006, 52–54).

36. Then again, pop music has always engaged with an awareness of market forces that observers often identify as cynicism. Diane Warren, the hugely successful writer of thousands of American pop songs, scandalized an interviewer by claiming that she had never had any personal experience with romantic love, but wrote songs by imagining what it would feel like (Cohen 2006).

37. This may help to explain why Egyptian pop music sounds so Western to many Egyptian listeners, yet vaguely foreign to Westerners who detect an unfamiliar substructure within the songs.

38. That is, singing with harmony, in which voices sing different notes at the same time. Arabic music has historically relied exclusively on monophony.

39. Writers have occasionally romanticized 'Abd al-Ḥalim's painful and debilitating illness on account of its disease vector as a peculiarly "Egyptian disease."

40. As opposed to pan-Arab.

41. Although scholars remark more often on the chilling effect these events had on Egypt's relations with the rest of the Arab world, Egypt's relations with Iran were also badly damaged; when the Islamic Revolution took over Iran, the new government formally severed all diplomatic and economic ties with Egypt, partly in retaliation for Camp David. Egypt–Iran diplomatic relations were not restored formally until 2012.

42. Marc Schade-Poulsen (1999) has described a similar trajectory for the Algerian pop genre of *raï*.

43. Charles Hirschkind (2004) has also noted the feasibility of such cassette duplication and distribution as a contributing factor to the popularity of Islamist sermons, and has compared the end of the musical Golden Age with the end of state-controlled religious media.

2. "Oh, My Brown-Skinned Darling"

1. Although the ambient lighting of the scene appears to change significantly throughout the video clip.

2. Or, more accurately, lip-synch the prerecorded lyrics for video purposes.

3. This term, *ḥabibi* in Arabic, is universally recognized in the Arab world to refer to the object of someone's affections before or after marriage.

4. I have heard rumors that Shirin has also had several cosmetic surgeries in order to present a suitably attractive face for the pop music industry. Although I have not been able to confirm this, it may well be so; the consensus among my acquaintances in Cairo was that plastic surgery is a given within the industry.

5. Marwa's ownership of her own car and a spacious, handsomely furnished apartment in the fashionable exurban satellite of Cairo called Shaykh Zayid City indexes her formidable economic privilege. She tacitly acknowledges this by emphasizing to her readers other, less financially onerous ways of pursuing greater independence from the expectations of families.

6. The phrase is borrowed wholesale from English, and is known in Arabic as *niyu luk.*

7. During the period of my doctoral research, the director Nadine Labaki herself became a well-known example of Lebanese glamour, after writing, directing, and starring in the film *Caramel* (2007). It is perhaps worth noting that the film was well received in Egypt, despite many critics' complaints that the romantic and sexual plot lines of the film were too daring and morally inappropriate for the Arab world—for example, Labaki's character is a single woman carrying on an affair with a married man.

8. 'Ajram performed on Lebanese television as a child, some years before she came to international attention.

9. Dissolution *(dub)* is a common thematic image in Arabic popular music, in both *musiqa al-ṭarab* and *shababiyya.*

10. Such ideals of female beauty in the Arabic-speaking world go back many centuries. As one interlocutor pointed out to me, the widely read pre-Islamic poet 'Antara ibn Shaddad celebrated the fatness of his lover as an index of her desirability.

11. I use the term "girl" here and elsewhere throughout the book because in Arabic, speakers generally avoid describing a female as a "woman" *(mar'a)* until she has married and, by implication, legitimately acquired sexual knowledge. Perhaps because of this association with sexuality, even the word "woman" itself can sound vaguely insulting in ECA; every Egyptian I know prefers to speak of a woman as a "lady" *(sayyida)* unless they intend the negative connotation.

12. The masculine inflection of the word for "dark-skinned"; *samra* is feminine.

13. I am not alone in my outsider's perception of Tamir: an American colleague of mine in Cairo once told me that she found Tamir so erotically attractive that billboards advertising his latest album tended to distract her while walking down the street. Needless to say, I have never observed any Egyptian so moved by his visage.

14. Such a singing style, while so common as to pass unnoticed in Western pop music, is highly unusual and even scorned in traditional Arabic music (see introduction).

15. That is, good for someone who otherwise evinces no talent for singing.

16. One may reasonably hypothesize that she represents the vamp to Lebanese people as well, but that assertion must be left to a researcher with the requisite ethnographic data. Moreover, since Negra discusses Pola Negri as a specifically *foreign* vamp, the comparison with Hayfa's reception in Egypt is more apt.

17. On her father's side, at least; Hayfa is Egyptian on her mother's side. Even some Cairene music fans who cannot tolerate her music spoke with grudging admiration of her beautiful command of Egyptian Colloquial Arabic.

18. It is worth noting here that Khulud is a Coptic Christian, and thus does not perceive Lebanese people as ethnically different on account of being non-Muslim.

19. Marwa made this utterance in English, and the context suggests that the first word that came to her mind, which she rendered as "local," was *baladi.*

20. The comparison, I acknowledge, is not a perfect correspondence, since Egyptian racial discourse differs greatly from its U.S. counterpart.

21. Compared to most female *shababiyya* singers, Shirin dresses very modestly in concerts and, to a slightly lesser degree, in some of her video clips. Interlocutors specifically pointed out to me that she wears long (and loose) trousers or gowns, and tops with sleeves that cover her shoulders and arms. And, at a concert that I attended, Shirin performed in a flowing floor-length gown as modest as anything that Umm Kulthum wore.

22. The Western musicological term for the octave represented by a person's ordinary speaking voice.

23. In 2009, Ṣabri broke professionally with Ruby, apparently in reaction to the commercial failure of her second album. As of this writing, culture industry gossips wonder publicly how Ruby's career will develop without his oversight.

24. I had met Khulud in the same way, in fact.

25. The recently built residential area is named for the Sheraton hotel near the airport, one of the more convenient landmarks in the area.

26. Christopher Stone argues intriguingly that the Lebanese Fairouz, whose public image has intertwined thoroughly with Lebanese nationalist metaphorical discourses, worried so much about sexualizing her body in her performances that she solved the problem by standing stock-still while singing in concert (2007, 148–49).

27. The lyrics reflect a very simple *shababiyya* approach to composition, which I shall discuss in the following chapter.

28. See my later discussion on this term.

29. Literally, "veiled." In Cairo, the term usually denotes a Muslim female who covers her hair and possibly frames her face with a scarf.

30. I acknowledge a degree of uncertainty here, since it is quite possible that some of my female interlocutors were hesitant to delve into physical preferences that might index their erotic desires in conversation with a male researcher.

31. The expression *khalli balak* in ECA can signify variously "be mindful," "be wary," "pay attention," and "watch out." Armbrust translates the film's title as *Pay Attention to Zuzu,* which best captures the sense intended.

32. Karyuka was married a staggering fourteen times, compared to Su'ad Ḥusni's four, and danced professionally for decades, which makes her public acclaim (if not adoration) perhaps even more remarkable nowadays than Ḥusni's.

33. Viola Shafik notes that this scene is symbolically charged with social determinism as well as the more overt gendered and classed public humiliation (Shafik 2007, 219). While I would not argue this point, I would add that if the scene posits an insurmountable gulf between rich and poor, it also presents the poor as possessing considerably more human decency and dignity, especially in the hands of a populist writer like Ṣalaḥ Jahin. In addition to filling in as the dancer, Zuzu also reintegrates her mother into the act via their well-honed call-and-response stage patter.

34. Nightclub engagements represent both the most potentially lucrative and the most morally suspect venue for belly-dancers.

35. This impression persists for me despite Bolton's documented ability to poke fun at himself and his image as a belter of romantic power ballads (Lonely Island and Bolton 2011).

36. Cairene critics of *shababiyya* habitually denigrate its female singers as "singers of seduction" (*mughanniyyat al-ighra'*).

37. In the video clip of Hayfa's song *Mush qadra astanna* ("I can't wait"; Saade 2007), the viewer is presented with a montage of genuine tabloid headlines and photographs that treat Hayfa as an object of intense interest based upon her physical beauty and desirability. In addition, several interlocutors told me of a

television interview they had seen in which Hayfa deprecated her own voice and averred that her fans love her only because she knows how to create a pleasing spectacle.

38. The modes that comprise traditional Arabic musical theory.

39. See chapter 3 for more on the nationalist perceptions of the contrast between Egyptian and Turkish musical forms.

40. I am, of course, aware that one could say a great deal more to complicate these categories, but this comparison will serve for present purposes.

41. And, as Lila Abu-Lughod (1999, 44–49) has noted, the Bedouin of the Western Desert traditionally call themselves Arabs rather than *Egyptians,* the latter term connoting for them sexual incontinence, poor moral caliber, and lack of honor, all of which they regard as the natural condition of the inhabitants of the Nile Valley.

42. A major thoroughfare in the Muhandisin neighborhood within Giza, just across the Nile from Cairo, and an area that in Cairene cultural geography is closely associated with dissolute Arabian Gulf expatriates on holiday (see Wynn 2007).

43. Like many young women in Cairo, Zaynab was expert at keeping her skin out of sight while simultaneously showing off her figure.

44. I refer here to the broad historical territory known to Egyptians as "the Sudan," rather than the political state of Sudan that, as of 2011, was formally divided into the Republic of Sudan and the Republic of South Sudan.

45. The country's name itself derives from the exonym *bilad al-sudan,* meaning "land of the black people" in Arabic.

46. Khulud made a passing remark to me once to the effect that I looked somewhat Egyptian because I was not white. This caught me off-guard: I have dark hair and eyes, and slightly olive-toned skin, but in America, the assumption of my whiteness is not usually questioned. When I asked her how she would describe my skin tone, she promptly answered, "You are wheaten!"

47. Much like ʻAbd al-Ḥalim Ḥafiẓ, Shadiyya sang "lighter" *musiqa al-ṭarab* compositions that partially resemble and presage *al-mụsiqa al-shababiyya* in their architecture.

48. It should be noted that this is not a satirical poetic device, since the imagery may put Western readers in mind of Shakespeare's Sonnet 130.

49. Many Cairenes who declared their preference for *musiqa al-ṭarab* expressed their particular admiration for Fairouz, who currently inhabits a position akin to elder stateswoman in Arabic popular song.

50. In fact, as a matter of ethnographic honesty, I must confess that I still have little taste for either one of them. While I felt some professional shame in the field for my apparent inability to appreciate such canonical singers as much as seemed expected, I often bonded with my interlocutors who reacted in the same way to the stars of their grandparents' generation.

51. ʻAbd al-Ḥalim died in 1977.

52. Many *musiqa al-ṭarab* recordings were in fact musical arrangements of poems written in Egyptian Colloquial Arabic.

53. To what extent the contemporary male stars of *musiqa al-ṭarab*–inflected *shababiyya* are necessarily associated with the non-Egyptian Arab world is a research question all of its own to which I have no answers.

54. More specifically, trademarked *musiqa al-ṭarab* techniques inserted into *shababiyya* performances.

55. Ihab Tawfiq's moral sensibility was further impugned, in the eyes of many fans, when the 2011 revolution began and he chose to speak out against the protesters. For this political choice, his likeness was depicted in a large poster excoriating pop culture celebrities who sided with the Mubarak regime against the people (see chapter 4).

3. "The Hardest Thing to Say"

1. *Ḥurriyya,* in standard transcription.

2. Since Baligh lived in the dense urban environment of ʻAbdin, one of the central neighborhoods of Cairo, it was relatively easy to navigate and direct others by means of landmarks. At the same time, his friends considered it mildly humorous that he had never bothered to ask his parents the address of the flat in which they lived.

3. Although it may seem counterintuitive to Western readers, the advanced age of some *shababiyya* singers does not bother youthful Cairene fans in the slightest.

4. A non-Arab ethnic minority group of Egypt and Sudan, who are noticeably darker-skinned than the majority of Egyptians.

5. Islamist objections rested ostensibly upon an understanding of the song's title and refrain as seeking direct intercession from the Prophet Muḥammad—a blasphemous impossibility, according to some strict Islamic theologians. Underneath that putative reasoning, however, also lay the fact that Munir was an outspoken proponent of secular nationalism, a political ideology diametrically opposed to the Muslim Brotherhood's goal of an Islamic state.

6. It was perhaps easy for Munir to make this claim in 2008, by which time he was a well-established musician with a strong fan base. It is well to note also that, when he began performing, Egypt was far more monolithically dominant in the pop music world than it is now, and even a relatively provincial Egyptian musician stood a reasonable chance of being heard throughout the Arab world.

7. Muḥammad Munir has been nicknamed "the king" by his fans, after his boastfully entitled album *al-Malik huwa al-malik (The king, he is the king).*

8. This album's release date of 1981 indexes the fact that Ḥassan is about ten years older than the bulk of my interlocutors.

9. All personal quotations are from this interview, listed in the bibliography as Munir 2008.

10. Munir and his assistants collectively glossed this word, which literally means "propaganda," in context to me as "positive provocation," in the sense of benevolent propaganda or polemic. This gloss is more easily understood when the reader is aware of Munir's positioning as a public proponent of peaceful civil society and secular nationalism.

11. And, by implication, why even I as a wayward *amrikani* should consider following his lead.

12. Music listeners often utter this as an expression of aesthetic appreciation at concerts.

13. This is not to suggest that Muḥammad Munir does not sing love songs; on the contrary, he has recorded dozens of them, such as *Qalb faḍi,* and most of his albums are named for his more romantic and even sensual songs.

14. The exact nuance of the phrase *masakin sha'biyya* lies somewhere between "working-class neighborhoods" and "public housing projects." In any case, the phrase implies a neighborhood where common folk live, rather than a rarefied preserve of the elite.

15. On the other hand, even Wusṭ al-Balad's video clips, such as the one for their song *Qarrabili,* make use of some gratuitous footage of beautiful women wearing tight clothing amid the shots of the (all-male) band performing.

16. Adham is known as a specialist in traditional *musiqa al-ṭarab* singing style, while Hani has greater expertise in Western rock-style singing.

17. The oblique language that Adham and I both used indexes the oppressive political atmosphere in 2007, when the conversation took place.

18. Inevitably, directly beneath a large "no smoking" sign.

19. Although traveling around Cairo via taxi is a marker of some midrange socioeconomic status, it is not nearly as prestigious a form of transportation as driving one's own car—or, for the extremely wealthy, being chauffeured in one's own car.

20. Charles Hirschkind (2006) describes numerous such encounters with taxi drivers who not only consumed cassette sermons avidly but engaged passengers in discussion about the merits of the preacher or the theological analysis of a particular topic.

21. See, for example, my encounter at the recording studio in chapter 1.

22. Culture Wheel, the most common performance venue for Wusṭ al-Balad, is located in the neighborhood of Zamalik, itself strongly associated with old money and political privilege. Since the 2011 revolution, Culture Wheel has also developed a reputation for booking Egyptian "alternative" musical acts who have become known for political music coming out of the revolution (Almadhoun 2011; Metwaly 2011).

23. One is tempted to use the term "inoffensive," but since the eroticism of the video clip form is highly offensive to many people in these countries, that term seems inadequate to the situation.

24. The rueful humor of this remark turned not only upon the relative tastelessness of the newer cooking fat, but also upon its status as a Western import.

25. No doubt Shannon's interlocutors in Aleppo, a city closely identified with greatness in traditional *musiqa al-ṭarab,* would take some issue with this claim.

26. Note that both Dr. 'Abd al-Laṭif and Aḥmad 'Umran, the *'ud* player in Wusṭ al-Balad, seem especially prone to exclude anything that they perceive to be "Turkish" (see chapter 2). Egyptian nationalism has long held up Turkish culture, as well as English and French culture, as a colonizing Other that must be distinguished from indigenous, autochthonous Egyptian culture.

27. It was a decidedly strange moment for me when I realized that I knew the melody that Munir had adapted from a klezmer recording I had purchased fifteen years earlier.

28. This aesthetic criterion is in some ways analogous to the phenomenon of "cultural intimacy" that Stokes (2010) describes as an aspect of the Turkish popular music industry. Since the situation Stokes describes invokes a very different national history and in particular a different set of relations between state and music industry, however, I do not consider the term appropriate to the Egyptian context.

29. 'Abd al-Ḥalim also recorded a good number of nationalist songs, not one of which anyone of the contemporary youth generation ever mentioned to me at all, except during the burst of nationalist pride that occurred for several weeks after Mubarak's ouster. His current reputation among young listeners rests almost entirely upon his corpus of love songs.

30. Like a great many Arabic abstract nouns, Aṣala can also be a personal name. Thus, this discourse finds itself mocked on an accidental level by the international popularity of a Syrian singer named Aṣala Naṣri, who changed her musical style from *musiqa al-ṭarab* to *shababiyya* to maintain her popularity as a concert performer, often sings in Egyptian Colloquial Arabic, and has undergone enough cosmetic surgeries that her face now appears in her video clips as all but immobilized.

31. What is more, this situation obtained even before the 2011 revolution, after which critiques of government censorship grew considerably more pronounced.

32. Jessica Winegar has described a similar ontological phenomenon among successive generations of Egyptian artists: shaped by the differences in growing up under Nasser's socialist modernization ideology and growing up under Sadat's market liberalization policies, the respective generations held clearly divergent views on the proper role of artists as nation-building public intellectuals and the relationship between artists and the state (Winegar 2006, 186–211).

33. And, for Arab and especially Egyptian philosophers and intellectuals, the question of cultural authenticity as part of constructive and liberatory political subjectivity has loomed large for decades (Kassab 2010, 116–72).

34. The Syrian emphasis on pan-Arab difference from the West, as suggested by the phrase "oriental spirit," contrasts tellingly with my interlocutors' nationally circumscribed emphasis on Egyptianness.

35. In this context, it is easy to understand the outrage and interest that simultaneously greeted 'Ala' al-Aswani's book *The Yacoubian Building* (2004), which portrays a variety of illicit sexual and romantic relations among an-all Egyptian cast of characters.

4. "A Poem Befitting of Her"

1. Astute readers will notice that this was Christmas Day in the Coptic Orthodox rite. Alice's family seemed to retain the festival as a day for a private family gathering, despite belonging to a Protestant denomination that follows a Western rite and celebrates Christmas on December 25.

2. When in Cairo, Elaine boarded at a Christian girls' dormitory.

3. Note that this was the same word that Shannon heard applied to Umm Kulthum's later recordings, with the implication that she was "phoning it in" (see introduction).

4. The power dynamic extended beyond the usual professor-student relations. Since Bushra worked at a state university, she was herself a state employee of some rank, and Elaine may have been wary of provoking someone who held a personal stake in the regime.

5. This phrase has become popular among Egyptian Christians since the former Pope Shenouda III began to promote it in his writings decades ago (Ramzy 2011).

6. And, as my instructor of media Arabic observed to me in 2004, the language is reinforced through repetition, since the decades-long stagnation of Arab-world politics meant that reporters necessarily repeated phrases, and sometimes repeated entire articles, over and over.

7. This practice was especially widespread with regard to periodicals published in ECA during the late 1800s and early 1900s that ceaselessly lampooned the occupying British forces and their Egyptian collaborators (Fahmy 2011, 32–36).

8. This was one of the more commonly estimated sums of Mubarak's profits from corruption, at the time of the protests. The actual figure may never be known, since the Mubaraks had ample time to arrange complicated investment portfolios to disguise their holdings, and foreign countries in whose banks Mubarak and his family had deposited much of their wealth were slow to freeze their assets after the president's ouster (Hope 2012; Loveluck 2012).

9. This pageantry did not hold for protests throughout all of Egypt in 2008: notably, the industrial city of Maḥalla al-Kubra briefly broke free from government control on April 6 of that year, amid intense antigovernment protests led by striking textile workers.

10. This slogan is especially notable as a consciously secularized reworking of the long-standing Islamist slogan of political change, "Islam is the solution."

11. Somehow the feminine gender inflection of his utterance made the situation more real and immediate to me. I suspect it is due to the tendency in Arabic to use the masculine inflection as the generic form: the inflection of Mohyeldin's interjection indexed the fact that he was pleading with a specific female colleague near the door to keep it locked.

12. An Arabic-language satellite channel, based in Dubai and funded primarily by Saudi Arabia.

13. It is possible that the news personnel were physically unable to leave the building at certain points, given the sporadic battles between security forces and protestors for this key location.

14. Politically active friends of mine in Cairo refer in exasperation to the apolitical masses as *ḥizb al-kanaba* (the Couch Party).

15. The elder son of the former president.

16. A wealthy and privileged Egyptian protestor, who became famous during the uprising for being detained by security forces after setting up a Facebook page memorializing Khalid Saʿid that came to serve as a bulletin board for revolutionaries (see Mackey 2011). See below for more on Khalid Saʿid.

17. A wealthy suburban district in the southern part of the Cairo metropolitan area.

18. In the *shababiyya* industry, albums are financed according to a private-investment model, very similar to the way in which feature-length films acquire financial backing (see Frishkopf 2010, 17–18).

19. The common term in Egypt to describe the boundaries of acceptable political discourse.

20. While few people in Arab countries, much less their leaders, held any sympathy for the notoriously unstable and politically fickle al-Gaddafi on a personal level, the NATO campaign appeared to many Arabs as yet another Western colonial intervention in an Arab and Muslim-majority state, and the participation of other Arab states in the campaign was a diplomatic sore point.

21. See my discussion of this topic in chapters 2 and 3.

22. Speaking of the attempt to work out one's politics in a way that facilitates creating pop music, Muḥammad Munir commented recently, "Every day I have another answer" (Giglio 2012).

23. More commonly transcribed as Hany Adel and Amir Eid, respectively.

24. Many protestors, in the expectation that they would be killed or maimed in

some fashion, took the precaution of writing contact information for their next of kin on their clothing before attending demonstrations.

25. A few of these channels are Mazzika, Mazzika Zoom, Melody Arabia, Melody Hits, Rotana Clip, Rotana Musica, Rotana *Nagham,* and *Shababiyya,* among many others originating in various locations around the Arab world.

26. I am indebted to fellow anthropologist John Schaefer for suggesting this term to me (Schaefer 2011, personal correspondence).

27. This claim was refuted by a number of witnesses who had been at the Internet café where Sa'id was seized by police.

28. Hilal's official YouTube channel uploaded a recording of the song *sans* video imagery on February 11, and followed up with the video clip on February 12.

29. The majority of lyricists in the Arab pop music industry are Egyptian. I suspect that this form of citation is meant to draw upon the associations in the Arab world of Palestinians with liberatory civil disobedience and resistance to political oppression.

30. That rage boiled over many times soon afterward, as the military junta attempted to consolidate its power by a near-continuous exertion of police violence, sometimes with the overt participation of the army.

31. An elegiac double-entendre: "moon" is a common poetic metaphor in Arabic for an ideally beautiful or admirable person.

32. As Abu-Lughod (2005) explores in her multisited ethnography, this ambiguity is sometimes an evasion tactic by producers against censorship, and sometimes the result of unanticipated reception by consumers who do not interpret narratives as the producers intend.

33. A particularly important criterion in a country with limited literacy rates.

34. Despite building his career on anarchic comic roles that often thumbed their noses at the Egyptian state's national modernity project, 'Adil Imam has since the early 1990s increasingly taken roles in films that either reflect a more progovernment perspective or actually support that same national modernity project. His 1993 film *The Terrorist* was so stridently progovernment that many filmgoers assumed that the Egyptian state had funded it as a propaganda effort (Armbrust 1998, 296).

35. In contrast, a number of independent or local artists more distanced from the corporate music industry made respected names for themselves among the revolutionaries by putting their music into the service of the revolution. See *inter alia,* Almadhoun 2011, el-Noshokaty 2011, DeGhett 2012.

36. That is, if one assumes honest intentions on the part of the NGOs to remedy human rights abuses in the Palestinian Territories. One could also interpret such nominally apolitical inaction as a coherent (and hostile) political statement.

37. Until then, he had been known generally as an ordinary pop singer and an actor in light comedies.

38. Indeed, as suggested above, the lyrics of Hilal's song (written by Malik 'Adil) do not spell out any of these questions that Sirag al-Din raises.

39. Video clips created and distributed on YouTube by independent artists, however, have not only continued to commemorate martyrs of more recent protests, but also articulate far stronger political stances than the earlier crop of martyr pop video clips ever took. This wide-ranging subject is beyond the scope of this chapter.

40. It is possible, though, to complicate this comparison by making a distinction between Egyptians and Arabs, as Zayn did in the introduction to this book.

Epilogue

1. Evidence suggests that the senior officers who comprised SCAF decided to depose Mubarak when it became clear to them that the junior officers deployed to major protest sites were more sympathetic to the protestors than to their own military superiors, and were likely to mutiny outright if ordered to shoot peaceful and unarmed protestors (Bou Nassif 2012, 20–21).

2. *Tamarrud*, in standard transcription. The word is an imperative in Modern Standard Arabic, not a noun, as many English-language media sources supposed.

3. For practical purposes, the Grand Imam and the Coptic Pope are the national leaders of their respective faiths, although only the Pope is formally delegated such authority by his office.

4. Despite contemporary critical assessments of Nasser's rule from a variety of perspectives among supporters as well as opponents, there has hovered around Nasser an aura of nostalgic fondness for some years, and especially so since the January 25 uprising, during which Nasser's image was often held aloft by protestors as an icon.

5. While no one disputes the idea that most Copts were opposed to Islamist political goals, it is patently absurd to imagine that this religious minority was somehow capable of acting as puppetmaster.

6. At time of writing, there is strong evidence that at least a few pro-Mursi protestors in the camps were indeed armed. The question of who fired first is considerably more difficult to answer, given the rampant propaganda and obfuscatory accusations hurled by both sides in the conflict.

7. As a number of my Egyptian friends have lamented ever since the runoff elections of 2012 between Muḥammad Mursi and Aḥmad Shafiq, their electoral options seemed to mirror the American binary system of one political party or the other.

Glossary

aṣala authenticity, originality, realness
asmar(ani) brown-skinned
baladi of a country, of a land; rural; crass, vulgar
fulul lit. remnants; members of Hosni Mubarak's ousted regime
ḥigab Islamic headscarf
ḥilyat lit. ornamentations; vocal embellishments on a basic melody line or note
infitaḥ lit. openness; the economic liberalization policies instituted by Anwar Sadat in the 1970s.
maqam(at) the scales or modal progressions upon which much of traditional Arab music is structured
mizmar a double-reeded oboe-like instrument
mufta'al(a) artificial, insincere
muḥaggaba a female who wears an Islamic headscarf
mutawasiṭ middle, medium
muthaqqaf cultured, educated; sophisticated, urbane
muwazzi' lit. arranger; the producer of a studio music recording
nay an end-blown flute often associated with *musiqa al-ṭarab*
raḥḥimahu allah "May God be compassionate to him"; common Arabic equivalent to the English "God rest his soul."
rumansi(yya) romantic
salafi a fundamentalist interpretation of Islam that espouses an Islamic state
samra see *asmarani*
sha'bi(yya) of the people, of the masses, popular
shababi(yya) of youth, of the young people, of the time of youth
Sprechgesang a half-singing, half-speaking style of vocal performance
ṭabaqa socioeconomic class
takht full instrumental ensemble associated with *musiqa al-ṭarab*

ṭarab emotional ecstasy
turath heritage
'ud a variety of lute frequently employed in *musiqa al-ṭarab*
wasṭa political connections, unofficial influence channels
wiḥsha ugly, plain-faced

Bibliography

‘Abbud, Khazin. 2004. *Al-musiqa wa-l-ghina’ ‘inda al-‘Arab.* Beirut: Dar al-Ḥarf al-‘Arabi.

‘Aṣi, Usama. 2011. *Ṣawt al-shahid.*

Abdel Aziz, Moataz. 2010. “Arab Music Videos and Their Implications for Arab Music and Media.” In *Music and Media in the Arab World,* ed. Michael Frishkopf, 77–89. Cairo: American University in Cairo Press.

Abu-Lughod, Lila. 1999. *Veiled Sentiments: Honor and Poetry in a Bedouin Society.* Updated ed. Berkeley: University of California Press.

———. 2005. *Dramas of Nationhood: The Politics of Television in Egypt.* Chicago, Ill.: University of Chicago Press.

Adham Sa‘id. 2007. Interview by Daniel J. Gilman.

Adorno, T. W., and Max Horkheimer. 2002. “The Culture Industry: Enlightenment as Mass Deception.” In *Dialectic of Enlightenment,* ed. J. Cumming, 31–41. Stanford, Calif.: Stanford University Press.

Allen, Lori A. 2009. “Martyr Bodies in the Media: Human Rights, Aesthetics, and the Politics of Immediation in the Palestinian Intifada.” *American Ethnologist* 36, no. 1: 161–80.

Almadhoun, Hani. 2011. “The Indie Music Revolution in Egypt.” *KABOBfest.* http://www.kabobfest.com/2011/06/the-indie-music-revolution-in-egypt.html.

Alt, Casey, and Hannah Fairfield. 2008. “Young and Jobless.” *New York Times.* February 15. http://www.nytimes.com/interactive/2008/02/15/world/middleeast/.

Amrani, Issandr El. 2011. “Three Decades of a Joke That Just Won’t Die.” *Foreign Policy.* January/February. http://www.foreignpolicy.com/articles/2011/01/02/three_decades_of_a_joke_that_just_wont_die.

Andeel. 2013. “A Dab Hand: Straight from Rifle to Heart.” *Mada Masr.* August 4. http://madamasr.com/content/dab-hand-straight-rifle-heart.

Armbrust, Walter. 1996. *Mass Culture and Modernism in Egypt.* New York: Cambridge University Press.

———. 1998. “Terrorism and Kabab: A Capraesque View of Modern Egypt.” In *Images of Enchantment: Visual and Performing Arts of the Middle East,* ed. S. Zuhur, 283–99. Cairo: American University in Cairo Press.

———. 2011. “The Revolution against Neoliberalism.” *Jadaliyya.* February 23. http://www.jadaliyya.com/pages/index/717/the-revolution-against-neoliberali.

———. 2012. “The Ambivalence of Martyrs and the Counter-Revolution.” *Cultural Anthropology.* http://www.culanth.org/?q=node/491.

Aswani, 'Ala' al-. 2004. *The Yacoubian Building.* Trans. Humphrey Davies. Cairo: American University in Cairo Press.

Badawi, el-Said, and Martin Hinds. 1986. "Asmar." *A Dictionary of Egyptian Arabic.* Beirut: Librairie du Liban.

Badrakhan, Aḥmad. 1940. *Dananir.* Studio Misr.

Baguri, Hadi al-. 2011. *Izzay.* Baguri/Munir. YouTube.

Barakat, Henry. 1947. *Ḥabib al-'umr. Aflam Farid al-Aṭrash.*

———. 1957. *Banat al-yawm. 'Abd al-Wahhab and Aflam Barakat.*

Barker, Hugh, and Yuval Taylor. 2007. *Faking It: The Quest for Authenticity in Popular Music.* New York: W. W. Norton.

Baron, Beth. 1994. *The Women's Awakening in Egypt: Culture, Society, and the Press.* New Haven, Conn.: Yale University Press.

Baum, Bruce. 2006. *The Rise and Fall of the Caucasian Race: A Political History of Racial Identity.* New York: New York University Press.

BBC News. 2008. "Arab TV Broadcasters Face Curbs." *BBC News.* http://news.bbc.co.uk/2/hi/middle_east/7241723.stm.

BlancoTV CH. 2011. "Aziz Elshafhi & Ramy Gamal—Ba7ebak Ya Belady—YouTube." *YouTube.* February 9. http://www.youtube.com/watch?v=_HmKf3Br47I&feature=youtu.be.

Bou Nassif, Hicham. 2012. "Why the Egyptian Army Didn't Shoot." *Middle East Report* 42, no. 4: 18–21.

Bourdieu, Pierre. 1984. *Distinction: A Social Critique of the Judgement of Taste.* Trans. Richard Nice. Cambridge, Mass.: Harvard University Press.

Braddock, Bobby. 2007. "Bobby Braddock: Spelling Success with Country Songs." Interview by Terry Gross. Radio. http://www.npr.org/templates/transcript/transcript.php?storyId=129550239.

Buchanan, Donna A. 2007. "'Oh, Those Turks!' Music, Politics, and Interculturality in the Balkans and Beyond." In *Balkan Popular Culture and the Ottoman Ecumene: Music, Image, and Regional Political Discourse,* ed. Donna A. Buchanan, 3–54. Lanham, Md.: The Scarecrow Press.

Burkhalter, Thomas. 2013. "New Sounds from Cairo." *Norient.* May 3. http://norient.com/video/cairo2013/.

CBS News. 2011. "Lara Logan Breaks Silence on Cairo Assault." *CBS News.* http://www.cbsnews.com/stories/2011/04/28/60minutes.

Chabal, Patrick, and Jean-Pascal Daloz. 1999. *Africa Works: Disorder as Political Instrument.* Bloomington: Indiana University Press.

Clifford, James. 1988. *The Predicament of Culture: Twentieth-Century Ethnography, Literature, and Art.* Cambridge, Mass.: Harvard University Press.

Cohen, Arianne. 2006. "I Belong to Me." Sex and Culture. *Nerve.* http://www.nerve.com/screeningroom/music/dianewarren.

Cole, Jennifer. 2005. "The Jaombilo of Tamatave (Madagascar), 1992–2004: Reflections on Youth and Globalization." *Journal of Social History* 38, no. 4: 891–914.

———. 2011. "A Cultural Dialectics of Generational Change: The View from Contemporary Africa." *Review of Research in Education* 35 (March): 60–88.

Cole, Juan. 1981. "Feminism, Class, and Islam in Turn-of-the-Century Egypt." *International Journal of Middle East Studies* 13: 387–407.

———. 1999. *Colonialism and Revolution in the Middle East: Social and Cultural Origins of Egypt's 'Urabi Movement.* Cairo: American University in Cairo Press.

Colla, Elliott. 2005. "Sentimentality and Redemption: The Rhetoric of Egyptian Pop Culture Intifada Solidarity." In *Palestine, Israel, and the Politics of Popular Culture,* ed. Rebecca L. Stein and Ted Swedenburg, 338–64. Durham, N.C.: Duke University Press.

Conant, Benjamin. 2010. "The Changing Face of Horreya." *Egypt Independent.* July 3. http://www.egyptindependent.com/news/changing-face-horreya.

Danielson, Virginia. 1996. "New Nightingales of the Nile: Popular Music in Egypt since the 1970s." *Popular Music* 15, no. 3: 299–312.

———. 1997. *The Voice of Egypt: Umm Kulthum, Arabic Song, and Egyptian Society in the Twentieth Century.* Chicago, Ill.: University of Chicago Press.

———. 1998. "Performance, Political Identity, and Memory: Umm Kulthum and Gamal 'Abd al-Nasir." In *Images of Enchantment: Visual and Performing Arts of the Middle East,* ed. S. Zuhur, 109–22. Cairo: American University in Cairo Press.

DeGhett, Torie Rose. 2012. "The Rhythms of Egypt's Revolutionaries." *Jadaliyya.* http://www.jadaliyya.com/pages/index/4545/the-rhythms-of-egypts-revolutionaries.

Denis, Eric. 2006. "Cairo as Neoliberal Capital?" In *Cairo Cosmopolitan: Politics, Culture, and Urban Space in the New Middle East,* ed. Diane Singerman and Paul Amar, 47–71. Cairo: American University in Cairo Press.

Fadel, Leila. 2013. "Egypt Is Under a State of Emergency." *NPR.* August 15. http://www.npr.org/2013/08/15/212198304/egypt-is-under-a-state-of-emergency.

Fahmi, Muṣṭafa, Muḥammad Khalifa, and Muḥammad Shakir. 2011. *Ṣawt al-ḥurriyya.* YouTube.

Fahmy, Khaled. 1997. *All the Pasha's Men: Mehmed Ali, His Army and the Making of Modern Egypt.* Cairo: American University in Cairo Press.

———. 2013a. "Weimar Republic or 18 Brumaire?" *Ahram Online.* March 16. http://english.ahram.org.eg/NewsContent/4/0/66962/Opinion/Weimar-Republic-or—Brumaire.aspx.

———. 2013b. "On Fascism and Fascists." *Ahram Online.* July 21. http://english.ahram.org.eg/NewsContentP/4/76987/Opinion/On-fascism-and-fascists.aspx.

Fahmy, Ziad. 2011. *Ordinary Egyptians: Creating the Modern Nation through Popular Culture.* Stanford, Calif.: Stanford University Press.

Faramawi, Muṣṭafa al-. 2011. Interview by Daniel J. Gilman.

Fox, Aaron A. 2004a. *Real Country: Music and Language in Working-Class Culture.* Durham, N.C.: Duke University Press.

———. 2004b. "White Trash Alchemies of the Abject Sublime." In *Bad Music: The Music We Love to Hate,* ed. Christopher J. Washburne and Maiken Derno, 39–61. New York: Routledge.

Frishkopf, Michael. 2001. "Tarab ('Enchantment') in the Mystic Sufi Chant of Egypt." In *Colors of Enchantment: Theater, Dance, Music, and the Visual Arts of the Middle East,* ed. Sherifa Zuhur, 233–69. Cairo: American University in Cairo Press.

———. 2010. "Introduction." In *Music and Media in the Arab World,* ed. Michael Frishkopf, 1–64. Cairo: American University in Cairo Press.

Frith, Simon. 1996. *Performing Rites: On the Value of Popular Music.* Cambridge, Mass.: Harvard University Press.

Gans, Herbert J. 1999. *Popular Culture and High Culture: An Analysis and Evaluation of Taste.* Rev. ed. New York: Basic Books.

Ghobashy, Mona el-, Jeannie Sowers, Mervat Hatem, Joshua Stacher, Paul Sedra, and Elliott Colla. 2013. "On Egypt's Day of Infamy." *Middle East Research and Information Project.* August 20. http://www.merip.org/egypts-day-infamy.

Giglio, Mike. 2012. "Can Egypt's Arab Spring Revolution Produce Great Art?" *Newsweek.* http://www.thedailybeast.com/newsweek/2012/01/15/can-egypt-s-arab-spring-revolution-produce-great-art.html.

Gilman, Daniel J. 2005. "Muhammad Ali, Gamal Abdel Nasser, and the Military in Egyptian Nationalist Historiography." Master's thesis, University of Texas at Austin.

———. 2009. "Flirting with Respectability: Gender Relations in the Private Public Sphere." *Text Practice Performance* 7: 80–93.

———. 2011. "Why Tamer Hosny Won't Go Away." *Jadaliyya.* April 19. http://www.jadaliyya.com/pages/index/1290/why-tamer-hosny-wont-go-away.

Goodman, J. David. 2011. "Anderson Cooper among Journalists Attacked in Cairo." *New York Times.* http://www.nytimes.com/2011/02/03/world/middleeast/03journalists.html.

Gordon, Joel. 2000. "Nasser 56/Cairo 96: Reimaging Egypt's Lost Community." In *Mass Mediations: New Approaches to Popular Culture in the Middle East and Beyond,* ed. W. Armbrust, 161–81. Berkeley: University of California Press.

———. 2002. *Revolutionary Melodrama: Popular Film and Civic Identity in Nasser's Egypt.* Chicago, Ill.: Middle East Documentation Center.

Grippo, James R. 2006. "The Fool Sings a Hero's Song: Shaaban Abdel Rahim,

Egyptian Shaabi, and the Video Clip Phenomenon." *Transnational Broadcasting Studies* 2, no. 1: 93–111.

———. 2007. "'I'll Tell You Why We Hate You!' Sha'ban 'Abd al-Rahim and Middle Eastern Reactions to 9/11." In *Music in the Post-9/11 World,* ed. Jonathan Ritter and J. Martin Daughtry, 255–75. New York: Routledge.

———. 2010. "What's Not on Egyptian Television and Radio! Locating the 'Popular' in Egyptian Sha'bi." In *Music and Media in the Arab World,* ed. Michael Frishkopf, 137–62. Cairo: American University in Cairo Press.

Haeri, Niloofar. 2003. *Sacred Language, Ordinary People: Dilemmas of Culture and Politics in Egypt.* New York: Palgrave Macmillan.

Hakim, Tawfiq al-. 1985. *The Return of Consciousness.* Trans. Bayly Winder. Second ed. New York: New York University Press.

Ḥamdi, Ghada. 2012. *"Ḥamada Hilal: Arfaḍ al-sukhriyya min ughniyya '25 Yanayir'." Al-Masry al-Youm.* http://www.almasry-alyoum.com/article2.aspx?ArticleID=327834.

Ḥarbi, Tamir. 2011. *Shuhada' 25 Yanayir.* YouTube.

Hartigan, John. 1997. "Unpopular Culture: The Case of 'White Trash.'" *Cultural Studies* 11, no. 2: 316–43.

Hashim, Ṭariq. 2004. *Al-ughniyya al-miṣriyya al-jadida: Misaḥat mudi'a; Dirasat li-ẓahirat al-ta'lif wa-l-talḥin wa-l-ada' min 1975 m ḥatta 2000 m.* Cairo: Dar al-Amin li-l-Nashr wa-l-Tawzi'.

Hellyer, H. A. 2013. "Egypt's Public Relations Disaster." *Foreign Policy.* April 1. http://mideast.foreignpolicy.com/posts/2013/04/01/egypts_public_relations_disaster.

Hilal, Ḥamada. 2011. *"Ḥamada Hilal—Shuhada' 25 Yanayir." YouTube.* February 11. http://www.youtube.com/watch?v=JHGGNe-Cw70.

Hirschkind, Charles. 2001. "The Ethics of Listening: Cassette-Sermon Audition in Contemporary Egypt." *American Ethnologist* 28, no. 3: 623–49.

———. 2004. "Hearing Modernity: Egypt, Islam, and the Pious Ear." In *Hearing Cultures: Essays on Sound, Listening, and Modernity,* ed. Veit Erlmann, 131–51. New York: Berg.

———. 2006. *The Ethical Soundscape: Cassette Sermons and Islamic Counterpublics.* New York: Columbia University Press.

Hope, Bradley. 2012. "Mubarak Family Worth Hundreds of Millions, Not Billions, Investigators Say." *The National.* October 23. http://www.thenational.ae/news/world/africa/mubarak-family-worth-hundreds-of-millions-not-billions-investigators-say.

Hourani, Albert. 1991. *A History of the Arab Peoples.* First ed. New York: Warner Books, Inc.

Ḥusni, Tamir. 2011. *Shuhada' 25.* YouTube.

Imam, Ḥassan al-. 1972. *Khalli balak min Zuzu.* Ṣawt al-Fann.

Jackson, Jr., John L. 2005. *Real Black: Adventures in Racial Sincerity.* Chicago: University of Chicago Press.

Jami'i, 'Abd al-Mun'im Ibrahim al-. 2005. *Taṭawwur al-musiqa wa-l-ṭarab fi Miṣr al-ḥaditha.* Cairo: Maṭbu'at Barzim al-Thaqafiyya.

Jankowski, James. 2001. *Nasser's Egypt, Arab Nationalism, and the United Arab Republic.* Boulder, Colo.: Lynne Rienner Publishers.

Kamil, Muṣṭafa. 2013. *Tislam al-ayadi.* Istudyu Risala.

Kassab, Elizabeth Suzanne. 2010. *Contemporary Arab Thought: Cultural Critique in Comparative Perspective.* New York: Columbia University Press.

Khalidi, Rashid. 1991. "Arab Nationalism: Historical Problems in the Literature." *The American Historical Review* 96, no. 5: 1363–73.

Khashaba, Ghaṭṭas 'Abd al-Malik. 2008. *Mu'jam al-musiqa al-kabir.* Cairo: Al-Majlis al-A'la li-l-Thaqafa.

Kraidy, Marwan. 2005. *Hybridity, or the Cultural Logic of Globalization.* Philadelphia: Temple University Press.

———. 2010. *Reality Television and Arab Politics: Contention in Public Life.* Cambridge: Cambridge University Press.

Labaki, Nadine. 2003. *Akhaṣmak ah.* Migastar/Relax-In Music.

———. 2007. *Caramel.* Les Films des Tournelles.

Lagnado, Lucette. 2007. *The Man in the White Sharkskin Suit.* New York: Ecco.

Lamont, Michèle. 1992. *Money, Morals, and Manners: The Culture of the French and American Upper-Middle Class.* Chicago: The University of Chicago Press.

LeVine, Mark. 2008. *Heavy Metal Islam: Rock, Resistance, and the Struggle for the Soul of Islam.* New York: Three Rivers Press.

Lohman, Laura. 2009. "'The Artist of the People in the Battle': Umm Kulthum's Concerts for Egypt in Political Context." In *Music and the Play of Power in the Middle East, North Africa and Central Asia,* ed. Laudan Nooshin, 33–53. London: Ashgate.

———. 2010. *Umm Kulthum: Artistic Agency and the Shaping of an Arab Legend, 1967–2007.* Middletown, Conn.: Wesleyan University Press.

Lonely Island, The, and Michael Bolton. 2011. *Jack Sparrow.* New York: Universal Republic.

Loveluck, Louisa. 2012. "Investigators Track Mubarak's Wealth." *The Bureau of Investigative Journalism.* Nov. 5. http://www.thebureauinvestigates.com/2012/11/05/investigators-track-mubaraks-wealth/.

Mackey, Robert. 2011. "Subtitled Video of Wael Ghonim's Emotional TV Interview." *New York Times.* http://thelede.blogs.nytimes.com/2011/02/08/subtitled-video-of-wael-ghonims-emotional-tv-interview.

Mahdi, Aḥmad al-. 2007. *Kul ma niqarrab.* Rotana.

Mahfouz, Naguib. 1991. *Palace Walk.* Trans. William Maynard Hutchins and Olive E. Kenny. New York: Anchor Books.

Maḥrus, Naṣr. 2002. *Garḥ tani.* Free Music.

Majid, Anouar. 2000. *Unveiling Traditions: Postcolonial Islam in a Polycentric World.* Durham, N.C.: Duke University Press.

Manuel, Peter. 1993. *Cassette Culture: Popular Music and Technology in North India.* Chicago: University of Chicago Press.

Marcus, Scott L. 2007. *Music in Egypt: Experiencing Music, Expressing Culture.* Global Music Series. New York: Oxford University Press.

Massad, Joseph. 2005. "Liberating Songs: Palestine Put to Music." In *Palestine, Israel, and the Politics of Popular Culture,* ed. Rebecca L. Stein and Ted Swedenburg, 175–201. Durham, N.C.: Duke University Press.

McCall, Michael. 2004. "Pro Tools." *Nashville Scene.* http://www.nashvillescene.com/nashville/pro-tools.

McCormick, Neil. 2004. "The Truth about Lip-Synching." *The Age.* http://www.theage.com.au/articles/2004/10/12/1097406567855.html.

Messiri, Sawsan el-. 1978. *Ibn al-Balad: A Concept of Egyptian Identity.* Leiden: E. J. Brill.

———. 1982. "Self-Images of Traditional Urban Women in Cairo." In *Women in the Muslim World,* ed. L. Beck and N. Keddie, Fourth ed., 522–40. Cambridge, Mass.: Harvard University Press.

Metwaly, Ati. 2011. "The Egyptian Revolution's Rhythms." *Ahram Online.* http://english.ahram.org.eg/~/NewsContent/5/33/8101/Arts—Culture/Music/The-Egyptian-Revolutions-rhythms.aspx.

Middleton, Richard. 1990. *Studying Popular Music.* Philadelphia: Open University Press.

Miller, Flagg. 2007. *The Moral Resonance of Arab Media: Audiocassette Poetry and Culture in Yemen.* Cambridge, Mass.: Harvard Center for Middle Eastern Studies.

Mitchell, Timothy. 2002. *Rule of Experts: Egypt, Techno-Politics, Modernity.* Berkeley: University of California Press.

Mourad, Sara. 2011. "Songs of Revival." *Al-Ahram Weekly.* http://weekly.ahram.org.eg/2011/1078/ee2.htm.

Muḥy al-Din, Ḥazim. 2011. *Baḥibbik ya biladi.*

Munir, Muḥammad. 2005. *Qalb faḍi.* Imbariḥ kan 'umri 'ashrin. Cairo: Mirage.

———. 2008. Interview by Daniel J. Gilman. Digital recording.

Nabawi, Maha el-. 2013. "Egypt's Musical Nationalism, and a Little George Orwell." *Mada Masr.* August 20. http://www.madamasr.com/content/egypt%E2%80%99s-musical-nationalism-and-little-george-orwell.

Nashat, Aḥad. 2011. *Bashabih 'alayk.* Fo2sh.TV.

Negra, Diane. 2001. *Off-White Hollywood: American Culture and Ethnic Female Stardom.* New York: Routledge.

Nieuwkerk, Karin van. 1995. *A Trade like Any Other: Female Singers and Dancers in Egypt.* Austin: University of Texas Press.

Noshokaty, Amira El-. 2011. "True, Passionate and Popular." *Al-Ahram Weekly.* http://weekly.ahram.org.eg/2011/1078/ee1.htm.

Peterson, Mark Allen. 2011. *Connected in Cairo: Growing Up Cosmopolitan in the Modern Middle East.* Bloomington: Indiana University Press.

Ra'fat, Muḥammad. 2011. *Maṣr qalit.* Nay for Media.

Racy, Ali Jihad. 1976. "Record Industry and Egyptian Traditional Music: 1904–1932." *Ethnomusicology* 20, no. 1: 23–48.

———. 1982. "Musical Aesthetics in Present-Day Cairo." *Ethnomusicology* 26, no. 3: 391–406.

———. 2003. *Making Music in the Arab World: The Culture and Artistry of Ṭarab.* Cambridge: Cambridge University Press.

Rakha, Marwa. 2008. *The Poison Tree: Planted and Grown in Egypt.* Cairo: Malamih Publishing House.

Ramzy, Carolyn. 2011. "Martyrs for Christ: Coptic Christian Revival and the Performative Politics of Song" presented at the American Research Center in Egypt, May 11, Cairo.

Rifaat, Mohammed. 1947. *The Awakening of Modern Egypt.* New York: Longmans, Green.

Rizk, Philip. 2013. "The Necessity of Revolutionary Violence in Egypt." *Jadaliyya.* April 7. http://www.jadaliyya.com/pages/index/11073/the-necessity-of-revolutionary-violence-in-egypt.

Saade, Yehya. 2007. *Mush qadra astanna.* Haifa Wehbe Productions.

Ṣabri, Sharif. 2007a. *Mashit wara iḥsasi.* Yellow/Delta Sound.

———. 2007b. *Mush ḥatiqdar.* Yellow/Delta Sound.

Said, Edward. 1991. *Musical Elaborations.* New York: Columbia University Press.

———. 2001. "Farewell to Tahia." In *Colors of Enchantment: Theater, Dance, Music, and the Visual Arts of the Middle East,* ed. Sherifa Zuhur, 228–32. Cairo: American University in Cairo Press.

Salem, Mahmoud. 2008. "Trying To Stop the Signal." *Rantings of a Sandmonkey.* http://www.sandmonkey.org/2008/02/13/trying-to-stop-the-signal/.

Salim, 'Abd al-Sattar. 1999. *Funun al-waw, al-mawwal, al-muwashshaḥ: Dirasa naqdiyya.* Cairo: Dar Zawil li-l-Nashr.

Sayf, Samir. 2006. *Al-Sindirila.* Sharika al-'Adl Grub.

Sayigh, Yezid. 2012. *Above the State: The Officers' Republic in Egypt.* The Carnegie Papers. Washington, D.C.: Carnegie Endowment for International Peace.

Schade-Poulsen, Marc. 1999. *Men and Popular Music in Algeria: The Social Significance of Raï.* Austin: University of Texas Press.

Schaefer, John. 2011. "Martyr Pop." February 17.

Schielke, Samuli. 2009. "Being Good in Ramadan: Ambivalence, Fragmentation, and the Moral Self in the Lives of Young Egyptians." *Journal of the Royal Anthropological Institute* 15, no. 1: S24-S40.

Shafik, Viola. 1998. *Arab Cinema: History and Cultural Identity.* Cairo: American University in Cairo Press.

———. 2007. *Popular Egyptian Cinema: Gender, Class, and Nation.* Cairo: American University in Cairo Press.

Shakir, Muḥammad. 2011. *Ya al-midan.* YouTube.

Shannon, Jonathan H. 2003. "Emotion, Performance, and Temporality in Arab Music: Reflections on Tarab." *Cultural Anthropology* 18, no. 1: 72–98.

———. 2006. *Among the Jasmine Trees: Music and Modernity in Contemporary Syria.* Middletown, Conn.: Wesleyan University Press.

Shawan, Salwa el-. 1980. "The Socio-political Context of al-Musiḳa al-'Arabiyyah in Cairo, Egypt: Policies, Patronage, Institutions, and Musical Change (1927–77)." *Asian Music* 12, no. 1: 86–128.

Shawan Castelo-Branco, Salwa el-. 1987. "Some Aspects of the Cassette Industry in Egypt." *World of Music* 29, no. 2: 32–48.

Sillitoe, Sue, and Matt Bell. 1999. "Recording Cher's 'Believe'." *Sound on Sound.* February. http://www.soundonsound.com/sos/feb99/articles/tracks661.htm.

Skinner, Ryan. 2009. "Artistiya: Popular Music and Personhood in Postcolonial Bamako, Mali." Dissertation, Columbia University.

Soueif, Ahdaf. 1992. *In the Eye of the Sun.* London: Bloomsbury.

Stack, Liam, and Neil MacFarquhar. 2011. "Egyptians Get View of Extent of Spying." *New York Times.* http://www.nytimes.com/2011/03/10/world/middleeast/10cairo.html.

Stewart, Susan. 1993. *On Longing: Narratives of the Miniature, the Gigantic, the Souvenir, the Collection.* Durham, N.C.: Duke University Press.

Stokes, Martin. 2009. "'Abd al-Halim's Microphone." In *Music and the Play of Power in the Middle East, North Africa, and Central Asia,* ed. Laudan Nooshin, 55–73. London: Ashgate.

———. 2010. *The Republic of Love: Cultural Intimacy in Turkish Popular Music.* Chicago: University of Chicago Press.

Stoller, Paul. 1989. *The Taste of Ethnographic Things.* Philadelphia: University of Pennsylvania Press.

Stone, Christopher. 2007. *Popular Culture and Nationalism in Lebanon: The Fairouz and Rahbani Nation.* New York: Routledge.

Swedenburg, Ted. 2012. "Egypt's Music of Protest." *Middle East Research and Information Project.* http://www.merip.org/mer/mer265/egypts-music-protest.

Tawy, Ayat al-. 2013. "Churches Torched across Egypt in Anti-Coptic Violence by Morsi Loyalists." *Ahram Online.* August 15. http://english.ahram.org.eg/NewsContent/1/64/79124/Egypt/Politics-/Churches-torched-across-Egypt-in-antiCoptic-violen.aspx.

Vatikiotis, P. J. 1991. *The History of Modern Egypt: From Muhammad Ali to Mubarak.* Baltimore, Md.: Johns Hopkins University Press.

Wagdi, Anwar. 1949. *Ghazal al-banat.* Sharika al-Aflam al-Muttaḥida.

Wallach, Jeremy. 2008. *Modern Noise, Fluid Genres: Popular Music in Indonesia, 1997–2001.* Madison: University of Wisconsin Press.

Washburne, Chris, and Maiken Derno. 2004. "Introduction." In *Bad Music: The Music We Love to Hate,* ed. C. Washburne and M. Derno, 1–14. New York: Routledge.

Weismantel, Mary. 2001. *Cholas and Pishtacos: Stories of Race and Sex in the Andes.* Chicago: University of Chicago Press.

White, Bob W. 2008. *Rumba Rules: The Politics of Dance Music in Mobutu's Zaire.* Durham, N.C.: Duke University Press.

Williams, Raymond. 1977. *Marxism and Literature.* Oxford: Oxford University Press.

Winegar, Jessica. 2006. *Creative Reckonings: The Politics of Art and Culture in Contemporary Egypt.* Stanford, Calif.: Stanford University Press.

———. 2011. "Egypt: A Multi-Generational Revolt." *Jadaliyya.* http://www.jadaliyya.com/pages/index/703/-egypt_a-multi-generational-revolt.

Worth, Robert F. 2008. "Despite Infighting, Meeting of Arab Leaders Gets Under Way in Damascus." *New York Times.* http://www.nytimes.com/2008/03/30/world/middleeast/.

Wynn, Lisa L. 2007. *Pyramids and Nightclubs.* Austin: University of Texas Press.

Yano, Christine R. 2002. *Tears of Longing: Nostalgia and the Nation in Japanese Popular Song.* Cambridge, Mass.: Harvard University Press.

Young, Angelo. 2013. "Bassem Youssef, Egypt's Version Of Jon Stewart, Released on Bail; Faces Charges of Insulting President Mohammed Morsi, Ridiculing Islam and Reporting False News." *International Business Times.* March 31. http://www.ibtimes.com/bassem-youssef-egypts-version-jon-stewart-released-bail-faces-charges-insulting-president-mohammed.

Zuhur, Sherifa. 2000. *Asmahan's Secrets: Woman, War, and Song.* Austin: University of Texas Press.

Index

Stewart, Susan, 152
Stokes, Martin, 67–68, 223n28
Stone, Christopher, 219n26
Studio Misr, 46, 49
subjectivity: authenticity of Egyptian music and, 159–65; mediation of sound and, 193–98
Sudan: Egyptian attitudes concerning, 116–24, 220n44
Sulṭan, Baha', 45
Sulṭan, Huda, 56
Supreme Council of the Armed Forces (SCAF): Mubarak and, 37; musical commentary on, 179; transitional government of, 203–9, 227n1. *See also* state security forces
Syria: Arab League and, 40, 214n7, 234n34; Egyptian merger with, 36; French colonialism in, 47; *musiqa al-ṭarab* and, 156–57, 216n35; wars with Israel and, 34

Tagammu' party, 43
taḥriḍ (dream of better life), 132–34
takht ensemble, 51; early use of, 9; in Ruby's recordings, 105; technological mediation, 66–67; in Umm Kulthum recordings, 121
Tamarod (Rebel) protest movement, 206–9, 227n2
tamsiliyyat (Ramaḍan television serials), 190, 212n16
Ṭanṭawi, Muḥammad Ḥusayn, 213n4
ṭarab (enchantment/engagement): in Egyptian music and culture, 6–7, 10, 64, 140–41, 149; Egyptian view of American pop music and, 110–11; in Munir's music, 134–38
Tawaḍrus II (Pope), 206
Tawfiq, Ihab, 123, 206, 221n55
taxonomies of music: aesthetics of Egyptian music and, 125–65; American popular music, 142–44; Arabic-language music industry, 5–16; class identity linked to, 140–44; Egyptian nationalism and, 150–53
Taylor, Elizabeth, 107
Taylor, Yuval, 160
al-Ṭayyib, Aḥmad, 206
teaching: socioeconomic status of, 40–43
technological mediation: in Egyptian pop music, 63–64, 215n31, 216n32; of production and consumption, 66–73
television news: Egyptian politics and, 169–71; Egyptian Revolution of 2011 and, 171–74; sound vs. vision in, 195–96; strategic political ambiguity in, 190–93
10:00 PM (television show), 200
theater: popularity in Egypt of, 47
Tin Pan Alley industry, 72
Tislam al-ayadi ("Kiss the hands") (video clip), 206–7
Tomei, Marisa, 99
Tunisia: Arab League and, 39–40; revolution in, 170
turath (heritage): definitions of, 5–6
Turkish musical traditions: in Egyptian pop music, 112, 150–51, 223n26, 223n28

'ud: generational attitudes concerning music of, 42–43; scales tuned to, 9–10; technical reproduction vs. real-life sounds of, 64–65, 73
Umm Kulthum: apolitical music of, 190; authenticity in music of, 162; cultural heritage associated with, 81–82, 97, 107, 112; death of,

75; Egyptian music industry and, 46–47; Egyptian youth criticism of, 57–61, 120–21; high modernism of, 10; historical background on, 34; *musiqa al-ṭarab* and, 5–9; nationalism and music of, 19–20, 44–45, 56, 214n19; physical appearance of, 80–81, 100; prerevolutionary success of, 50; sexuality in music of, 13; singing style of, 68; technology and career of, 66, 69, 224n3; vocal technique of, 93, 120–21
'Umran, Aḥmad, 111–12, 127, 142, 223n26
underground music: Egyptian revolution of 2011 and, 16–19; technology and increased production of, 75; Wusṭ al-Balad (band) and, 139–40
United Arab Republic, 36
United States: coverage of Egyptian Revolution by, 172–74; Egyptian state and, 156
'Urabi, Aḥmad, 159
Üsküdar'a gider iken ("While going to Üsküdar") (Turkish folk song), 150–51

vamp image: of Hayfa Wahbi, 93–95; of Ruby, 100, 104–5
video clips: of counterrevolution, 206–7; Egyptian revolution and, 45–46, 175–78; of Hayfa Wahbi, 93–95; narrative characterization in, 78–80; New Look standard of beauty in, 85–89; political ambiguity in, 189–93; postrevolution politics in, 179–82; of Ruby, 102, 105; sex and race issues in, 78, 157–58, 223n23; *shababiyya* music in, 16; by *sha'bi* performers, 141; standards of beauty in, 157; terminology of, 211n2. *See also* music videos
visual aesthetics: authenticity and, 163–65; in Egyptian pop music, 77–78
vocal quality: technological mediation and, 66–73
"voice of the martyr, The" (song), 185

Wahbi, Hayfa, 46, 89–90, 92–95, 111, 122, 158, 218nn16–17, 219n37
al-Walid bin Ṭalal (Prince), 118
Warren, Diane, 216n36
wars: 1967 War, 34; 1973 War, 34–35
Washburne, Christopher J., 17–19
Wasuf, George, 122–24
Weismantel, Mary, 77
Western pop music: Autotune software use in, 70, 216n37
Winegar, Jessica, 212n19, 223n32
women in *shababiya* music, 13–14
Wusṭ al-Balad (band), 127–29; Egyptian youth view of, 111, 127–29; musical aesthetics of, 145–47, 222n15, 222n22; nationalism and work of, 45; political criticism of, 146–47; postrevolution music by, 179–82; *shababiyya* music and, 104–5, 138–42; taxonomic classification of, 141–42; technical mediation used by, 66

Ya al-midan ("O Square") (song), 180–82
Ya banat iskandariyya ("O girls of Alexandria") (folk song), 149–51
Yacoubian Building, The (al-Aswani), 224n35
Youssef, Bassem, 204

DANIEL J. GILMAN is assistant professor of anthropology at DePauw University.